Praise for

"*Psychic Psychology* is an elegant synthesis of several great teaching traditions, combining the wisdom of the Seth material with the structural elements from Eastern and Western approaches to energy healing. You can skim this book, learn a lot, and enjoy it thoroughly. But then to benefit from its depth and true power, I suggest treating it as a workbook to be experienced over the course of several months, serving as a catalyst for your personal transformation.

"This book is a hands-on guide to the mechanics of the mysticism in everyday life; by describing the nuts and bolts of energy flow in relationships, both present and past, the book shows the reader how, literally, to create your own reality. Infused by the very attitudes that Hemsher and Friedlander advise the reader to adopt—openness, playfulness, and curiosity—the book is both challenging and entertaining, and is guaranteed to broaden any reader's understanding of the nature of personal reality."

—ERIC LESKOWITZ, MD, author of *Transpersonal Hypnotherapy: Gateway to Body, Mind, and Spirit;* board-certified psychiatrist with the Pain Management Program and director of the Integrative Medicine Project at Spaulding Rehabilitation Hospital in Boston, Massachussetts; and faculty member at Harvard Medical School

"John Friedlander and Gloria Hemsher give you a universe you can believe in, but more than that: a universe that believes in you, a universe you always secretly knew was there."

—ROB BREZSNY, author of *Pronoia Is the Antidote for Paranoia: How the Whole World Is Conspiring to Shower You with Blessings*

"At the core of each of us are pathways into deeper, more profound, more gratifying ways of living than those cultivated by a culture that cherishes materialistic gain, instant gratification, and maintaining a competitive edge. *Psychic Psychology* gently and effectively teaches those who will take the time and exert the effort to enter hidden realms that have been known to wisdom traditions throughout time. Through ninety-eight highly practical and wonderfully accessible exercises, it systematically builds your connection with the psychic energies that surround you and brings you into the eternal moment, where our deepest joy and most authentic living dwell."

—DONNA EDEN, author (with David Feinstein) of *Energy Medicine: Balancing Your Body's Energies for Optimal Health, Joy, and Vitality*

"*Psychic Psychology*, invitingly warm and clearly written, is a book that needs to be read slowly ... enjoyed and savored, tasting each layer, one bite at a time. Chapters on advanced grounding techniques and other life skills continue to bring me and my students to a deeper place of understanding, balance, and strength within our hatha yoga and meditation practice. The practical skills taught in this book allow us to engage in the world and capably experience life as a spiritual journey."

—LILIAS FOLAN, "First Lady of Yoga," PBS host of *Lilias!*
Yoga and You, and author of *Lilias! Yoga Gets Better with Age*

"In this beautiful and very important book, John Friedlander and Gloria Hemsher share knowledge to expand your understanding of the cosmos and practical tools with which to improve your life. A fascinating and deeply insightful exploration of what it means to be a soul having a human experience. There is great wisdom here."

—ROBERT SCHWARTZ, author of *Your Soul's Plan: Discovering the Real*
Meaning of the Life You Planned Before You Were Born

"John Friedlander is the truth. There is the big picture, so-called, and then another big picture framing *it*. That one is not only invisible, operating at a different vibration from our perceived consciousness state, but flashes of its recognition change everything, put us back into a hospitable universe. The *big* big picture takes the darkest aspects of our crisis and despair, locates them rightly in a larger congruence, and makes us calm and whole. There is a great deal of work ahead, some hard yoga, but John provides a few of the key tools that we will need. This is a teaching ahead of its time by perhaps a thousand years, but it is completely imbued with our time because it is the background against which all our foregrounds curtsy and pay homage."

—RICHARD GROSSINGER, author of *Embryos, Galaxies,*
and Sentient Beings: How the Universe Makes Life and
2013: Raising the Earth to the Next Vibration

"John and Gloria have elevated the work of psychic and spiritual development to entirely new levels. The skills and exercises are practical, insightful, and they leverage the best of all of us—our curiosity, imagination, and playfulness. All in the pursuit of self-awareness and healing. Female grounding is a worthy practice in and of itself—for all over-committed, harried, nurturing women everywhere. Read this book and learn to female ground!"

—JILL LEIGH, founder and director of the
Energy Healing Institute, Boston, Massachussetts

Psychic Psychology

Energy Skills for Life and Relationships

John Friedlander
and Gloria Hemsher

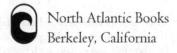

North Atlantic Books
Berkeley, California

Published by

North Atlantic Books	Cover art by Benny H. V. Anderssen
Huichin, unceded Ohlone land	Cover design by Brad Greene
aka Berkeley, California	Book design by Suzanne Albertson

Illustrations on pages 59, 64, 74, and 101 are reprinted courtesy of the publisher from *Basic Psychic Development: A User's Guide to Auras, Chakras & Clairvoyance* by John Friedlander and Gloria Hemsher (York Beach, ME: Samuel Weiser, Inc., 1999). Illustration on page 195 by Brian Greminger.

Printed in Canada

Psychic Psychology: Energy Skills for Life and Relationships is sponsored and published by North Atlantic Books, an educational nonprofit based in the unceded Ohlone land Huichin (aka Berkeley, CA) that collaborates with partners to develop cross-cultural perspectives; nurture holistic views of art, science, the humanities, and healing; and seed personal and global transformation by publishing work on the relationship of body, spirit, and nature.

North Atlantic Books' publications are distributed to the US trade and internationally by Penguin Random House Publishers Services. For further information, visit our website at www.northatlanticbooks.com.

Library of Congress Cataloging-in-Publication Data

Friedlander, John.
   Psychic psychology : energy skills for life and relationships / John Friedlander and Gloria Hemsher.
     p. cm.
   Includes bibliographical references (p.).
   ISBN 978-1-55643-997-1
   1. Interpersonal relations—Psychic aspects. 2. Parapsychology—Social aspects.
I. Hemsher, Gloria. II. Title.
   BF1045.I58F75 2011
   133.8—dc23   2011018800

5 6 7 8 9 10 MQ 25 24 23 22 21

To Jane Roberts and Lewis Bostwick

Twelve years ago we dedicated our book *Basic Psychic Development: A User's Guide to Auras, Chakras & Clairvoyance* to Jane and Lewis. Since then we have studied and been enriched by other systems and have had our horizons expanded by life, family, friends, students, and our guides. And yet, just as the sun and moon stay right with you on a long journey, Jane and Lewis are right here. Their systems and lives seem even more exemplary and supportive, their embrace of everyday life as the center of an eternal spiritual journey ever more inspiring and relevant.

Contents

Acknowledgments   xix

Introduction: The Dance of Life as an Ecstatic Conversation
with Everyday Reality   xxi

Part One:
Psychic Skills for Life and Relationships 1

CHAPTER 1: Openness, Playfulness, and Curiosity:
The Attitudes That Work Best   3

CHAPTER 2: Perceiving Energy   5

Perceiving Emotions   7

    EXERCISE 1: Noticing Your Emotions   7

    EXERCISE 2: Exploring How You Know What Your
      Emotions Are   7

    EXERCISE 3: Seeing, Hearing, and Feeling an Emotion   8

Om   9

    EXERCISE 4: Experiencing the Energy of Om   10

Neutral Earth and Cosmic Energy   10

    EXERCISE 5: Experiencing Golden Cosmic Energy   11

    EXERCISE 6: Experiencing Green Earth Energy   12

CHAPTER 3: Whose Energy Is It? An Elegant Path to a
New Kind of Authenticity   15

Distinct Energy   17

    EXERCISE 7: Comparing Your Energy with Someone
      You Respect Enormously   18

Is It Your Energy?   19

    EXERCISE 8: Comparing Your Energy with
      Different Consciousnesses   19

Be Respectful and Gentle with Your and Other People's Energy 21

Collecting Your Energy and Sorting Out Others' 21
  Separating from Energy Enmeshment with a Parent 22
    EXERCISE 9: Discerning Your Father's Energy 22
  Two Basic Methods for Separating Energy 23
    EXERCISE 10: Separating Your Energy from Your Father's 23
    EXERCISE 11: Giving Your Mother a Rose 25

Advanced Energy Concepts 29
  Boundaries 32
  You Are Not a Mere Victim 33
  Matching Energies 34

No Matter Where You Go, There You Are 36
    EXERCISE 12: Pulling Your Energy Out of Someone's Space 36

Exploring Pain 37
    EXERCISE 13: Separating Pain Energy 38

CHAPTER 4: Pictures 41

Present Time or Current Time 42

Exploding Pictures 43
  The Tools and Process for Exploding Pictures 44
    EXERCISE 14: Exploding Pleasant and Unpleasant Pictures 45
  If You Find Exploding a Picture Too Abstract ... 47
    EXERCISE 15: Breathing Your Energy Out of a Pet-Peeve
    Picture 48
    EXERCISE 16: Dissolving the Picture of a Moderately
    Difficult Event 49

More on Pictures 50

CHAPTER 5: Grounding and the Center of the Head 55

Creating a Grounding Cord 58
    EXERCISE 17: Creating Your Grounding Cord 60
    EXERCISE 18: Quick Grounding 62
    EXERCISE 19: Creating a Mental Image of a Grounded You 63

Center of the Head 64
    EXERCISE 20: Finding the Center of Your Head 65

CHAPTER 6: The Energy of Biological Differences 67

The Divine Complexity of Women, the Divine Simplicity of Men,
and the Skills to Appreciate Both 67

Male and Female Grounding 69

Male Energy: An Elegant Simplicity 71
    EXERCISE 21: Creating a Male Grounding Cord 71

Female Energy: An Elegant Complexity 72
    EXERCISE 22: Creating a Female Grounding Cord 74
    EXERCISE 23: Intentionally Challenging Your Female
       Grounding 76

Discovering and Appreciating the Beauty and Strength of
Your Gender's Biological Energy 78
    EXERCISE 24: Acknowledging Your Exquisite Complexity 78
    EXERCISE 25: Acknowledging Your Exquisite Simplicity 79

Observing and Appreciating the Biological Energy of the
Other Gender 80
    EXERCISE 26: Acknowledging Your Female Complexity
       and Male Energy Simplicity 80
    EXERCISE 27: Acknowledging Your Male Simplicity and
       Female Energy Complexity 82

Two Drives: Responsibility and Supporting "Potential" 83

Male Grief and Female Guilt 87
    EXERCISE 28: Female Grounding for Male Grief in a
       Woman's Space 90
  Male Clarity 91
    EXERCISE 29: Cultivating Male Clarity 91
  Female Guilt 92
    EXERCISE 30: Female Guilt 93
  Male Rage 94
    EXERCISE 31: Male Rage 95

A Reminder: Explore These Ideas with a Playful Curiosity   96

Recap   97

CHAPTER 7: The Seven Major Western Chakras: Psychic Centers
of Awareness and Healing   99

Chakra Placement   102

Chakra Functions   104

    First Chakra: Grounding, Preservation, and Manifestation   104

    Second Chakra: Emotions, Boundaries, and Creativity   104

    Third Chakra: Success in Everyday Life, Understanding
      Self and Others   106

    Fourth Chakra: The Heart Chakra—Love and Affiliation   108

    Fifth Chakra: Communication, Listening, Inner Identity,
      and Telepathy   109

    Sixth Chakra: Beliefs, Clairvoyance, Center of the Head,
      and Neutrality   110

    Seventh Chakra: Knowingness, Seniority, and Connection
      with Your Path   111

    Feet Chakras: Grounded Mobility   112

    Hand Chakras: Healing and Communication   112

Opening and Empowering the Chakras   113

    EXERCISE 32: Opening and Empowering the Seven
      Major Chakras   116

Mantra Meditation   120

    EXERCISE 33: Mantra Meditation for Each Chakra   121

CHAPTER 8: Tools for Large-Scale Changes   123

Creating and Destroying Roses   124

    EXERCISE 34: Second Chakra—Creating and Destroying
      Roses   125

Vacuuming Energy   127

    EXERCISE 35: Fourth Chakra—Vacuuming Energies   127

*Grounding an Energy Out of Your Body and Aura with
Your Grounding Cord*   128

EXERCISE 36: Full Aura Clearing Using Your
Grounding Cord   129

Cords: Limitations on Communication and Autonomy   129

A Few Important Exceptions   134

Three Methods for Removing Cords   134

EXERCISE 37: Third Chakra—Removing Cords   135

The Power and Freedom of Healthy Boundaries   137

EXERCISE 38: Fifth Chakra—Exploding Roses,
Vacuuming Energy, and Removing Cords   138

More on Designing Your Daily Practice   138

CHAPTER 9: Opening to Life As It Is: Resistance and Neutrality   141

EXERCISE 39: Observe the Space of Anger, Happiness,
Impatience, and Love   143

EXERCISE 40: Comparing How Emotions Occupy Space   145

EXERCISE 41: Giving Your Mild Anger All the Space
It Naturally "Wants" to Unfold   146

EXERCISE 42: Observing If a Difficult Emotion
Is Compressed or Taking Its Space   147

EXERCISE 43: Noticing That You Are Not
Your Emotions   148

Resistance   149

EXERCISE 44: Dwelling on Someone or an Ideology
You Really Dislike   150

Seniority   151

EXERCISE 45: Seniority   152

Intentionally Lighting Yourself Up   152

EXERCISE 46: Intentionally Lighting Yourself Up   153

EXERCISE 47: Non-Judgmentalness: Letting Someone
Be Who He or She Is   154

Seeing All Experience as Sacred and Meaning-Filled   155

EXERCISE 48: Seeing Experience as Sacred and an
Opportunity to Grow   155

Two Approaches for Cultivating Neutrality: In-the-Body and
Out-of-Body   156
   In-the-Body Neutrality   156
      EXERCISE 49: A Golden Crown in Ten Seconds   157
      EXERCISE 50: Bringing Your Crown to Gold
        with a Clearing   157
      EXERCISE 51: Moving Something Further Away   157
      EXERCISE 52: Making Your Challenge Smaller   158
      EXERCISE 53: Changing the Color of a Challenge   159
   Going Out-of-Body to Gain Neutrality   160
      EXERCISE 54: Go to Your Crown or Just Above   160
      EXERCISE 55: Go Back Behind Yourself to View
        Something   161
      EXERCISE 56: Going Up into the Corner of the Room   162
      EXERCISE 57: Going to the Edge of the Universe   163

   Perfect Pictures   164

   Spiritual Freedom   166
      EXERCISE 58: Running the Colors of the Rainbow
        through Your Aura   167

Part Two:
The Mysticism of Everyday Life 171

CHAPTER 10: What Is the You That Creates Your Reality?   173

CHAPTER 11: Humanity Has Chosen to Have a
   Self-Reflective Ego   177

CHAPTER 12: What's New About the New Age? Enlightenment,
   Mastery, and the Spacious Ego   183
   The Value of Personality   185
   The Limitations of Enlightenment   187

CHAPTER 13: Rambunctious Multidirectional Time   193

CHAPTER 14: The Reincarnational Process and the
Eternal Validity of the Personality   199

    After Death   201

    The Co-Personality   202

CHAPTER 15: The Limitations of the Ego and the Assets
Available to It   207

CHAPTER 16: Desire and Trust   213

    If You Could Make Your Desires Come True   214

       EXERCISE 59: Imagine You Could Make Someone Love
       You According to Your Design   214

       EXERCISE 60: Consulting Inner Wisdom   216

    What to Trust   217

       Two Examples of the Imperfection of Intuition   217

       Getting Your Desires Is Not a Good Predictor
       of Happiness   220

CHAPTER 17: Creating Your Own Reality According
to Your Aura   221

CHAPTER 18: Matching Pictures and Unconditional
Responsibility   231

       EXERCISE 61: Brainstorm About Beliefs That Might
       Bring Seemingly Different Groups Together   234

       EXERCISE 62: Finding Matching Pictures by Revisiting
       an Unfair and Unpleasant Interaction   235

    Matching Picture Issues Don't Require Proportionality   236

    Accepting People as They Are   236

CHAPTER 19: Pain and Punishment   239

    Guilt and Pain   240

    Pain Doesn't Actually Originate in the External World   240

CHAPTER 20: Pleasure, Happiness, and Joy   243

    Happiness and Joy as Functions of Meaning   244

Joy   245

There Is Always a "You" That Is More Intrinsic   246

    EXERCISE 63: Finding Your Intrinsic You   247

    EXERCISE 64: Finding Meaning—Observe the Same
    Event from Two Perspectives   248

    EXERCISE 65: Brainstorming with Someone You Trust
    to Find Meaning in an Event   249

Finding the Larger Context of Experience   250

    EXERCISE 66: Finding Your Meaning Space About
    Three Inches Above Your Crown   250

    EXERCISE 67: Finding an Event's Essential
    Meaningfulness   251

    EXERCISE 68: Finding Happiness Through Meaning   252

Everything Is Full of Meaning   253

Part Three:
Practical Wisdom 255

CHAPTER 21: Internal Awareness: A Bridge to Change   257

Becoming Aware in Current Time   257

    EXERCISE 69: Noticing Your Breathing, Sensations,
    Emotions, and Thoughts in Current Time   257

    EXERCISE 70: Becoming Aware of Your Energy Field
    in Current Time   258

Becoming Aware in Past Time   259

    EXERCISE 71: Reconnecting with Your Past Thoughts,
    Feelings, and Sensations from Today   259

    EXERCISE 72: Reconnecting with Your Thoughts,
    Feelings, and Sensations from Your Distant Past   260

    EXERCISE 73: Reconnecting with Your Thoughts,
    Feelings, and Sensations from Various Times in
    Your Life   260

Monitoring Your Whole Aura: A Core Skill   261

EXERCISE 74: Observing Your Aura's Response to
Making One Change 262
EXERCISE 75: Observing the Effect of Anxiety on
Your Aura 263

*Becoming Aware of How Your Aura Changes in Specific
Situations* 264
EXERCISE 76: Pure Imagination—Be Angry About the
Weather 264
EXERCISE 77: Imagining How Someone Would Respond
and Your Own Internal Response 265

CHAPTER 22: Self-Talk and Stories: Conversation vs. Commands 269
EXERCISE 78: What Is Your Self-Talk Telling You? 270
EXERCISE 79: Exploring Your Self-Talk Regarding
Parents or In-Laws 271

Stories Are How We Tie Our Self-Talk Together 271
Stories Organize the Energy Field of the Personal Aura
What Happens to the Personal Aura When Someone,
Gritting Their Teeth, Says, "I Am Loving, I Am Loving,
I Am Loving…"? 274
Two Kinds of Stories: Feeling Tone and Self-Talk 274
Indulging Self-Righteousness for a Moment 274

Stories Are the Gatekeeper 276
EXERCISE 80: Finding Feeling Tones 277
EXERCISE 81: Explore the Standard Interpretations You
Believe About Life 277
EXERCISE 82: Exploring and Changing Your Inner
Landscape 278

CHAPTER 23: Anger 281
Becoming Skillful with Anger 281
More on the Mechanics of Anger 283
EXERCISE 83: Breaking Your Grounding to Explore
Ungrounded Anger 285

EXERCISE 84: Exploring Second-Chakra Enmeshment
and Anger   286
EXERCISE 85: Finding Hidden Anger and Resentment—
Throwing Purple Light at Something to Light It Up   287
EXERCISE 86: Clearing Anger and Resentment from
Your Spleen and Liver   287

Compressed Emotions: "I'm So Over It!"   288
EXERCISE 87: Freeing Hidden and Compressed Emotions   289

Conscious Breathing   290
EXERCISE 88: Counting Your Breath to Reduce
Stress Quickly   290
EXERCISE 89: Counting Your Breath Extended
Meditation   290

CHAPTER 24: Self-Evaluation   293

You Engage the World, Making the Best Choices You Can Make   293

Mistakes   295
EXERCISE 90: Accepting a Personal Mistake and
Exploring Its Meaning   295
EXERCISE 91: Clearing Punishment Energy Out of
Your Aura   297

CHAPTER 25: Difficult Conversations   299

A Paradoxical Goal   300
EXERCISE 92: Exploring Your Anger at Not Getting
What You Felt Entitled To   300
EXERCISE 93: Exploring Why Someone Behaved As
They Did   302
EXERCISE 94: Bring into Current Time a Specific,
Subtle Energy Related to Desire—Turning Off
Your Perfect-Picture Energy   303

Chapter 26: Affirmation and Visualization   307

Chapter 27: Manifestation   309

      EXERCISE 95: Letting a Goal Light You Up So You
         Can Clear Pictures   309

      EXERCISE 96: Sorting Out Energies from Your Goal   310

      EXERCISE 97: Vibrating Your Goal Throughout
         Your Aura   310

      EXERCISE 98: Releasing Your Goal into the Dreamstate
         for Manifestation   311

Chapter 28: A Good Life   315

Notes   321

Index   333

About the Authors   347

Illustrations

Figure 1: Grounding and Meditation Posture   59

Figure 2: The Center of the Head   64

Figure 3: Female Grounding   74

Figure 4: The Seven Major Western Chakras   101

Figure 5: The Seven Planes of Consciousness   195

Acknowledgments

In great appreciation we'd like to thank ...
Our guides whose voices we hope form the foundation of this book, our deepest gratitude.

The two people without whom this book wouldn't have been written: Richard Grossinger and JoAnn Wess. Richard Grossinger for his belief in this work, his invitation to John to write this book, and important early criticism. JoAnn Wess for her laughter and copious transcribing.

With deep gratitude to our project editor Hisae Matsuda for her gentle patience and expertise, and copyeditor Kathy Glass for her penetrating, restrained, and effective editing. All the knowledgeable and caring folks at North Atlantic Books.

To all our students and clients who have been so adventurous, courageous, helpful, and encouraging. We continue to learn from you every day. To Gilbert, Deborah Cowan, Brian Greminger, Carole and Russ Smiley, and Violeta Viviano for their tremendous behind-the-scenes expertise, love, and support.

From Gloria: With love and appreciation to my husband, Gilbert, for his tireless support of all phases of this work and our shared spiritual journey, thank you. With love to my children, Narayan and Sarah, for their computer wizardry, beautiful humor, and loving encouragement. To my parents and my brother Patrick, who taught me generosity and that life is an adventure. And to my treasured friends of the Cincinnati Practice Group for sharing many years of laughter, tears, playfulness, and courage in exploring the unknown together, thank you.

From John: With love to my partner in every way, my wife Pamela. To my dear departed friend and collaborator, Dennis Drake, and my other principal collaborators, Art Giser and Linda Saurenmann, to the friends and students who have supported me and shared our joint explorations, deep gratitude. To my parents who taught me unconditional responsibility, and to my brothers, Shlomo and Charlie, who have always been there for me.

And to you, adventurous readers, for sharing your spiritual journey with us. Thank you.

The Dance of Life as an Ecstatic Conversation with Everyday Reality

"Darn, I had thought that being psychic meant you had a voice that gave you all the right answers."

—A student

Desire has such wild yet subtle creativity that when you engage it with courage and unconditional responsibility, it leads you from the surface of your longing to the depths of meaning.

In *Psychic Psychology* we embrace the uniquely personal, joyous, and meaningful events of everyday life and relationships. As humans, we are enticed into the psychological life of everyday life and relationships through our desires, and in psychic psychology we welcome our desires as a divine attraction, neatly and sometimes not so neatly drawing us into all the adventures and lessons of human life. Still, reliable happiness does not come from the fulfillment of desires, it comes from the richness that can only result from real-life experience. Everyday life presents us with a dazzling array of subtle and specific interactions that offer spiritual, even mystical, opportunities to develop happiness, kindness, and generosity. Souls incarnate as humans because the sharp focus of space, time, and desire generates experiences, meaning, and understanding that the soul cannot generate by itself in its own higher soul plane. In time and space we enter into conversation with our desires, our own humanity, with others, and with the world. This conversation is ineradicably open-ended. Life constantly surprises us, and whether it delights or disappoints, it always offers back more than we knew or could have known before encountering it.

Many excellent systems give psychic/spiritual advice on how to attain your desires. Psychic psychology brings the powers and pleasures of psychic awareness into your life so you can use your ever-growing awareness effectively. In this book we explore and use a system whereby when our desires are congruent and we create the aura space for those desires, we obtain our goals. However, though most of us tend to imagine that great power will inevitably lead to the fulfillment of our desires and therefore to happiness, life is too rich and deep to be tamed or solved by any technique.

Like all spiritual/mystical paths, this one involves paradox. Without paradox you could program your life into a computer. You would speak and the world would obey. It's the open-endedness of paradox that generates a never-ending conversation in which you bring newness to the world and it brings newness to you. Two paradoxes in particular are important. The first one we've been alluding to already. Our desires are the passageway to embracing life, but reliable happiness comes from much deeper sources than satisfying our desires. Life is so unstoppably creative and spontaneous that following our desires inevitably takes us in unexpected directions.

For example, all of us know that we have longed for things that in retrospect didn't make us happy, or that would have brought pain if we'd gotten that desire; yet most of us think that we now know what will make us really happy. In a way, we are all like adolescents in our desires. An adolescent lacks the experience to even imagine what love is or to understand that it doesn't just drop out of the sky; love develops over the span of years and through the power of committed engagement with ourselves and the loved one. Since by its very nature desire anticipates experience, there is inevitably a naiveté and shallowness in our desires compared to the depth of experience and transformation that the pursuit of our desires can bring. In this book, we explore powerful means of finding what is authentic and true in our desires, yet even so, it is a good idea to be open to the unexpected directions that desire inevitably takes.

The second centrally important paradox is this: you create your reality but cannot absolutely control it, no matter how powerful or aligned you become. The external world has a life of its own; when we engage it, it engages us back with spontaneity, creativity, and surprise. Our inability to pin down the external world is part of the very fabric of reality and meaning of existence. Were it otherwise, there would be nothing to be gained by life experience. It would be a puzzle to be solved that would quickly become as predictable as tic tac toe, and as deadly as the life King Midas discovered when he turned everything he touched into gold, even his daughter. Reality's intrinsic uncontrollability is an essential precept of wisdom teachings from ancient Taoism and Buddhism right down to the modern Seth, originator of the phrase "You create your own reality."

The price we pay for being in a world we create but do not control is that life inevitably involves an interplay of pleasure and pain. We can learn to engage the dance of pleasure and pain with practical skills like those taught in this book. Such skills allow us to engage the world capably, achieving more of our goals. Still, there is something even more fundamental, more core than competency. All life expands in all directions; everything is ultimately redeemed in an underlying unobstructed and sublime awareness (technically called nondual awareness). It is the nature of desire to *resist* change so that we can rest eternally in the pleasure we anticipate such desire will bring, but it is the purpose of desire to *engage* us in the unceasing change of life expanding in all directions. What is most essential is learning to engage life with a courageous open-heartedness that welcomes unbridled creativity and generates happiness.

There are many paths to that open-hearted happiness. The path we explore in this book focuses on skillfully engaging everyday life and relationships through a combination of psychic skills, understanding the big picture, and practical wisdom. Psychic psychology approaches everyday life and relationships through a fun, exciting, and easily learned system of psychic development that is uniquely psychological and relationship-based. But being psychic is not enough by itself to generate life and relationship skills. Thus there are two other equally important aspects of life covered in this book which, when integrated with psychic skills, do reliably generate life and relationship skills, and more fundamentally, do reliably generate happiness. These other two aspects are: 1) the "big picture," or understanding our place in the world and the purpose of desire and life experience itself; and 2) practical wisdom, or the ability to engage complex real-life situations that have no single right answer.

Part One of this book explains how to develop psychic abilities that are particularly focused on everyday life and relationships. The psychic skills we each develop can enhance our own psychological well-being. Using these skills we become more self-aware, authentic, kind, and generous, and more understanding of others.

Two simple kinds of awareness are the basis from which a rich assortment of psychic skills grows. First you learn to sense psychic energy, something surprisingly easy for most people. In particular, you learn to sense what energy is yours and what energy is another's. It is true that underneath all manifestation there is a fundamental unity, so from that point of view there is just the one energy of All That Is. But within manifestation, that is, within your life as a human, life's purpose is to learn how to engage the utter uniqueness of all the manifested world, particularly that of each human being. As a psychic you can explore your uniqueness by identifying and learning to use the energy that is uniquely yours. That unique energy has an intrinsic directionality, that is, a desire or impulse towards action in your unique authentic direction. When you act skillfully using your own energy, you move and act naturally and spontaneously. Acting naturally and spontaneously out of your intrinsic uniqueness is "authenticity."

The second kind of awareness or psychic skill out of which all others emerge is the skill called "being in current time" or simply "current time." Ideally, moment by moment, your aura is free to vibrate through the entire range of human actions, emotions, and thoughts and thus respond to whatever you turn your attention to. However, in any given moment there is a tendency for portions of your aura to be stuck in past reactions to life. Where the aura is stuck it vibrates in an unresponsive fixed pattern called a picture. Having stuck pictures in your aura is much like having a muscle with a cramp in it or a guitar string with knots tied in it; the stuckness limits your ability to be open to, active in, and responsive to the present. Your ability to have new experiences is degraded. This book teaches a powerful method for psychically releasing the stuckness so you become more open to the present.

Once you learn to recognize your own energy (which generates authenticity) and learn how to free your aura of pictures (which allows you to be open to whatever is happening now), a world of powerful psychic abilities opens up.

Part Two of this book explores the big picture: how you create your reality, the purpose of human experience, and how to find happiness. Some traditions address the uncontrollability of the external world by trying to rise above desire. While rising above desire can reliably generate a kind of happiness, we the authors are committed to a path of engaging the world through our humanity and our relationships. Desires particularize experience and trigger the spontaneous creativity and surprise inherent in life. Desire is the way one commits to life.

The second part explores what creating your reality means, what you can and cannot do, and where desire fits in. Here is discussed the surprising fact that not only your soul but also your personality is eternal. One needs to look in a usually unexplored psychic direction to see that the personality survives and continues to grow into finding its own sublime and unobstructed consciousness. The personality isn't lost in further incarnations, though further incarnations usually happen; nor is the personality gobbled up by the soul. As illustrated in Chapter 14 through the experience of John's deceased friend Will, a personality grows and powerfully transforms, yet retains what seems most precious and individual. Understanding that the personality continues and grows eternally after this life, and understanding the personality's eternal relationship with the soul, helps us comprehend the sometimes-mysterious complexity of desire. We close Part Two by exploring the nature of happiness—what it is and how to attain it.

Part Three delves into practical wisdom, sometimes called knowhow. We can use psychic abilities and techniques to help us create the reality we want, but every day moments defy formulation. What do you do when your spouse says you're spending too much money? We explore how to use all you've learned to have a meaningful discussion when neither of you are probably at your best. You're both probably vying to prove your point rather than deeply engaging your own concerns and those of your partner. Practical wisdom is the ability to address the tension inherent in the dance of polarities that underlies all manifestation, even to use that tension as a vital part of the unbridled creativity of all life. Yes, there is an intrinsic underlying harmony to all of the universe, but too many of us try to repress the irrepressible other voice that lies outside our ego self. With practical wisdom we move from trying to repress the external world so that it adds nothing of its own, to engaging the spontaneous creativity of All That Is.

Part Three, then, offers practical skills such as: how to relate to and work skillfully with anger, how to integrate the insights of psychology and communication theory with psychic abilities, and how to pursue your goals in ways that enhance your overall clarity, kindness, and generosity.

Hindu iconography portrays life as an ecstatic, chaotic dance. The world of psychic psychology takes us directly into a skillful engagement with this dance. Engaging this dance is the most authentic of spiritual journeys. Our spiritual state grows through and is most powerfully reflected in our responses to everyday life—a baby crying, the demands of work, an unexpected promotion, a parent's death, a wedding, heavy traffic, grocery shopping, a baby laughing. If the everyday life of a human weren't deeply meaningful and enriching, we would never incarnate in the first place. The opportunity to know oneself more authentically and more joyfully is present in every breath.

Our goal is to engage life with practical wisdom and a sense of adventure, to know that life is a spiritual journey, and to know that each of us (and no other) holds the key to our own happiness. Seeing life as an adventure and staying open through its ups and downs with authenticity, practical wisdom, kindness, and generosity is a reliable way to cultivate happiness.

Part One

Psychic Skills for Life and Relationships

CHAPTER I

Openness, Playfulness, and Curiosity: The Attitudes That Work Best

Learning to be more psychic can be a lot of fun. Perhaps you are experienced and already using your psychic abilities. We hope this material helps you put it all together and to best utilize your abilities for communication and self-change. Perhaps you are an experienced meditator, yet unfamiliar with a system of development centered in everyday life, especially in relationships and boundaries between people. Over time you can use these techniques to deepen your ability to engage real-life situations, not just with kindness and generosity, but with an authentic recognition of differences as well as similarities between you and others. You can also increasingly recognize your own personal energy, both the energies you approve of and the energies you might wish, sooner or later, to transform. Engaging all your energies adds a physical and emotional vitality that really opens your relationship with life as it is. Perhaps you are new to this material or "not very psychic." We have endeavored to present the material so that you can learn it by yourself at your own pace.

The three words *openness, playfulness,* and *curiosity* help convey the attitude most beneficial both for your developing psychic perception and your encounters with daily life. To develop psychic perception, it is useful to cultivate an open, relaxed, adventurous, and playful attitude. Such an attitude helps you pay attention to a wider spectrum of sensations, emotions, and thoughts than you do when you narrow your attention with stress. You can learn to focus without shutting off the wide spectrum of awareness that opens you to the spontaneity of psychic perception. This focus with an open, relaxed, and adventurous mind is what we refer to as "playfulness" or "amusement."

When you are stressed or very sad, you may find it difficult or impossible to be playful. Even then, you can be as open as possible to all aspects of the moment by cultivating a curiosity and even a reverence for your experience.

Throughout this book, we will often suggest that you "acknowledge" your experience as you explore the various exercises—meaning that you take a moment to attend to your perceptions, emotions, and thoughts, letting go of resistance or judgment. This helps you assimilate all experience for subsequent use.

Please have fun, proceed at a comfortable speed, and be open to letting your experience unfold at its own natural pace.

CHAPTER 2

Perceiving Energy

This chapter features a progression of exercises to help you learn to perceive and utilize the energy of your personal aura. Some readers already know how to work with aura energy and will breeze through this chapter. Many new practitioners will learn to perceive and utilize energy fairly directly and easily, while other people will require more time to learn. Regardless of your current skill level, you'll find it most effective to be open and patient with your progress.

The process of learning to perceive energy is more like the subjective experience of falling in love than the objective experience of solving an algebra problem. The awareness of both falling in love and perceiving energy emerge over time. The initial sense of either falling in love or becoming psychically aware can seem slight and ambiguous. "Do I love her or him?" It's best not to jump to a hasty conclusion about love but to continue to explore the relationship; and so it is with psychic perception.

There are two parts of the brain involved in engaging the process of psychic perception: 1) the part that facilitates your feelings, and 2) the part that facilitates your imagination. The ability to perceive energy rises from the same part of the brain you use to check your feelings. The ability to do something with the energy you perceive—to move energy, e.g. to clear obstructions in your energy—rises from the same part of the brain used as your imagination. Neither of these parts (emotional and imaginative) are areas of the brain that most of us were taught to use to find answers in school. So some (but by no means all) highly educated people (or, as John refers to himself, *overly* educated) require time and practice to learn how to perceive energy.

The exercises in this book will help you perceive and utilize psychic energy, whether you find it easy or challenging. We see that a large percentage of people start to perceive energy at some point while practicing the first ten exercises. Please practice each exercise several times. Find your own rhythm. If you perceive the relevant energies easily, you may choose to fly though the exercises. Some people will require more time. You can choose to go through the exercises more slowly, picking one or two to practice in depth for a week or two.

A few people will still doubt their perceptions after practicing slowly for a few weeks. If this is your experience, here are several suggested options:

- You can continue practicing patiently. Most people find that with regular practice their perceptions grow, though perhaps more slowly than they'd like.
- You can focus on the more conventional ancient meditation exercises. The advantage of the ancient meditations is that they give you something to concentrate on that doesn't already require perceptual abilities. Even for the highly educated person who might be locked into trying to use an incompatible part of the brain for psychic perception, a month to several months of traditional meditation practice will teach you how to open the psychic part of your brain and nervous system as a whole. Useful ancient meditations are contained in Exercise 4, "Experiencing the Energy of Om"; Exercise 33, "Mantra Meditation for Each Chakra"; and Exercise 89, "Counting Your Breath Extended Meditation." (To practice the Mantra Meditation, please read the accompanying text and Chapter 7 on the chakras. It would be worthwhile to have read the earlier material also.)
- Another suggestion for extra help is to listen to the seven-CD companion set to this book, *Psychic Psychology: Practicing Your Energy Skills for Life and Relationships*, which explains the system (with a slightly different emphasis). It also contains guided meditations that many people find helpful in developing the necessary perception.

- You may also want to read our first book, *Basic Psychic Development: A User's Guide to Auras, Chakras & Clairvoyance* (Samuel Weiser, Inc., 1999), which offers extensive exercises on building perception.

Perceiving Emotions

The following three exercises explore perceiving your emotions, which may seem so simple that you could easily miss the point. But it is from just these kinds of beginnings that the most powerful abilities will grow. The first exercise is to simply notice your feelings in the moment.

EXERCISE 1: Noticing Your Emotions

1. Sit comfortably straight in your chair, feet flat on the floor, arms and legs uncrossed.
2. With a sense of openness, relax, close your eyes, and breathe gently into your belly.
3. Look within and notice what you feel emotionally: happy, sad, eager—whatever your emotions are, just notice.
4. What steps take place? Is your recognition instantaneous or does it take time?
5. Take a few refreshing breaths and, when you are ready, stand up and gently stretch.
6. You may find it useful to make some notes of your experience.

EXERCISE 2: Exploring How You Know What Your Emotions Are

The next exercise is more subtle. It's actually quite abstract, so if you find it too subtle, simply move on to the next exercise, and come back to this one at another time.

1. Sit comfortably straight in your chair, feet flat on the floor, arms and legs uncrossed.
2. With a sense of openness, relax, close your eyes, and breathe gently into your belly.

3. Look within and explore the question, "How do I know what my emotions are?"

4. See if you can detect how you know what your emotions are. Where do you put your attention? What steps take place? Is your recognition instantaneous or does it take time?

5. Take a few refreshing breaths and, when you are ready, stand up and gently stretch.

6. You may find it useful to make some notes of your experience.

Noticing emotions is not a deep or mystical experience, nor is the evaluation of your internal feelings something you could prove to a skeptical outsider. When you perceive energy you will be utilizing the same awareness you already use to notice your emotions.

In noticing energy your sense will usually be a feeling, a sound, a visual image, or a simple knowing—all unprovable. The meaning you attribute to your sense of energy will, like the meanings you attach to your emotions, be useful or not, depending upon your maturity, judgment, and training such as you'll learn in this book. The next exercise may again seem so easy that it could appear you accomplished little, yet again, it is from just these kinds of distinctions that powerful abilities grow.

EXERCISE 3: Seeing, Hearing, and Feeling an Emotion

Choose an emotion you'd like to explore. Then imagine that it has a shape in your body, and even outside your body. Imagine you can see the emotion, letting your imagination display or somehow indicate what color(s) it would have, and then do the same with sound and kinesthetic sensation/feeling. For example, if you choose anger, check to "see" where the anger seems to be in or around your body. What would be its shape? Is it hot or cold? Different people will often prefer different sensory systems, usually visual, tactile, or auditory. A person might "feel" the energy clearly but see or hear little. Many find they naturally use some combination of those three. If you've never done this before, you may be surprised at how easy it is.

1. Sit comfortably straight in your chair, feet flat on the floor, arms and legs uncrossed.
2. With a sense of openness, relax, close your eyes, and breathe gently into your belly.
3. Choose an emotion that you are now feeling to explore.
4. Look within and "see" where you find your emotion in or around your body.
5. Notice its visual characteristics such as shape, size and/or color.
6. Next, listen within and hear where your emotion resonates in or around your body.
7. Notice its auditory characteristics such as tone, loudness, disharmony, or harmony.
8. Sense where you feel your emotion in or around your body.
9. Notice its tactile characteristics such as temperature and texture.
10. Take a few refreshing breaths and, when you are ready, stand up and gently stretch.
11. You may find it useful to record some notes of your experience.

You may not yet know what to make of this information, but it is a good beginning to experiencing energy. The next three exercises are intended both to benefit you by improving the functioning of your aura and to help you continue familiarizing yourself with perceiving energies. Once you can perceive the difference in as few as two psychic energies, the entire world of psychic perception eventually opens up, even the most advanced levels.

Om

Most people reading this book will already be familiar with the lovely energy of the mantra "Om," known worldwide. It is the indescribable vibration of creation that underlies all existence. In the following exercise we encourage you to explore how you experience its vibration by repeating "Om" either aloud or silently to yourself and noticing its resonance and effects on your body, well-being, energy, and awareness.[1]

EXERCISE 4: Experiencing the Energy of Om

1. Sit comfortably straight in your chair, feet flat on the floor, legs and arms uncrossed.
2. With a sense of openness, relax, close your eyes, and breathe gently into your belly.
3. Repeat the mantra "Om" aloud or silently to yourself for 3 to 5 minutes.
4. As you rest in Om's embrace see, feel, or hear its vibration.
5. Notice where and how the energy resonates in your body, even beyond it, and how it affects your well-being, energy, and awareness.
6. Take a few refreshing breaths and, when you are ready, stand up and gently stretch.
7. You may find it useful to make some notes of your experience.

Neutral Earth and Cosmic Energy

In the beginning of your psychic work it's often easier to clear your aura using neutral energy rather than your own energy. The aura can be so congested with pain and programming that it can end up resisting your efforts. John's teacher, Lewis Bostwick, referred to this as "the body's resistance." Eventually, after you've cleared sufficiently, you will primarily run your own energy, but you'll also continue to utilize some neutral energies. Everything is composed of multiple energies, and since the body is part of the Earth and solar system it requires a certain amount of earth and cosmic energies in its normal functioning.

All consciousness, all energy, has its own unique directionality, which is constantly growing and changing. The large consciousnesses that we call neutral energy have such an expansive directionality that it doesn't impinge on any human in a way that changes his or her choices in directionality. Thus, these neutral energies are supportive, perhaps especially for the physical body, but they are neutral in the sense that they impart no directionality to our choices.

The following two exercises allow you to familiarize yourself with the two powerful and unconditionally supportive energies that you will work (and play) with throughout this book: neutral golden cosmic energy and neutral green earth energy. For comparative purposes, it is helpful to do the exercises back to back. We'll begin with neutral golden cosmic energy.

EXERCISE 5: Experiencing Golden Cosmic Energy

To bring cosmic energy into your body, imagine a stream of lovely golden cosmic energy (also called golden sun energy) from well above your head, gently flowing down through the top of your head (hereinafter referred to as the crown chakra—see Figure 4, "The Seven Major Western Chakras," page 101), down through your neck, throughout your body, and out into your entire aura. Then you'll rest in its nurturing energy for a short while, noticing all that you can sense about it. You can continue to bring more cosmic energy in from time to time as you feel like doing so.

Since you will be bringing energy into the body you'll want to be sure to release any excess, so at the conclusion of the exercise you'll *reverse polarities*, which means you'll bend forward at the waist, allowing any excess energy to flow out of your crown chakra and arms into the earth.

1. Sit comfortably straight in your chair, feet flat on the floor, legs and arms uncrossed.
2. With a sense of openness, relax, close your eyes, and breathe gently into your belly.
3. When ready invite a stream of loving golden cosmic energy to gently flow down from well above your head into your crown chakra, then throughout your entire body and aura.[2]
4. Continue replenishing for 3 to 5 minutes.
5. Notice if you can see, feel, hear, imagine, or sense its energy in some manner.
6. Take a few refreshing breaths and, when you are ready, stand up and gently stretch.
7. Reverse polarities: Slowly bend over at the waist and release any excess energy from your head and arms into the earth.
8. You may find it useful to make some notes of your experience.

EXERCISE 6: Experiencing Green Earth Energy

To familiarize yourself with neutral earth energy, invite unconditionally loving, neutral green earth energy to simply flow up from the very center of the Earth, up through your feet and legs, then throughout your entire body and aura. As with the golden cosmic energy, simply rest in its supportive energy for several minutes, noticing all that you can sense about it.

1. Sit comfortably straight in your chair, feet flat on the floor, legs and arms uncrossed.
2. With a sense of openness, relax, close your eyes, and breathe gently into your belly.
3. When ready, invite unconditionally loving, neutral green earth energy to flow up from the very center of the earth, gently up through your feet and legs, gently into and throughout your entire body and aura.
4. Continue to replenish with green earth energy.
5. Rest in Mother Earth's gentle nurturance for 3 to 5 minutes.
6. Notice if you can see, feel, hear, imagine, or sense this energy in some manner.
7. After you have experienced the earth energy, take a few moments to contemplate your experience of the golden cosmic energy and compare and contrast the two.
8. Thank your body for being willing to explore.
9. Take a few refreshing breaths and, when you are ready, stand up and gently stretch.
10. Reverse polarities: Slowly bend over at the waist and release any excess energy from your head and arms into the earth.
11. You may find it useful to make some notes of your experience.

Often it isn't until people compare earth and cosmic energies that they can acknowledge that they are beginning to discern energies. If you are not yet certain that you've perceived energy, you might look for any way that you may feel different: perhaps more open to your experience, more curious, or more refreshed. Sometimes the first indication of your growing perception is a simple recognition that you have somehow changed, even if you cannot articulate exactly how.

CHAPTER 3

Whose Energy Is It? An Elegant Path to a New Kind of Authenticity

In August of 1972, John returned to law school after finishing his summer job. He walked into the ashram (a meditation-focused yoga community) where he lived during the school year and was immediately greeted by his fellow residents with "Wait until you read the Seth books that Will has!" Everyone in the house seemed to have read and become excited by these new books delivered by Seth, an especially high and wise being who spoke through his medium, Jane Roberts. John immediately read the two Seth books that were in publication and was galvanized by them, as were large parts of the community of spiritual seekers both within his organization and beyond. The Seth books overturned, with a convincing clarity, much of what had been the conventional spiritual wisdom.

After reading the books, John wrote to Jane Roberts and received permission to attend one of her classes. John had already traveled to India seeking wisdom; he was eager to sit at Seth's knee, as it were, and be instructed in the right path of life. At the time John was wavering in his desire to be a lawyer and was considering becoming a psychologist instead. He expected, and was eager to be told by Seth, which choice was better. So the following February John skipped his law classes and attended one of the Tuesday night Seth classes given by Jane Roberts in her home in Elmira, New York.

The Seth class was very exciting, with maybe twenty people gathered around Jane, who sat in her rocking chair. The class members chatted about some of Seth's writings and how they applied to their lives. From time to time Jane would take off her glasses and change her posture, and out would come Seth's booming voice teaching with a confident, astonishingly articulate, and intelligent insight. For any person with meditation experience, it was clear from the energy vibration that filled the room when Seth channeled through Jane that the class was talking with a "different energy personality," a phrase Seth uses to describe himself in his books. His wonderful, powerful energy filled the room.

John was convinced both from Seth's writings and his distinctive energy that Seth was a "master," so when John had his first opportunity, he asked Seth what to do—practice law or study psychology. Seth immediately responded with exuberant good humor and kindness, "If you knew me better, you would not ask that question." Seth went on to explain that John's life had its own purpose; it was important that he, John, make his own choices and that he, Seth, not steal John's opportunity to make choices and sometimes mistakes, even serious mistakes. Only then would John learn how to engage the energies and experiences of his unique and personal everyday life.

In 1973 Seth's position was a radical one. The books and other authorities that John and his friends consulted, of both an Eastern and Western orientation, all seemed to stress the importance of rising above the fallibility of personal choices. They communicated that the correct answer for every occasion lay with obtaining cosmic consciousness or masterhood; and they conveyed the importance of consulting a master so you could avoid error and rise above your fallibility to eventually become a master yourself. Later, when he moved near Elmira to study long-term with Seth, John came to understand that Seth was blending spiritual or psychic skills and insights in a fundamentally new way.

Seth centered the human spiritual journey in the human personal reality. He explained an energetic universe in which every part is sacred and meaningful; in which the meaning and path of your personal self is to encounter and engage the personal, the psychological. Of course, each of us is part of greater wholes or energy gestalts, and those greater energy gestalts are sacred and meaningful too. But for Seth, the personal is just as sacred, just as eternal (see Part Two, Chapters 10 through 20), and is only accessible through an authentic engagement with what is personal and unique in us.

Distinct Energy

The uniqueness that Seth so values in each individual's personal experience is visible as identifiably distinctive energies in one's personal aura. The distinctiveness arises from a threefold collaboration among All That Is, your soul, and your personality.

This threefold collaboration set up your incarnation such that these three aspects of you can experience the universe from the unique point of view of your personality. (The way the personality originates and contributes to setting up the incarnation itself is explained in Chapter 14, "The Reincarnational Process and the Eternal Validity of the Personality.") That unique point of view arises and plays out in each person's aura. The interplay of those three generate a unique quality that expands eternally, and which throughout your life gives a personal and distinct quality to the natural energy of your aura. It is true that the particular kind of uniqueness and separateness that is experienced in the human personality is only applicable at the outer level of human consciousness where normal perception operates. At deep inner levels, humans are interconnected with one another and with other consciousnesses, larger and smaller. Human personal consciousness, as generated and experienced in one's personal aura, could not stand without that interdependence with other consciousnesses. Nevertheless, the cultivation of human uniqueness is a major part of the business and joy of being human, and that uniqueness is written in the distinctiveness of your own personal aura energy as compared to anyone else's energy.

When your life rises out of your natural energy, you'll engage it authentically—not perfectly, but authentically. You'll be in your natural flow. Your authentic energy is uniquely yours; it contains your information and holds the key to your next step. So, if you were to use someone else's energy—no matter how powerful, elegant, or loving—you would not actually be in your authentic flow or *dharma*. This psychic approach, probably drawn from Western mystical traditions but developed in a new way, we think, by Lewis Bostwick, has a surprising implication. For the personal aura, it isn't a question of whether an energy is good or bad, just is it yours or not. If it's yours, it will naturally direct you towards what is true for you, and if it is not your energy, even if it is a saint's, it will not serve as a long-term fuel for your growth. When you are lost and mired in other people's energy, the saint's might help you reconnect with your own, but for the long term, only your own energy will do. (In energy ranges below or above the personal aura, which are not the subject of this book, the question of better or worse reemerges.)

EXERCISE 7: Comparing Your Energy with Someone
You Respect Enormously

In this exercise choose someone you respect enormously in order to experience his or her supportive energy, as well as to compare his or her energy with your own. Two of our favorites are His Holiness the 14th Dalai Lama and the Hugging Saint Ammachi, Mata Amritanandamayi Devi. We choose them because we cannot imagine anyone being more wonderful. Yet, in the final analysis, even the Dalai Lama's and Ammachi's energy is no long-term substitute for your own.

1. Sit comfortably straight in your chair, feet flat on the floor, legs and arms uncrossed.
2. With a sense of openness, relax, close your eyes, and breathe gently into your belly.
3. Allow your awareness to rest lightly behind your eyes.
4. Being mindful to maintain a respectful boundary, invite the energy of the person you respect enormously to surround you and permeate you.
5. Rest in that energy for 2 to 5 minutes; feel yourself unconditionally supported.
6. Next, notice how—even though his or her energy is unconditionally supportive of you and your journey—his or her energy does not contain your pertinent information or your authentic impulse. Therefore, while you can learn from the person you respect, in this system you would not run his or her energy in any significant way in your personal aura.
7. Thank the person you have chosen, and intend that his or her energy return to him or her.

8. Take a few refreshing breaths and when you are ready stand up, gently stretch, and reverse polarities.
9. You may find it useful to make some notes of your experience.

Is It Your Energy?

You might assume it would be easy to recognize your own energy. Often it is, but some of the energy in your personal aura can be someone else's, and occasionally it can be hard to tell. The process doesn't proceed step by step with clearly defined instructions. It isn't like putting together a toy airplane. It's more like learning to ride a bike; you learn by doing. With a little time and practice you find yourself getting better at discerning what energy is uniquely yours. While you're learning, you'll make mistakes. In most circumstances, when you turn your psychic awareness to the question of whose energy you're evaluating, you'll get an accurate answer, though sometimes you may be so accustomed to an energy that it can take years to recognize that it isn't you. In all circumstances it helps to have a sense of humor, to avoid taking yourself too seriously, and to cultivate some humility so that you recognize more quickly when you go off track.

Recognizing your energy, or any energy, calls for nuance. The following three exercises will help you begin to build a more nuanced awareness that will aid you in recognizing your unique energy and the distinctive characteristics of other energies.

EXERCISE 8: Comparing Your Energy with Different Consciousnesses

In the following meditation you'll explore the differences, one at a time, between your energy and five other consciousnesses. If your natural mode of perception is "seeing," begin by imaging each consciousness like a picture. If your natural mode of perception is "feeling," compare your energy at a feeling level. With a sense of play, explore the differences in as much detail as possible. Once you can discern three or four differences, simply let the image or feeling go.

1. Sit comfortably straight in your chair, feet flat on the floor, legs and arms uncrossed.
2. With a sense of openness, relax, close your eyes, and breathe gently into your belly.
3. Allow your awareness to rest lightly behind your eyes.
4. See or feel the difference between your energy and an inanimate object such as a rock or even your favorite car with as much detail as possible.
5. When you can discern three or four differences, simply let the image or feeling go.
6. See or feel the difference between your energy and a favorite tree with as much detail as possible.
7. When you can discern your energy from that of the tree, let that image or feeling go.
8. See or feel the difference between your energy and a particular animal—a particular dog, cat, or horse—with as much detail as possible.
9. When you can discern your energy from that particular pet, let the image or feeling go.
10. See or feel the difference between your energy and your best friend with as much detail as possible.
11. When you can discern your energy from your best friend's, let that image or feeling go.
12. See or feel the difference between your energy and an authority figure with as much detail as possible.
13. When you can discern your energy from the authority figure, let that image or feeling go.
14. Replenish your entire body and aura with a lovely golden cosmic energy.
15. Take a few refreshing breaths and when you are ready stand up, gently stretch, and reverse polarities.
16. You may find it useful to make some notes of your experience.

Be Respectful and Gentle with
Your and Other People's Energy

Until now you've explored your perception of energies and noted how various energies affect your body, aura, and sense of well-being. Next you will begin to explore the energies of relationship more intimately and develop a powerful healing skill: the ability to clarify your aura by moving other people's energy out of your space. Because you will engage and, in some sense, handle other people's energy, the skill calls for a nuanced awareness of boundaries and a respectful handling of the energies. As you explore your relationships and encounter their respective energies, please remember to treat your and others' energy with respect and gentleness. As always, cultivating an adventurous and playful attitude works the best.

Collecting Your Energy and Sorting Out Others'

There is no confusion in physical reality as to whose body is whose. Each person's physical body is stably separate. You don't wake up one morning with another person's arm on your body.

Your personal aura is sometimes called your *energy body*. It is similar in one way to your physical body and very different in another. Your energy body or personal aura is similar in that it has one central location: the bubble of energy that surrounds you. But unlike your physical body, portions of your energy body can leave your aura and get intermixed with other people's auras. When you are in resistance your energy crosses boundaries and gets stuck in other people's auras and vice versa.[1]

This movement of bits of your energy body into other people's auras and theirs into yours is problematic because every bit of personal aura energy has emotion and an impulse or directionality, i.e., intention of the person to whom it belongs. When you get enmeshed with another person, your energy, emotions, and intentions and their energy, emotions, and intentions get intermixed.

When this mixing takes place each person suffers two losses: 1) Each, when feeling and thinking, will experience the other's feelings and intentions as their own; and 2) Each loses access to the energy information that has left their own aura and entered the other person's (for as long as that energy remains outside the aura of the person to whom it belongs).

Part of your developmental task is to retrieve your energy from wherever you've left it, assimilate it, and bring your experience into current time. To illustrate what it means to collect your energy while releasing other people's we'll begin by exploring parental enmeshment. All of us still have at least some enmeshment with our parents or parental figures. It's natural, even inevitable, because they were your first models for engaging the world.

Regardless of the status of your current relationship with your parents—challenged or easy-going, whether they are living or deceased—the following three exercises will help you increase your ability to understand your relationship with your parents much more deeply.

Separating from Energy Enmeshment with a Parent

We suggest that you eventually do the following three exercises with all who play or have played parental roles in your life, but we'll begin with your father figure. In the first exercise you'll take a few moments to compare and contrast your energy with your father's.

EXERCISE 9: Discerning Your Father's Energy

1. Sit comfortably straight in your chair, feet flat on the floor, legs and arms uncrossed.
2. With a sense of openness, relax, close your eyes, and breathe gently into your belly.
3. Allow your awareness to rest lightly behind your eyes.
4. Imagine your father sitting about 20 feet in front of you.
5. See, feel, or imagine your father's energy and compare and contrast it with your own.
6. Replenish your body and aura by imagining yourself surrounded by a golden cosmic energy.
7. Take a few refreshing breaths and when you are ready stand up, gently stretch, and reverse polarities.

8. You may find it useful to make some notes of your experience.

For the following exercise continue to work with your father. Without having to intellectually understand the concept, you'll imagine that you can gently pull your energy out of his space and send it back to him.

There are two major ways that you might play with this: one is kinesthetically-feeling the energy; the other is clairvoyantly-seeing the energy. It can often be a combination, and there is no one right way to perceive and experience energies. All five senses can be used. See, feel, hear, taste, know, allow, or imagine. Acknowledge and affirm what seems to be your most natural approach.

Two Basic Methods for Separating Energy

Before proceeding to the next exercise please take a few moments to familiarize yourself with two basic methods for disentangling energy: breathing your energy back and seeing your energy return to you. Choose the technique that seems to work best for you in Exercise 9 above ("Discerning Your Father's Energy"). You can, of course, use both techniques if that seems natural for you. Many people do.

To breathe your energy back: First, imagine someone with whom you feel you have an enmeshment. Then inhale gently and breathe your energy back into your body and aura from their aura. With each exhalation, intend to gently release the person's energy from your body and aura to return to them. Repeat the process three or more times, or until you feel a comfortable separation.

To see your energy return to you: First, imagine someone in front of you with whom you feel you have an enmeshment. Next, see your energy as having a color or colors and call it back into your body and aura. And last, imagine his or her energy as having a color or colors and allow it to release from your aura and return to them. Repeat the process three or more times, or until you feel a comfortable separation.

EXERCISE 10: Separating Your Energy from Your Father's

If you are kinesthetic—meaning that you feel energy—or if you are not certain of your natural mode of perception, we suggest that you begin by working with your breath. Gently inhale your personal energy back from your father's aura, then gently exhale, letting his energy return to him. It may be subtle at first, but you'll probably feel something distinguishable about his energy as you compare and contrast it with your own. But even if you cannot sense his energy, you will probably notice a palpable difference in your own body and aura after releasing it—perhaps less stress, or simply a sensation of more space.

For those who are naturally clairvoyant: You might see your personal energy as color streaming back from your father to you, and see your father's energy as color streaming back to him. Take your time and notice how the energies look, how they are similar and different. You may even perceive multiple colors and textures. Look for something distinguishable about his energy, even if his energy and your energy appear as the same color. Two different energies can be the same color and still have subtle visual qualitative differences in sheen, saturation, texture, or other qualities. Even if you cannot see your father's energy very well, you may notice your own colors more vividly or discern a palpable difference in your body and aura—maybe less stress, or an awareness of more space.

Repeat for several rounds until you feel or recognize a difference in your energy. It usually takes at least three to seven rounds to sense a difference and a comfortable separation. Please keep an awareness of appropriate boundaries; be gentle and respectful with your own and your father's energy whether you have a great relationship with him or a challenging one.

1. Sit comfortably straight in your chair, feet flat on the floor, legs and arms uncrossed.
2. With a sense of adventure, relax, close your eyes, and breathe gently into your belly.
3. Allow your awareness to rest lightly behind your eyes.
4. Imagine that your father is sitting in a chair about 20 feet in front of you.

If you feel energy: Gently inhale your energy out of your father's space back to you, and as you exhale, gently and with respect send his energy back to him. Take your time, repeating for three or more rounds, or until you notice a shift. As you finish, thank your father.

Or if you see energy: See your personal energy gently streaming back from your father to you, and with a playful respect see his energy gently streaming from you back to him. Take your time, repeat for three or more rounds, or until you notice a shift. As you finish, thank your father.

5. Replenish your body and aura by imagining yourself surrounded by a golden cosmic energy.
6. Thank your body for being willing to change.
7. Take a few refreshing breaths and when you are ready stand up, gently stretch, and reverse polarities.
8. You may find it useful to make some notes of your experience.

EXERCISE 11: Giving Your Mother a Rose

Another very effective and charming technique for giving someone their energy back is to present it to them in a rose. Western mystics have used the rose symbol for thousands of years because of its rich archetypal value, somewhat similar to the way the lotus is treated in many contexts in the East. Throughout this system we use several variations of the rose as tools for meditation.

As part of the next exercise you will create a rose and empower it to "hold" energy for you. Your rose will provide a stage, a location for your vision or imagination, and give you the ability to move energy outside your aura to work with it as well as to perceive it more clearly. Please practice creating a rose briefly before proceeding to Exercise 11, "Giving Your Mother a Rose."

To create a rose: Imagine a rose in front of you 3 to 6 inches in diameter. Give it a color and as much detail as you can. Let it dissolve and repeat until you feel comfortable with the process. Next, create a rose and empower it with the ability to pull energy out of your aura and hold it for you. Let it dissolve, and repeat until you feel comfortable with the process.

For the following exercise you'll work with the relationship you have with your mother. You'll create two roses, one to hold your energy and the other to hold your mother's energy. Empower your rose with the ability to gently pull some of your energy out of your mother's space. Empower your mother's rose with the ability to pull some of her energy out of your aura, which you will then present to her.

Be playful and gentle. To begin, simply intend to bring a little bit of your energy back from your mother's aura, and simply intend to let go of her energy that you are ready to release at this time. Her energies that you are "ready to release" represent the part of your relationship with your mother that you are ready to bring into current time.

1. Sit comfortably straight in your chair, feet flat on the floor, legs and arms uncrossed.
2. With a sense of openness, relax, close your eyes, and breathe gently into your belly.
3. Allow your awareness to rest lightly behind your eyes.
4. Create a rose out in front of you to hold your energy.
5. Give your rose the ability to pull out some of your energy that you've left in your mother's aura—from this or any lifetime— and return it to your rose.
6. When nicely filled, set this rose off to your left about a foot and leave it there.
7. Create a rose out in front of you for your mother's energy.
8. Give it the ability to gently pull your mother's energy out of your aura—from this or any lifetime—and let this energy of hers fill the rose.
9. When filled, set it off to your right about a foot and leave it there.
10. Compare and contrast your rose with your mother's rose, allowing it to simply be what it is.
11. When ready, thank her and give your mother her rose.
12. Allow your rose to dissolve and your energy to simply come into your body and aura.
13. Thank your body for being willing to change.
14. Replenish your aura by imagining yourself filled with a golden cosmic energy.

15. Take a few refreshing breaths and when you are ready stand up, gently stretch, and reverse polarities.
16. You may find it useful to make some notes of your experience.

Usually the last two exercises raise several important questions. We have compiled here the ones most often asked.

"Aren't I being mean or ungrateful by giving someone their energy back?"
Though giving someone their energy back could be misconstrued as an insult, it is in fact quite advantageous to the other person. Remember, a person's energy is their natural authentic impulse. Each bit of their energy contains some useful and important information or impulse for them. Since a person's energy is their information about their authentic path, when they don't have their information, a part of them is missing, like a piece of a puzzle.

"Is taking my energy back selfish?"
One of the greatest gifts we can give someone is to honor his or her uniqueness and boundaries. Your energy, no matter how good, no matter how well intended, cannot work well in another person's space. It's the wrong fuel, an inauthentic source for their power, and inevitably eventually creates disruption of their own natural impulses.

A real-life illustration: Many clients' first call to us for a reading or healing work is not for themselves but arises out of concern for their child's health or mental well-being. Before addressing the child's issue, we first address the parent's energy, which is unfailingly active in their child's space and seeking a solution. The parent is always surprised to learn that when their loving concern—their worry—is in their child's space, their child rarely experiences this energy as a message of love but rather as a resounding message that the child is broken. This message of brokenness can generate depression, anxiety, and anger in the recipient.

Gloria: "John and I were talking recently about how much better my children 'look' when I and my husband pull our energy out of their space. It reminded me of the first time John asked everyone in class to send any of his energy back that he might have left in their space—from this or any lifetime. He was astonished and a little dismayed. He said he knew they would look better without his energy; it was just a shock and surprise to see how much better they looked."

"What if the person doesn't accept their energy back?"

That happens, and there's no need to insist. It is important to understand that it's not your responsibility to see that the person whose energy it is accepts his or her energy back. In fact, insisting would be a breach of boundaries. Just because, abstractly, people are better off when they take their energy back doesn't mean that they have to choose to take their energy back. They, like you, are learning how to use and coordinate energy. If you are open to letting others make their own choices, their energy will find its way back to them naturally when they are ready.

When you find that someone doesn't want their energy back, acknowledge and celebrate your growing ability to perceive such information, acknowledge their choice, then simply intend that the energy go back to their guides, or to the Sun, or to the Earth to hold that energy for them. Remind yourself that it is another's choice when or if to assimilate their energy. Then let the matter go.

It frequently happens that certain people will want you to *keep* their energy. No one has the right to keep their energy in your space when you are ready to release it. Remember that their response will be spontaneous and unconscious; their energy may innocently try to return to you, or may even demand that you take it. But it's your space, your choice. It may take skill to make that choice, as we discuss in a few pages.

"If we don't have our energy in each other's space, how can we be intimate?"

The major strength and developmental direction of this spiritual journey is the cultivation of intimacy based upon uniqueness. While continuing to appreciate similarities, honoring boundaries allows you to be more aware of and in communication with another person's uniqueness.

In the movie *Groundhog Day,* Phil is stuck in a time warp. When the movie starts, he's in a small town reporting on the Groundhog Day festivities. Each night he goes to sleep, only to wake up to discover that he's repeating the same day over and over. Each day, he's at the beginning of Groundhog Day. As he repeatedly re-experiences the day he begins to slowly change what he does. He tries various experiments to make the best of the time warp he's powerless to escape. Through many false starts, he grows in wisdom. By the story's end, the once shallow and narcissistic Phil emerges as a lovable, wise, and generous person. The movie is a great metaphor for the entire reincarnational cycle, and for every day of your life.

Early in the movie Phil tries to establish a relationship with the girl of his dreams by finding out exactly what she likes and pretending that he too likes the exact same things. "I'm just like you" is a common invitation.

We are often taught to sustain and cultivate relationships narrowly through the lens of sameness. This tends to lead to enmeshment. For example, the melding of identity so often seen in the early bloom of romance often turns into a sense that one has lost oneself, resulting in the demand, "Let me be myself!"

Mature relationships grow from knowing who you are, observing skillfully and respectfully who the other person is, and communicating appropriately. So, in addition to giving somebody their information back when you return their energy, you're also setting up the possibility for a more authentic relationship than you would have otherwise.

Advanced Energy Concepts

There are at least three important ways to look at what energy is. While they aren't *obviously* equivalent to one another, they are. First, your energy is forever inextricably colored and imbued with your experience. Thus your energy is the information or grounding for all subsequent experience. Often we will call energy "information." Second, your energy, since it arises from your eternal spark of uniqueness, contains your authentic impulse towards your personal life. Third, energy is the source of your awareness or attention. We say that energy follows attention when we want to treat these as two separate aspects, but fundamentally your energy *is* your attention. When some of your energy is outside your aura, some of your ability to pay attention is temporarily lost. Understanding that all three of these points are true about energy in the personal aura will help in assimilating the often-subtle ideas below.

"How does my energy get into someone's aura? And how does their energy get into mine?"
Energy follows your thoughts. While you are actively talking to or thinking of a person, your energy will naturally go towards them. Because your energy arises from the spark of your uniqueness, it has a strong propulsion to return naturally back to your physical body and personal aura. The only thing that can disrupt the natural return of your energy is you. If part of your thought is stuck on a person with whom you have interacted or on what he or she represents, then some part of your energy will get stuck outside you. The energy techniques described earlier in this chapter are really ways to free your attention so that you can turn your awareness to whatever direction you wish.

Usually when your energy/attention is stuck on another person, your energy will lodge in his or her aura until you withdraw your attention, but it cannot lodge in his or her aura without his or her "collaboration." As is so often the case in talking about psychic energy or spirituality in general, one uses an ordinary word—in this case, "collaboration"—in an unusual, perhaps even puzzling way. Collaboration with someone here means meeting their energy in time and space with energy of your own that matches the frequency and quality of his or her energy. Your energy won't match all of his or her energy, just some relevant energy. This kind of "collaboration" is present, to some extent, whenever you interact with anyone in any way. Since you create your own reality, and since you can interact with another person only if you have some connection in time and space, then, at a minimum, you have collaborated in other dimensions to connect in time and space. This may seem to be a mere truism—of course you are meeting in time and space—but when you can see what goes on in those other dimensions, you see how actively and collaboratively even the bitterest of enemies work together as often as it takes (sometimes every night) to create the conditions in time and space for their battle. It's shocking how cordial the inner relations of the collaboration can be.

Understanding the collaboration required for your energy to stick in another person's aura or for theirs to stick in yours requires setting a foundation to understand one of the two or three hardest concepts in psychic psychology: what you resist you become.

Your body and aura by their nature are set up to contain and utilize your energy. No one else's energy can stick in your aura unless you "hold on" to it.[2] This holding on is an inner mechanism less like grabbing with your hand than being psychologically enmeshed. The enmeshment can come from either rigid attachment or aversion. In this system rigid attachment or aversion is called "resistance." Both are resistance to change. Chapter 9 pulls together a number of useful ideas and psychic skills to help you let go of resistance.

This brings us to a related concept we often encounter in this system and others. Since you create your own reality, you are never a mere victim. When you are victimized there is always a way in which you collaborated to create those circumstances, and consequently, there are always ways you can bring meaning for yourself and power to your situation. Parts Two and Three address these issues. Often people take a shortcut when talking about victimization, saying, "You are never a victim." Of course you can be a victim, of course you can suffer, when you relatively or wholly innocent. What the phrase is intended to mean is that collaboration is always present—a collaboration that always has meaning for you as an individual. Part Two of this book presents that case as part of its overall exploration of the mysticism of everyday life.

Thus your energy gets into other people's space following the often-unimagined implications of your beliefs. It is surprising to find that the most difficult energies to clear are usually the most well intended, and likely to be from a loved one, or someone close. Why? Often the well-intended person is convinced that they know what's best for you, or that they are entitled to something that you're not giving them. Again, it is not a conscious process. Look at another parental enmeshment example. Say that you feel that you are entitled to be treated like an adult by your parent—after all you're nineteen, or thirty-three, or fifty-five years old now. Unconsciously your energy will jump into their space to try to convince them to treat you respectfully. In the logic of spiritual engagement, not only does it not work, but jumping into their space to make them respect you actually makes it easier for their energy to then jump into your space with their opinions. (See Chapter 18, "Matching Pictures and Unconditional Responsibility.") You can learn to set boundaries and communicate without jumping into another person's space. Part Three of this book aims to help readers develop that skill.

Without some level of openness to your experience it would be easy to feel victimized when someone's energy is in your space. And sometimes it can feel emotionally or physically painful. Have you ever said, "So-and-so gives me a headache!"? Energetically that can be true. But it will also be true that you jumped into their space too.

The next time you think that someone is giving you a headache or other type of stress, consider the possibility that you are in their space unconsciously, perhaps even as a result of good intentions but unclear boundaries. Try pulling your energy out of their space and giving them back theirs. Separating your energies often works better and faster than ibuprofen.

Boundaries

The exploration of "Is it my energy" or "Whose energy is it" is first and foremost an exploration of authentic boundaries and the honoring of free will. Treating others with authenticity—communicating what you want and who you really are, with respect for the other's individual uniqueness—is the foundation of kindness and generosity. Pivotal to authenticity is the understanding that it is a violation to coerce another person with your energy, no matter how justified your wishes for them. They are separate individuals with their own path and their own issues. They may or may not behave as you want. If they misbehave it may be regrettable, even tragic, but coercion is not an answer.

The exploration of whose energy it is will gradually help you wean yourself from the delusion that you can legitimately control another person's behavior; and becoming sensitive to energy boundaries will improve your communication with people whose behavior you'd like to see change. There will be times when, even after you communicated effectively, the other person still has no openness to authentic communication, but learning to honor boundaries minimizes times where communication isn't effective.

We consider the exploration of communication to be one of the most important endeavors on the spiritual path, and we have become walking advertisements for the seminal book, *Difficult Conversations: How to Discuss What Matters Most*, written in 1999 by three members of the Harvard Negotiation Project. It contains a wealth of information, very well organized and easy to follow, about how to communicate with clear boundaries, authenticity, and a respectful, true kindness and generosity.[3] A more recent book, *Nonviolent Communication: A Language of Life* by Marshall B. Rosenberg, is another excellent read for the same reasons.[4]

You Are Not a Mere Victim

Even as you explore the concept of "my energy" in increasingly sophisticated and powerful ways, it's very easy to feel victimized. Someone else's energy can be annoying and uncomfortable. People naturally want to know why another person's energy is in their space, and often have the assumption that the other person intended it. Often nothing could be further from the truth. Almost all such energy flows are unconscious and unintentional. Intention, in the sense of a conscious choice, rarely drives those energies. What generates the movement of energy from one person's aura to another's is much like the process of electricity and magnetism. An extreme but frequent example will help illustrate this. You will often find energies in your space from people you have never even met. And you'll often find your energies in the space of other people whom you have never met. It happens by what is called *matching energy*. Matching energies is a hard concept to understand because it has many layers of subtlety, but for a beginning definition we'll say that matching energies are energies that resist each other and therefore attract each other. For more on matching energies see below and also Chapter 18, "Matching Pictures and Unconditional Responsibility."

Matching Energies

Say you climb onto a city bus while feeling a keen resentment for an international politician. And someone else is on the bus who really likes that same politician and deeply resents people criticizing that politician. You wouldn't even have to see them. There'd be an excellent chance that your level of judgment and their level of judgment would *match*, and both of your energies would jump into each other's space like water flowing from high ground to low ground. Though you probably wouldn't monitor it happening, you would likely experience it in some way, perhaps by feeling more resentful or tired. You might even experience the event as a sudden ache somewhere in your body. Keep in mind that you wouldn't even have had to speak to the person—the whole event would have been unintentional, unconscious, and automatic.

We understand that with this example some of you may wonder, "Why not just put up some kind of protection, such as surrounding myself in white light or some form of protective shielding?" Our goal is more long term: learning to become conscious of how our energy and beliefs affect and interact with others, and clarifying our identity. It is true that protection can be a quick fix and may occasionally be necessary, but that kind of white-light protection walls you off because it treats the other person's energy as a problem rather than addressing your own resistance.

How can you avoid matching energies? Resistance and judgment trigger aura enmeshment. You are going to have your opinions, you're meant to have your opinions, but you can learn to be less judgmental, less resistant to others with different opinions. Working on your resistance to other people's opinions is a powerful way to attend to your matching energies. If before boarding the bus you had meditated, or gone to a class where you worked on your judgmental tendencies, you might have then climbed onto the bus still disliking and opposing the international politician, but without the significant judgmentalness. In that case you would not match energies of judgment with your fellow passengers and your aura would stay clear.

It can be frustrating when someone's energy is in your space. Even so, it isn't skillful to consider yourself a victim and feel that you had no part in it. Instead, make some changes in your own aura.

Even if you have enough willpower to push someone's energy out of your space and keep it out by vigilance, the healing won't authentically hold. If you remain stuck on a polarity, energy will come in that matches your polarity. The answer is to change yourself by addressing the resistance and the consequential stickiness that attracts and holds that energy in your aura.

Often, even usually, you don't have to give conscious thought to removing that stickiness; the process of sending someone's energy back with openness and neutrality will remove the stickiness from your aura (see Chapter 9). You can address the stickiness indirectly by sending the energy back with neutrality; and you can address it directly by asking yourself what picture or belief generates the resistance in your aura and then clearing the picture.

But often the *most* effective way of getting someone's energy out of your space is to find what matching energy you have in their space; it's impossible for someone to have their energy in your space without your having a matching energy in their space.

Back to our political example—if your heart bleeds red politics and you're judgmental about blue's, and someone else's heart bleeds blue and they're judgmental about red's, to that extent when you're interacting consciously or unconsciously, your energies will flow into one another.

And matching energies can become much trickier in your interpersonal relationships. Bosses and workers can jump into each other's space, each thinking that the other owes them something. Specifically, a boss may think that a worker owes unquestioned obedience, and a worker may think the boss owes them respect.

One of our students laughingly said that he was happy and relieved to "discover" that an unsavory thought he had was his ex-wife's energy. That didn't mean that the unsavory thought wasn't his responsibility; whatever is in your aura is your responsibility. If you find an unsavory thought that you can attribute to someone else, it is a strong indicator that you have the same or a matching thought.

No Matter Where You Go, There You Are[5]

When you're stuck on a polarity you will very likely be drawn to situations where that polarity is magnified. Until you begin to take unconditional responsibility for your thoughts and your energy you will probably remain unaware of your unconscious participation in enmeshment. (See Chapter 18, "Matching Pictures and Unconditional Responsibility.")

You can usually pinpoint where you are stuck on a polarity by examining your uncomfortable patterns. If, for example, as an employee you have a continuous stream of unbearable bosses, that's a clue that you're missing a crucial point about yourself.

You may choose to leave a job to get away from an overbearing boss. But unless you genuinely and deeply understand why you attract unbearable bosses in the first place—until you've addressed your own boundaries, fear, difficulty with tense conversations, or resistance—you may simply step into a similar situation or, often, into the opposite but also deeply flawed situation.

If you're patient and resourceful you will eventually be able to disentangle yourself. The other person may never behave as you'd like, but you will be able to free yourself and move on. You'll also become better at communicating in that particular situation, and you may, in fact, find that you can reach an accommodation with the other person. It's all grist for an ever-growing openness to the world as it is.

We used to joke that if nothing else works to get someone's energy out of your space, try pulling your energy out of their space. Through the years this technique has proved so useful that we've stopped joking and we simply use it the first moment we have any difficulty with someone. The more annoying a relationship is, the more likely you will find your energy in the other person's space acting just as annoyingly. Recognizing that does tend to take the fun out of blaming others.

EXERCISE 12: Pulling Your Energy Out of Someone's Space

For the following exercise choose someone with whom you are having difficulty relating to or communicating with.

1. Sit comfortably straight in your chair, feet flat on the floor, legs and arms uncrossed.
2. With a sense of openness, relax, close your eyes, and breathe gently into your belly.
3. Allow your awareness to gently rest behind your eyes.
4. With openness and a sense of adventure, remind yourself that you are not a mere victim.
5. Create a rose out in front of you to retrieve and hold your energy.
6. Give your rose the ability to gently pull your energy out of the person with whom you are having difficulty, and let your energy return to your rose.
7. Allow your rose to dissolve and your energy to be assimilated back through your crown.
8. Replenish your entire body and aura with a golden cosmic energy.
9. Send an energetic thank you to the person.
10. Thank your body for being willing to change.
11. Take a few refreshing breaths and when you are ready stand up, gently stretch, and reverse polarities.
12. You may find it useful to make some notes of your experience.

Exploring Pain

Wherever you find pain or disease in a body, you will probably find someone else's energy. Saying this is not the same as saying that the other person's energy is the root cause of the pain or disease. Remember, everyone creates his or her own reality. The other person's energy is only present in your space if you have underlying restrictions that actively allow or trigger their energy to stick in your space. Otherwise their energy would naturally travel straight through your body and aura. Thus, while it's true that wherever you find pain in your body you'll find someone else's energy, it's important to understand that this other energy is a secondary cause of your pain. The root cause is your own beliefs or resistance to their energy. Your own beliefs or restrictions cause the stickiness in your aura that allows another person's energy to get stuck and cause you pain.

However, you often don't need to address the root cause. You can just clear the secondary cause, the other person's energy. When you clear someone's energy out of your space, the clearing will work because and only because you consciously or unconsciously change your underlying self and move out of resistance to the other person or people. The technique of clearing energy and all later techniques are merely elegant, powerful tools for working directly with your growing ability to let go of particular aspects of resistance to life as it is.

EXERCISE 13: Separating Pain Energy

For the next exercise, please find some pain or weakness in your body; create a rose and clear that part of your body of other people's energy.

1. Sit comfortably straight in your chair, feet flat on the floor, legs and arms uncrossed.
2. With a sense of openness, relax, close your eyes, and breathe gently into your belly.
3. Allow your awareness to rest gently behind your eyes.
4. With a sense of adventure, remind yourself that you are not a victim.
5. Create a rose out in front of you to retrieve and hold your energy.
6. Give your rose the ability to gently pull your energy out of each person's space whose energies are contributing to your pain. (You don't have to know who they are.) Let your energy return to your rose.
7. Allow your rose to dissolve and your energy to be assimilated.
8. Create a rose out in front of you for all the people whose energies are contributing to your pain. (Again, you don't have to know who they are.)
9. Give the rose the ability to gently pull their energy out of your aura—from this or any lifetime—and let their rose fill.
10. When ready, simply give their rose to the earth to recycle their energy back to them.
11. Replenish your aura by imagining yourself filled with a golden cosmic light.

12. Thank your body for being willing to change.
13. Take a few refreshing breaths and when you are ready stand up, gently stretch, and reverse polarities.
14. You may find it useful to make some notes of your experience.

POINTS TO REMEMBER

- Your energy holds your unique information and the key to your next step. At a personality level, only your own energy is authentic for you.
- When your life arises out of your unique energy—your natural impulse—you will engage life authentically, not perfectly, but authentically, more gracefully.
- Taking unconditional responsibility, an openness to "life as it is," is at the heart of this spiritual journey.
- The question is not which side of the polarity you're on; the question is whether or not you're stuck on a polarity.
- Enmeshment is not a conscious process.
- You are not a victim.
- You are a cocreator in any enmeshment.
- The exploration of "whose energy is it" will gradually help you wean yourself from the delusion that you can control, or have the right to control, another person's behavior.
- Whatever is challenging you, whatever is lit up, is your next spiritual step.

CHAPTER 4

Pictures

The vibrations of your aura are what create your reality and allow you to experience your reality. (Your aura must vibrate for your body to operate.) Different parts of the aura create different parts of our reality or experience by vibrating in a coordinated psychic structure called a *picture*. We naturally and unconsciously create pictures moment by moment, and in each moment numerous pictures are vibrating in our aura. They are called pictures because often when you look at the energy of the psychic structure clairvoyantly, you can see the event that was created or experienced through the picture/psychic structure. It could be a little confusing: the word "pictures" refers both to the psychic structure that organizes and vibrates the relevant portions of the aura, and to what a clairvoyant sees when he or she looks at that part of the aura.

Pictures are naturally created and destroyed in an automatic, flowing, and spontaneous process.[1] Ideally, as each experience passes, your pictures are processed and assimilated, and the pictures simply dissipate. It is only when you are in resistance to an experience that the related picture becomes problematic in two ways. First, since the picture structure freezes in time rather than naturally dissipating when it is no longer necessary, it becomes an obstruction in your aura, where it vibrates in an old, fixed pattern. Some part of you is stuck in the past in a perpetual loop. The part of your aura contained inside the picture is unable to change its repetitive vibration to create or experience new life. Second, as long as the experience is vibrating in a repetitive loop, your inner self cannot assimilate the experience and gather joy or wisdom from it.

We call pictures that don't dissipate *stuck* or *frozen pictures*, often referring to them as knots or blocks rather than pictures because clairvoyantly it is often difficult and unnecessary to see the underlying image of the stuck experience. The pictures will often look like little more than dark blocks or dust. Groups of pictures make small portions of your aura unable to vibrate smoothly and freely through its whole range. Eventually, if pictures continue to accumulate, there will be areas where the aura can no longer vibrate reasonably well because there are just too many knots. The flow of new energy is diverted around such areas, and sometimes stopped altogether.

As soon as you move out of resistance to a picture, that picture dissipates automatically, your aura is freed up, and the picture's information is assimilated. When your life is flowing, your aura will vibrate streams of new energy smoothly, continuously, and effortlessly through the entire range of that experience, and then the aura's responses will move smoothly on to each new experience.

Surprisingly, your response to either pleasant or unpleasant experiences can render your aura stuck in a picture or knot. It's probably easy to imagine that you could move into resistance to the next moment of your life when you are cringing from an unpleasant experience. It might be a little harder to imagine that grasping onto pleasant experiences places you in resistance also.

John likes to use an image of a kiss. He enjoys kissing his wife, and to do so, he has to pucker his lips. Walking through an entire day with his lips puckered would adversely impact his ability to eat, communicate, and get kisses. When you hold onto a pleasant picture, you limit the ability of your aura to respond to new events, or to support new pleasant experiences that vary and grow from earlier experiences (as all experience must).

Present Time or Current Time

That brings us to the concept of *present time* or *current time,* which in our practice does not refer to clock time but instead to the status of your aura. In our usage, when you are in present time your aura is able to vibrate freely and naturally in the moment. If your aura is vibrating freely, you are in present time whether you are focusing on the present moment or not. You can be in present time even if you're daydreaming about the past or the future, so long as your daydreaming vibrates reasonably freely as you do so. Pictures, by definition, do not vibrate freely, and so are not in current time.

Conversely and more subtly, you could be focused clearly in the present of clock time, but if you are *driven* to that focus by fixed pain or fear—that is, by a picture—your aura would not be vibrating freely and you wouldn't be in what we mean by "present time." In that case, you'd really be responding to some former event stuck in your aura as a picture, and consequently wouldn't be engaging the moment at hand.

Exploding Pictures

Exploding a picture is a magical way to free a picture's energy. When you destroy a picture you create the aura freedom that your next experience requires. It quickly and directly frees that portion of the aura cramped into a picture to once again vibrate freely. When you explode pictures you also send the message to your soul that you are ready to move on, ready to grow.

Though the technique may seem magical and automatic, it works because it helps generate an inner change. You are the key to its lasting effectiveness; you supply the magic. The technique's effectiveness rests on your openness to change and growth, e.g. your willingness to release your resistance to the old experience or to the letting go of it, and deeply open to your new experience as it is in the present moment.

To explode pictures, you use a kind of psychic energy that facilitates your clearing either resistance to an unpleasant experience or your resistance to letting go of a pleasant experience in order to move to the next experience. If you were to try to explode a picture because "It was so awful I will never let go of the horror," no matter how many times you exploded the picture, it would come back because you are holding on to the horror. If instead you explode the picture because it horrifies you, and you are willing to assimilate the horrible experience and to let it be just what it is now to you, exploding the picture will allow you to assimilate the experience and move on.

Letting go of resistance is not the same as letting go of your *response* to an experience; you will still find an experience unpleasant or pleasant. But exploding pictures increases your ability to respond to your experience and then be open to what comes next.

Neither is letting go of your resistance transcending your experience. Letting go allows you to embrace the actuality of an experience—it happened, it's now part of who you are—so it can then become the foundation for your next breath, your next step.

People often wonder if their experience is lost when they explode a picture. To the contrary. In the normal course, pictures dissipate almost immediately. Only when you haven't fully assimilated an experience does the picture or psychic knot last long after the experience itself has passed. Until you have exploded such a picture, it will remain undigested in the aura.

Only when your aura is no longer vibrating in the fixed pattern of the picture, only when your aura once again is free to vibrate to new experiences, will the information that had been locked there undigested be able to move into your psychic archives where it is assimilated. If you wish, you can always retrieve your memory of the experience from your archive and in an effortless process remember and enjoy it. A picture doesn't make an experience more available, it just renders your aura blocked and unavailable for the free experience of what's happening now.

The Tools and Process for Exploding Pictures

Golden cosmic energy: To explode a picture and free its energy, you'll use golden cosmic energy from the sun and the cosmos. Though golden cosmic energy flows everywhere, you can find it naturally above your head (above your crown chakra). The range of golden cosmic energy is the energy range of non-resistance, of openness to life as it is. When you explode a picture using the golden cosmic energy, the energy itself helps you unconsciously let go of your resistance.

A rose: You will again create a rose to hold your picture, which will give you a stage, a location for your picture, and the ability to move it outside your aura to work with it as well as to perceive it more clearly.

First you'll imagine a rose about 3 to 6 inches in diameter out in front of you.[2] Then intend for your picture to move out onto your rose. Next you'll imagine a big ball of golden cosmic energy (we also call it a golden sun), which you place over and all around the rose and the picture you intend to explode. Now imagine that both the picture and rose explode. Poof!

Once the picture explodes, your energy that had been stuck in the picture will become free, ready to return back into your aura where it originated. Intend that the freed energy effortlessly rise above your head and then flow down through the top of your head, your crown chakra. With no need to mentally follow it, just intend that it return to its appropriate location.

EXERCISE 14: Exploding Pleasant and Unpleasant Pictures

The next exercise will give you the experience of exploding both a pleasant and an unpleasant picture. For this exercise you'll recall two events. The reason we suggest that you work with both a pleasant and unpleasant event is to give you the opportunity to observe how resistance is present in any type of picture.

To begin we suggest that you choose a *slightly* unpleasant event rather than a very unpleasant event. A slightly unpleasant picture will provide plenty to work with. A very unpleasant event may stir up too much resistance before your technique has grown strong. However, in our classes there is always someone who doesn't want to wait. Usually they do just fine.

Note: While the next exercise calls for you to explode pictures, in the beginning you may not notice anything to explode. If so, you can just let the rose itself represent the experience. Then when you explode the rose, your unconscious will find any resistances you were holding to the experience and clear them.

1. Sit comfortably straight in your chair, feet flat on the floor, legs and arms uncrossed.
2. With a sense of openness, relax, close your eyes, and breathe gently into your belly.
3. Allow your awareness to gently rest behind your eyes.

Exploding your unpleasant picture:

4. Imagine a rose about 3 to 6 inches in diameter, about 6 feet out in front of you.
5. Allow your unpleasant picture to go out onto your rose and your perception to grow. Remember, it may or may not appear as a picture to you. It might just be a little chunk, or you might see it, you might feel it, you might hear it, or you might imagine it.
6. Spend a few minutes simply becoming aware of the energy of your unpleasant picture.
7. When ready, imagine a big golden sun coming down from above your crown and exploding the rose and your unpleasant picture.
8. Once you have exploded your unpleasant picture, imagine that the energy you've freed, that's currently out in front of you, effortlessly circles above your head and down through your crown. With no need to mentally follow it, just intend that it return to its appropriate location.
9. Breathe gently and deeply into your belly and relax.

Exploding your pleasant picture:

10. Recall your pleasant experience.
11. Create a new rose about 3 to 6 inches in diameter, about 6 feet out in front of you.
12. Allow your pleasant picture to go out onto your rose and your perception to grow. Remember, it may or may not appear as a picture to you. It might just be a little chunk, or you might see it, you might feel it, you might hear it, or you might imagine it.
13. Spend a few minutes simply becoming aware of the energy of your pleasant picture.
14. When ready, imagine a big golden sun coming from above your crown and exploding the entire rose and your pleasant picture.
15. Once you have exploded your pleasant picture, imagine that the energy you've freed, that's currently out in front of you, effortlessly circles above your head and down through your crown. With no need to mentally follow it, just intend that it return to its appropriate location.

16. Imagine that your entire body and aura are replenished with the fresh golden cosmic energy.
17. Thank your body for being willing to change.
18. Take a few refreshing breaths and when you are ready stand up, gently stretch, and reverse polarities.
19. You may find it useful to make some notes of your experience.

The technique becomes more powerful and more comprehensive with practice, but ideally you experienced a shift and release even during your first attempt. Remember to acknowledge your experience no matter how subtle, and your understanding and perceptions will grow.

Following the previous exercise, some people report a reluctance to explode their unpleasant picture because they didn't feel ready to let go of their resistance. Being able to observe your feelings like your reluctance is just the kind of skill this system intends to build. Acknowledging and exploring your reluctance is very important. There is no hurry. Asking the question "Why don't I want to let this go?" will automatically begin a healing process for you.

Often people have more difficulty exploding their pleasant picture, usually because they fear they will lose the experience, but sometimes because they're not ready to let it be what it was. Remind yourself that you won't lose the experience—it will be assimilated by your soul and remain ready for you to access whenever you want—and by exploding the picture you will often find new levels of meaning. Again, exploring your reluctance is very important.

If You Find Exploding a Picture Too Abstract...

Occasionally people initially find the practice of exploding pictures too abstract or too fast-moving for them. Following are two leisurely methods for freeing the stuck energy of a picture that are also very effective. The first is to simply *breathe your energy out of a picture,* and the second is to slowly *dissolve a picture with golden cosmic energy,* letting it take as long as it needs.

Both techniques give excellent results. Depending on the issue we are addressing or the atmosphere we'd like to create for a meditation, we'll choose the method best suited to the moment. For example, to clear a lot of pictures we find it very effective to explode them, but for particularly stubborn pictures we'll often use the breath.

If you find a picture that won't explode or if you simply want to sit quietly with a picture to contemplate and clear it, breathe your energy out of the picture, patiently letting it take as long as it takes. It may take several sessions, but breathing your energy out of a picture will eventually disassemble even the most stubborn picture.

EXERCISE 15: Breathing Your Energy Out of a Pet-Peeve Picture

Most of us have a pet peeve, and with pet peeves will inevitably come stuck pictures related to our resistance. For the next exercise choose a pet-peeve picture to clear by breathing your energy out of it. For this to work, you must be willing to let go of your judgments. (See Chapter 22, "Self-Talk and Stories: Conversation vs. Commands.") This exercise will help you do so.

1. Sit comfortably straight in your chair, feet flat on the floor, legs and arms uncrossed.
2. With a sense of openness, relax, close your eyes, and breathe gently into your belly.
3. Allow your awareness to rest lightly behind your eyes.
4. Recall your pet peeve.
5. Create a rose 3 to 6 inches in diameter, about 6 feet out in front of you.
6. Allow a pet-peeve picture to go out onto your rose and let your perception grow. Remember, it may not appear as a picture to you. You might see it, feel it, hear it, or just imagine it.
7. Spend a few moments simply being aware of the energy of your pet-peeve picture.
8. When ready, gently breathe your energy out of the picture until you feel a shift.
9. Imagine that as you breathe the energy out of your picture, you breathe the energy back through your crown. With no need to

mentally follow it, just intend that it return to its appropriate location.

10. Imagine that your entire body and aura are replenished with fresh golden cosmic energy.
11. Thank your body for being willing to change.
12. Take a few refreshing breaths and when you are ready stand up, gently stretch, and reverse polarities.
13. You may find it useful to make some notes of your experience.

You will find that utilizing your breath is a powerful technique for clearing your chakras and aura as well.

EXERCISE 16: Dissolving the Picture of a Moderately Difficult Event

Dissolving a picture with golden cosmic energy is another very effective way to free the energy in a picture, and also quite simple. As before, first ask a picture to go out onto a rose, then simply surround it in golden cosmic energy and let that energy dissolve the picture, allowing it to take all the time it needs. You might choose to dissolve the picture of a moderately difficult event.

1. Sit comfortably straight in your chair, feet flat on the floor, legs and arms uncrossed.
2. With a sense of openness, relax, close your eyes, and breathe gently into your belly.
3. Allow your awareness to rest lightly behind your eyes.
4. Recall your moderately difficult event.
5. Create a rose 3 to 6 inches in diameter, about 6 feet out in front of you.
6. Allow your picture to go out onto your rose and let your perception grow. Remember, it may not appear as a picture to you. You might see it, feel it, hear it, or just imagine it.
7. Spend a moment simply being aware of the energy of your picture.
8. When ready, invite a big ball of golden cosmic energy to surround your rose and picture.

9. Allow the golden cosmic energy to dissolve your rose and picture, leisurely taking as long as it needs. Repeat as many times as necessary.
10. Allow the freed energy to be assimilated back though your crown chakra.
11. Imagine that your entire body and aura are replenished with the fresh golden cosmic energy.
12. Thank your body for being willing to change.
13. Take a few refreshing breaths and when you are ready stand up, gently stretch, and reverse polarities.
14. You may find it useful to make some notes of your experience.

More on Pictures

Now that you have a sense of pictures, here are several refinements on what you will naturally begin to encounter as you work with them.

New levels of meaning: Often people discover new aspects of meaning in the original experience while exploding pictures. For example, if you explode a fond memory of a new baby, you may find yourself also releasing a lot of fear that was present but not in the foreground of your mind when you held your new baby. Or, if you explode an unpleasant experience with an old lover, you may also be able to see more balance in what you learned and to appreciate the warmth you once had for each other.

Spending time with pictures: Sometimes it's nice to take your time with a picture—to process your thoughts and feelings about it, and to clear your relevant beliefs and relationships. Instead of exploding a picture right away, you can place it on a rose in order to explore all your thoughts and feelings, and to see what other pictures light up as you explore this one. Then explode the rose when you are ready. Other times you may explode a hundred or a thousand pictures without even noticing what they each were about.

To help you become more aware of your pictures, try running energy through your aura, which will "light up" the pictures, allowing them to stand out from the background. Energy is light. Usually light will not shine through a picture. The picture's rigidity blocks the free flow of energy or light, and as the light bounces off or goes around the picture, the picture seems to "flare," making it easier to perceive.

When pictures aren't lit up, they render the part of the aura where they are located very dense. They passively but deeply affect your life creations. Remember, to the extent that your aura is vibrating harmoniously with your desires, those desires will manifest. If a part of your aura won't vibrate freely because it is knotted up by too many pictures, then your desires won't be able to vibrate and won't manifest.

Energy passing through the area of a picture not only lights it up, often the energy flow itself so vibrates a picture that it explodes. Each of us naturally and unconsciously explodes pictures as we assimilate our experience. Running energy helps us find and consciously explode the pictures that had become walled off from the natural cycle of creating and destroying pictures.

Getting lit up: *Getting lit up, lighting up,* and *being lit up* are terms that you will hear throughout this book. They mean that pictures are energized, awakened, and in some manner activated in your aura, which is the objective of running energy.[3] You don't have to intentionally run energy to get lit up. Every experience, every sensation, emotion, or thought generates at least some movement of energy in at least some part of your aura. When that energy movement vibrates at the same frequency as some of your pictures, those pictures will light up.

When you are lit up, your emotions (pleasant or unpleasant) will have a brittleness about them. Learning to recognize when you are lit up is an important skill.

A few examples of being lit up include embarrassment (especially if your face flushes) and when you are angry, anxious, envious, or even overly tired. If you can take advantage of such times by clearing the lit-up pictures, you can release hundreds of pictures quite easily. Also, when you learn to recognize the signs that you are lit up, you will be less likely to get thrown off balance by the sudden activation of pictures in your aura. You can simply ask your inner self to explode any pictures that are lit up, and later, when you have the time, you can sit down and do a more thorough clearing.

When more pictures light up: Often as you explode one picture you'll notice (feel, see, or hear) other pictures light up in your aura. When you find other pictures lighting up, congratulate yourself on the perception—that means your awareness is growing. There will always be other pictures beneath your conscious awareness. Playfully explode them when they arise.

Collections of pictures: Sometimes you will find a collection of pictures clumped together, which will usually represent a theme of some sort—anger, greed, impatience, fear, etc. If you are visual they might appear like a stack of newspapers or papers rolled into a tight log, a steamer trunk, or any number of ways. If you feel energy, it might feel like an impenetrable or dense space. It is helpful to remember your amusement and explode a few at a time. Again, you do not have to know what the pictures are in order to explode them.

Some pictures are easier, others are harder to explode: Sometimes you'll find pictures that are very easy to explode, and you might explode a hundred or a thousand in a sitting. If so, it usually means you have already come to some resolution of the underlying issue.

Other times you may be surprised to find a single picture that you never imagined could be very important that takes much longer to explode. If you cannot seem to explode it, breathe your energy out of it, patiently letting it take as long as it takes. That could be one or several sittings, occasionally even years. If you find such a pivotal picture and eventually do explode it, profound change can result.

Some pictures go through the interesting process of seeming to have already been cleared for years. Then, when you hit a deeper level, you once again find pictures of the event in question but this time resonating in deeper and different ways. Probably these renewed experiences are different pictures of the same event. In any case, you can revisit the event and explode the new level of the picture, thereby coming into current time.

Other people's pictures: Sometimes when a picture is hard to explode, it's because the picture is another person's picture, made of his or her energy rather than yours. People often throw their pictures into other people's aura when they want that person to agree with them. The simplest response is to pull your energy out of the other person's space (to clear any resistance you have to that person and their picture) and give them (or the earth, or their guide) back the picture. You don't have to know whose picture it is.

How exploding pictures works: Exploding pictures can work in interesting ways. Sometimes you'll notice that a few hours or a few days after exploding a picture you are thinking differently or feeling different than you did prior to exploding that picture. Not that you weren't intellectually capable of thinking or feeling that way, but for some reason it just never occurred to you. Or, if you had thought about it, that way of being seemed false and now, all of a sudden, it appears to be true—you see it in a different light. That's because the energy is flowing more freely through that part of your aura, and you have access to more of your natural thoughts and feelings.

Matching pictures: Matching pictures is one of those hard-to-define yet core concepts that is good to dive into and slowly let your understanding grow. In some ways the mechanics may seem simple: During your conscious or unconscious interactions with others there will be some pictures in your aura that will match and instantaneously light up in response to charged pictures in someone else's aura. Any interaction you have with any person is going to light up some matching pictures.

Matching pictures does not necessarily mean equal pictures. They can match by representing the same, similar, or even opposite ideas, events, energies colors, or emotions. Your matching pictures with someone will be unique and will arise out of your own history and beliefs.

A fairly simple example of matching pictures would be, for instance, three friends chatting, one relating a mishap that happened while he was backpacking: while he was sleeping by the campfire an ember popped out and burned a big hole in his sleeping bag. One friend finds it funny and remembers how in his family his "job" was to be the fire watcher when they went camping, and how seriously he took his responsibility. The other friend flashes back to when as a young boy he and his buddies were playing with fire in an empty lot, and the fire got out of control and accidently burned down a garage.

The whole concept of matching pictures can be quite confusing. For instance, someone's righteous stance on world peace could easily match someone's righteous determination to cause harm. We discuss the pivotally important issue of matching pictures in depth in Chapter 18.

A polarity of pictures and energy: There is a subtle and interesting point that's easy to miss. Pictures and whose energy it is are themselves two sides of an energy polarity. If you're operating by entirely utilizing *your* energy, you will not be in resistance to your own experience, and you won't create stuck pictures. If you are exploding your stuck pictures so that you're addressing your resistance, you will be operating utilizing your own energy. Sometimes it's easier to become unstuck by exploding pictures; sometimes it's easier by seeing whose energy it is. Generally you'll use a combination of the techniques.

IS IT MY ENERGY? IF IT'S MY ENERGY, IS IT IN CURRENT TIME?

We've devoted a lot of attention to these two core concepts of determining whose energy it is and whether or not it's in current time because they are the foundation of this spiritual journey of exploring the personal aura—everything grows directly out of them. With these two simple concepts alone you can accomplish great healings on yourself. As we employ additional techniques you'll find synergies developing, and the techniques will become increasingly comprehensive and powerful, but they are all based upon these two simple techniques. Should you encounter difficulty with any of the more advanced techniques you can always come back to either of the basic techniques. By using them patiently, you'll find that even the most stubborn barrier will crumble.

CHAPTER 5

Grounding and the Center of the Head

Addressing the two questions—Is it my energy, and if so, is it in current time?—works to clear the aura of obstructions in a general way. Clearing other people's energy and exploding pictures doesn't require any particular knowledge or orientation to the structure of the aura. Further skills do require that we orient to specific aura energy structures. Next we'll explore two orientations that are pivotal to this system: *grounding* and the *center of the head.*

One way to look at how you engage everyday life is as collaboration between your body, which is physical, and your soul, which is not. Together with a personal spark from All That Is, they give birth to your personality, which draws on both and is still utterly itself. (See Chapter 14, "The Reincarnational Process and the Eternal Validity of the Personality.")

The two orientations of grounding and center of the head allow the body, personality, and soul (which all vibrate in different energy ranges) to work together harmoniously by stabilizing the body and the personality, respectively. We stabilize our bodies as they address and engage psychic energies through the use of a *grounding cord,* and we stabilize the personality by engaging the soul's neutrality and openness to life through placing our awareness in the *center of the head.*

Depending on the purpose and the energy range in which a system works, there are numerous methods used to ground. The method we use is specifically designed for working with the personal aura.[1]

Your body's programming naturally supports the health of your physical body, while many of its systems allow it to collaborate with nonphysical energies. A grounding cord helps you stabilize and accurately tune your body to its physical aspects, even while the body is collaborating in a world where psychic non-physical energies directly and indirectly impact it. Once established, your grounding cord will help your body comfortably and skillfully tune to its natural frequency and stabilize there. It will also provide a powerful means for releasing stress and excess energies from your body and aura.[2]

Grounding allows you to be in your body. Without grounding there is a tendency for your psychic awareness to float out of the body.[3] Unless you are trained, you won't notice this floating; but the outcome of the floating is a distance between you and a direct encounter with everyday life. Your body consciousness, as a part of the great naturalness and spaciousness of the Earth's consciousness, has a natural unconscious joy that can easily get lost in the emotional give-and-take of your personal life. Grounding helps you separate the temporary fluctuations of your emotions from the stable knowingness of the body. You gain more access to your body's flexible balance in current time and to the body's own information and resourcefulness that lie outside your conscious awareness.

Earth energy: Earth energy is a relatively dense, comfortable, and stabilizing energy for the body. We use it to ground. It's not the only energy you'll run through your aura, but it is an essential energy. As you connect to the center of the Earth you will come to realize the magnitude of this relationship: how your body responds to earth energies, and how you relate to and grow out of the consciousness of Mother Earth. What we know of the physical world is only a tiny portion of Mother Earth's awareness. Earth's consciousness is infinite in range, beyond our ability to imagine.

Earth is your playground, supporting and maintaining a space of tremendous freedom for your spiritual adventure. You'll feel that freedom as an unconditional loving and neutral energy, an energy having no other agenda for you than supporting your exploration.

As you connect to Mother Earth you're more likely to find what is true and authentic for you, but she won't insist or push you into authenticity. You're given a magnificent and sometimes troubling freedom to play; there are boundaries to human experience, but they go far beyond any particular human's awareness. You essentially have complete freedom within the Earth playground to learn and play—to make mistakes, to make wise choices, and to grow constantly in authenticity, kindness, and generosity.

Colors and grounding: We suggest that you initially practice grounding using an earthy green energy because of its inherent healing properties and its natural association with Mother Earth. After you become comfortably familiar with earth energy, you can expand your exploration to the numerous colors and frequencies of earth energy.

Though gold is a lovely neutral energy, we do not recommend using it for your grounding cord as a general practice because it is challenging to sustain that frequency ("to hold it"). We do normally work with golden *cosmic* energy for replenishing the aura and neutrality. Gold is one of the highest-frequency colors you can run in your body and remain in your body; it is also the most neutral. If you do explore the golden earth frequencies you might begin with an earthy brassy gold.

Within the energy range of the personal aura, white is not an authentic energy for everyday life. It vibrates at such high frequencies that most people go out of their body, and from a psychic standpoint go unconscious.

White light is the color a lot of people use for protection. In a temporary emergency where we aren't comfortable with our other energy skills, we might use white light for protection. But white light vibrates most people out of their bodies, so that the challenge they are trying to escape from isn't really addressed, just transcended. Transcending life's challenges leaves a gap in understanding what triggered the challenge in the first place. Gaps in awareness generate pain. That pain continues vibrating in the body that you have jumped out of and transcended. Then, when you come back to a more physical level, your pain will still be waiting, unresolved, with all the additional problems that come from avoiding life as it is. Our hope is that people practice vibrating in the range of the personality and everyday experience where they can clear their pain and develop increasingly more of their humanity, authenticity, kindness, and generosity.

We do explore how to work with white light authentically in frequency ranges below and above the frequency range of the personal aura in our channeling, etheric, and seven-planes classes, and will also do so in future books.

There are other colors that don't work well for grounding. Silver is a very psychic color, but it can make you very spacey and tends to bring in a lot of ungrounded psychic chaos. Black plows into the unconscious and for the non-expert can bring in a lot of psychic chaos. And for most people, especially women, brown is too dense, too slow a frequency to use for a grounding cord. Occasionally, however, we will suggest mixing a little brown into someone's grounding when they are having difficulty becoming grounded (i.e., when they are very spacey).

Creating a Grounding Cord

To create your grounding cord you'll imagine connecting the base of your spine to the very center of the Earth with an earthy green cord, a beam of light, or a stream of energy.

The reason we ground to the center of the Earth is that it is completely neutral. If you were to extend your grounding cord only to a depth of a hundred feet or even ten miles, you'd be likely to encounter a lot of other people's anxiety energies.

We'll introduce three different ways for you to create a grounding cord. As you become more practiced, you will probably choose the fastest, simplest method. But while learning please take time to become as familiar with the process as possible, imagining each step in as much detail as you can. It can be helpful to visualize your grounding cord in earthy colors or textures, feel its strength and support for you, listen to the deep hum of the Earth and/or smell its earthy freshness.

We'll introduce the most detailed grounding method first. You'll imagine a 6-inch-diameter sphere of earthy green energy at the base of your spine, in your *first chakra*. (See Figure I, "Grounding and Meditation Posture," page 59.) There you'll let it gently spin for about 30 seconds or so. You'll then let it fall down to the center of the Earth, and as it is falling, you'll allow it to create a grounding cord for you. Imagine the cord as a green, flexible, open pipe of light about 6 inches in diameter.

Figure 1: Grounding and Meditation Posture

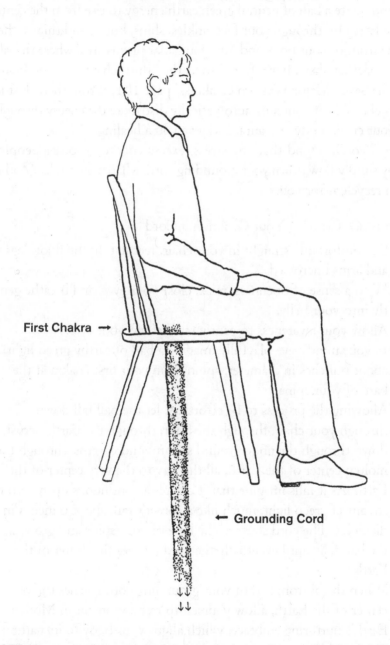

First Chakra ➡

⬅ Grounding Cord

NOTE: Your grounding cord extends from the base of your spine about 4,000 miles down to the earth's neutral center.

After you create your grounding cord, turn your attention to your feet and invite a ball of neutral green earth energy to rise from the center of the Earth up through your feet, ankles, shins, knees, and thighs, then up the front of your body and into your solar plexus area, where the ribs come together (hereafter referred to as the "third chakra"). (See Figure 4, "The Seven Major Western Chakras," page 101.) From there, just let the intelligence of your aura automatically distribute the energy throughout your entire body and aura, and give you a healing.

Last, you'll intend that any stress, excess energy, or other people's energy simply flow down your grounding cord, where you can let Mother Earth recycle it for you.

EXERCISE 17: Creating Your Grounding Cord
1. Sit comfortably straight in your chair, feet flat on the floor, legs and arms uncrossed.
2. With a sense of openness, relax, close your eyes, and breathe gently into your belly.
3. Allow your awareness to gently rest behind your eyes.
4. In your mind's eye playfully imagine a ball of earthy green light, about 6 inches in diameter, spinning in your first chakra at the base of your spine.
5. Allowing the process to be effortless, let the ball fall down through your chair, through the floor, through the Earth's crust, down through the underground streams and caverns, through the molten center of the Earth, all the way to the very center of the Earth. As it falls imagine that it creates a continuous open cord or stream of green light, much like a comet's tail, about 6 inches in diameter. The cord starts at the base of your spine and grows as the ball falls until eventually the cord reaches the center of the Earth.
6. When the bottom end of your grounding cord reaches the very center of the Earth, allow yourself to rest a moment in Mother Earth's nurturing embrace, which aligns your body to its natural comfortable frequency.

7. Then from the center of the Earth, invite a ball of green earth energy up into your feet; up through your ankles, shins, knees, and thighs; up through the front of your body and into your third chakra, at the solar plexus area—where the ribs come together in the chest. Let the intelligence of your aura automatically distribute the energy throughout your entire body and aura.

8. Allow any excess energy, or any energy that you're ready to let go of, to simply drop away, down your grounding cord, down to the center of the Earth where the Earth recycles it for you.

9. Invite a couple more balls of green earth energy up through your feet, ankles, shins, knees, and thighs, up through the front of your body into your third chakra, and from there allow the intelligence of your aura to distribute it throughout your body and aura.

10. Again, allow any excess energy, or any energy that isn't yours that you're ready to let go of, to fall away down your grounding cord, for Mother Earth to recycle.

11. Replenish your entire body and aura with the fresh golden cosmic energy.

12. Thank your body for being willing to change.

13. Take a few refreshing breaths and when you are ready stand up, gently stretch, and reverse polarities.

14. You may find it useful to make some notes of your experience.

Creating and destroying grounding cords: As a human you very capably sculpt psychic energy with your imagination all the time. To help you stay in current time, it's useful for you to become accustomed to the idea that you can freely and prolifically create and destroy certain images. Destroying your old grounding cord is just like exploding a picture; you put your grounding cord in a rose and explode it. Then you create a new grounding cord.

For most people we suggest using a grounding cord for everyday life.[4] Grounding is also a good way to stabilize the body and drain out chaotic energy before you go to sleep. To minimize any tendency for your grounding cord itself to get stuck in the past and hold you back from absorbing and assimilating experience, we suggest that you destroy your old grounding cord and create a new one any time you meditate or find yourself making a big shift.

EXERCISE 18: Quick Grounding

Once you've familiarized yourself with earth energy and can discern the difference between being grounded and not being grounded, you might enjoy practicing a faster way to ground. It's simple: from the center of your head, in one fell swoop, see a continuous stream or beam of light extending from the base of your spine to the center of the Earth. Or you can create it the other way around, flowing from the center of the Earth up to the base of your spine. With either approach the point is to see one continuous connection that you create in an instant. Also, if ever you find it hard to ground or be neutral, just ask Mother Earth to send up a grounding cord, and she'll be happy to oblige.

1. Sit comfortably straight in your chair, feet flat on the floor, legs and arms uncrossed.
2. With a sense of openness, relax, close your eyes, and breathe gently into your belly.
3. Allow your awareness to gently rest behind your eyes.
4. Put your old grounding cord in a rose and explode it with golden cosmic energy.
5. In one imaginative image, see or feel a continuous stream of energy or a cord connecting the base of your spine to the very center of the Earth, with a diameter of about 6 inches.
6. Allow any excess energy, or any energy that isn't yours, to fall away down your grounding cord, allowing Mother Earth to recycle those energies.
7. Replenish your entire body and aura with the fresh golden cosmic energy.
8. Thank your body for being so willing to change.
9. Take a few refreshing breaths and when you're ready stand up, stretch, and reverse polarities.
10. You may find it useful to make some notes of your experience.

EXERCISE 19: Creating a Mental Image of a Grounded You

The last grounding technique we'll cover will help you understand more deeply how your mental images themselves have power. As you become more skillful in the practices, you will often simply imagine something, and it will appear in your aura.

For the next exercise, about 6 feet out in front of your aura you'll imagine a mental picture of yourself sitting comfortably in your chair—legs uncrossed, hands uncrossed—then mentally see a connection from the base of your spine to the very center of the Earth. Almost magically, the act of creating the mental picture of yourself and the center of the Earth will generate your grounding cord. Practicing it a few times slowly, in as much detail as you can, will help you access it more easily later.

1. Breathing gently and deeply into your belly, sit comfortably straight in your chair, with your feet flat on the floor, legs and arms uncrossed.
2. Put your old grounding cord in a rose and explode it with golden cosmic energy.
3. About 6 feet out in front of your aura, create a mental picture of yourself seated comfortably in your chair with the base of your spine connected to the very center of the Earth via a grounding cord about 6 inches in diameter.
4. Allow any excess energy, or any energy that isn't yours, to fall away down your grounding cord, allowing Mother Earth to recycle those energies.
5. Imagine that your entire body is replenished with the fresh golden cosmic light.
6. Thank your body for being willing to change.
7. Take a few refreshing breaths and when you are ready stand up, stretch, and reverse polarities.
8. You may find it useful to make some notes of your experience.

You'll find an immediately increased ability to access and address your experience—especially any time you experience stress—by taking a gentle deep breath and creating a new grounding cord.

The Center of the Head

A powerful energy of genuine openness and neutrality can be found in the center of your head. The center of the head is located in the area of your pineal gland to about 2 inches behind and a little above. It's centered roughly at the top of the ears. All future meditations in this book will begin with grounding and bringing your conscious awareness into the center of your head. (See Figure 2, "The Center of the Head," below.)

Of course there are other placements for centering your consciousness. A favorite for many is in the heart area, which when done correctly and with subtlety can accomplish much the same thing. But centering authentically in the heart is trickier than most imagine, and requires an advanced and accomplished grounding. Otherwise one can tap into invisible conditioning, resistances, and delusions.

Please take a moment to playfully observe where your attention is centered at this moment. It might not be obvious. Ask yourself, "Where am I?" Look for what you call "yourself." Your answer will be found where "yourself" is located. You could also ask, "From where am I seeing or experiencing this moment?" Very often you'll be off to one side or

Figure 2: The Center of the Head

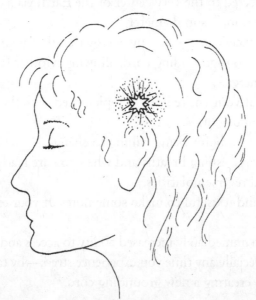

another; or buzzing around; or back behind a person that you're talking to, monitoring their opinion of you; or lost somewhere out in space; or stuck in your jaw thinking about the next thing you want to say. "You" can be in any of a number of places.

We have two suggested techniques for finding the center of your head. The first is to invite your consciousness to rest in the center of your head. The other is to measure the distance between you (that is, your awareness) and the center of your head. Somewhat magically, this act of measuring has the tendency to pull your awareness into the center of your head like a magnet. It works because the natural place for your awareness is in the center of the head. When you measure the distance, you simultaneously pay attention both to where your awareness is and to its natural location. Highlighted by your attention, there is an innate tendency for your awareness to jump back to its natural location for engaging personal life.

Few of us naturally "own" the center of our head. In the beginning you may find so much energy from other people in the center of your head that there seems to be little room for you. Or you may not easily find the center of your head, or you might find the center of your head only to pop back out. If so, you'll have plenty of company.

John: "If you find that to be the case, I can sympathize. I've spent thirty-eight years on this, and I still find lots of energies in the center of my head."

Even if you do find lots of energies in the center of your head, as you begin to add being in the center of your head into your grounding, you will rapidly increase your neutrality, resourcefulness, humor, and openness to life.

EXERCISE 20: Finding the Center of Your Head

1. Sit comfortably straight in your chair, feet flat on the floor, legs and arms uncrossed.
2. With a sense of openness, relax, close your eyes, and breathe gently into your belly.
3. Put your old grounding cord in a rose, explode it, and create a new grounding cord.
4. Take a moment to notice where your awareness is centered.

5. When ready, invite your awareness into the center of your head. Or measure the distance between you (your awareness) and the center of your head, and let this process gently pull your awareness into the center of your head like a magnet.
6. Spend a few minutes observing how that looks, feels, or sounds.
7. Practice letting your awareness rise to the ceiling and then inviting it back to the center of your head.
8. Repeat several times until you are reasonably confident that you know how it feels for your awareness to be in the center of your head.
9. Thank your body for being willing to change.
10. Take a few refreshing breaths and when ready stand up, stretch, and reverse polarities.
11. You may find it useful to make some notes of your experience.

Cultivating center-of-the-head awareness may take years. Even so, you will find immediate benefit each time you practice this skill.

With these two simple skills of grounding and locating the center of the head, you now have an easy and powerful way to engage the world. To begin your day, ground and bring your awareness into the center of your head.

Please note: Any time you make a physical, emotional, mental, or spiritual change it is helpful to update your grounding. In most exercises throughout this book we suggest that you cut off your old grounding cord and create a new one twice within the same exercise. The first time you create your grounding cord is to prepare you for the psychic work you'll do during the exercise, and the second time is to help your body assimilate the work you just completed.

CHAPTER 6

The Energy of Biological Differences

The Divine Complexity of Women, the Divine Simplicity of Men, and the Skills to Appreciate Both

John: "For the first ten or so years I knew about male and female grounding, I thought it couldn't possibly be true, that it sounded like sexist nonsense. This was back in the '70s and '80s when we were strongly ideologically committed to the idea that there weren't any important intrinsic differences between men and women. As I've grown in psychic awareness, and as the prevailing ideologies have changed, I've come to understand the gender differences and grounding more deeply. The women of my acquaintance find female grounding to be their most valuable tool, and in fact Gloria, my coauthor, has a saying we now use all the time. It's a little tongue-in-cheek, but it's only the tiniest exaggeration, if an exaggeration at all: 'The answer to practically every challenge a woman faces is to female-ground.'"

One of the gifts that comes from the fact that men and women are different is that it forces us, if we're to be successful in life, to learn to interact well with people who are simply different from us. Men's and women's auras are different in ways that affect how each gender engages the world and engages the other sex. Other things being equal, a woman's aura will be higher in frequency and about 2 feet larger in radius than a man's due to the energy that supports her ability to bear children. This is true whether or not a woman chooses to have children, and whether she is heterosexual, lesbian, or even transgendered born with a female body. Viewed clairvoyantly, very little of a man's aura energy is generated by his reproductive system, whereas large parts of a woman's emerge from the energy of her ovaries, uterus, and breasts and from differences in several glands such as the pituitary (a woman's pituitary gland is about four to five times larger than a man's).

Gender energies are palpable, particularly the female energies. (We're using "gender" to refer to biological differences, not differences due to social programming.[1]) It's helpful to be aware of those gender energies, as they are key to understanding and treating your personality as real and important. There are transcendent states where gender is irrelevant, but at the personality level gender plays an essential part in your embodied humanity. Learning to be male- or female-grounded will effectively and gracefully address the balancing of your gender energies, as well as help you acknowledge your unique strengths and challenges.[2]

The main tool for grounding is the creation of a male or female grounding cord, each of which has slight adjustments to the grounding cord you learned to create in Chapter 5. Male or female grounding helps open a clear line of communication for your personality and your body to engage your soul more easily. At a body and emotional level it greatly reduces gender-driven stress, clarifies your energy, helps you maintain healthier boundaries, and balances the gender energies that can unconsciously tax your relationships. It also helps enormously in understanding and communicating with the other sex.

The energies and drives we'll discuss in this chapter are beautiful and natural drives. We can imagine the possibility that someone might misunderstand and think we are demonizing one or the other gender, but nothing could be further from the truth. The better we all understand these natural drives and energies, the more we'll all celebrate our differences as well as our similarities. And the more skillful we'll all become in communicating with each other—our own sex as well as the other sex. Nor are we saying that any person must conform to any gender expectations. There are biological differences which are discrete and which experience convinces us are best addressed. Personality is free to vary, though the body energies might seem to promote another direction.

Male and Female Grounding

Men's and women's bodies vibrate in different energy ranges, each with a biological programming unique in quality and characteristics. This is true whether or not they are heterosexual. Our programming naturally and strongly conditions us to behave differently in several important ways. (We use the word "differently" intentionally, as opposed to "better or worse.") Women are strongly conditioned biologically to be responsible for nurturing, not only children but often anyone who might appear to need help. Men's biological conditioning lends itself to a simpler approach to life—to view some problems as theirs to solve and some problems as not theirs to solve. Of course, this distinction simply refers to a qualitative difference in style and attitude, not to an inability to care for others.

To the psychically aware, a woman's body energy will have an exquisite complexity, while a man's body energy will have an exquisite simplicity. Gender grounding helps men and women to understand and function more skillfully with their distinctive gender conditioning, to better comprehend and honor each other's boundaries, and to cultivate a deeper understanding and appreciation of the other gender's natural programming and approach to life. As you male- or female-ground and play with these concepts, even a little, you will find it much easier to be less judgmental and to give the other gender space to be who they are, with more appreciation, kindness, and generosity on your part.

We are often asked, "Don't we all have aspects of both sexes? Shouldn't we develop and balance aspects of both sexes?" And sometimes essentially, "Why can't my husband be more like a woman?" The answer is, we all have aspects of both sexes, and it is part of our spiritual journey to learn how to use the energies that we associate with both genders. Please understand that androgyny doesn't apply to the behavior we are discussing in this chapter because these specific energies arise from that portion of the energy spectrum that underpins the natural *differences* in our physical bodies.

Thus while it is important for a man to learn how to communicate with and support women, it's not part of a man's journey to learn how to run female creative energies though his energy body in the frequency range we are discussing. To say otherwise would be like suggesting that a man would be better if he had ovaries *and* testicles. And that is just not true.

Male grounding is far less of an issue for men than female grounding is for women. For example, when a man is not male-grounded it may manifest as passivity or aggression, certainly important issues. But since a woman's reproductive energy involves so much more total energy and programming than a man's reproductive energy (thus extending her aura 2 feet further than a man's), the consequences are greater when she isn't female-grounded. For example, it is easier for her to inadvertently over-step boundaries, or even worse, be judged as out of control or hysterical, and not in the comical sense. Have you ever noticed how people, perhaps even you, will often stop listening to a woman if she raises her voice? Both men and women have a tendency to tune out a woman who is not female-grounded, though men tend to have a more exaggerated response: anger or even rage. Fair or not, it's often the case that a woman will be dismissed if she is not female-grounded. If she is female-grounded she can raise her voice *and* be heard.

Later in this chapter we introduce skills that will allow you to recognize and clear gender enmeshment energies: where you've placed your biological energy in someone's aura, as well as when you have someone else's gender energy in your own aura. Unrecognized, the other gender's energies can cause overwhelming sadness in a woman, and rage in a man. Because it is easy to forget, we remind you that any energy in your space is there by your invitation, whether explicit or implicit.

After learning how to establish your male or female grounding cord, we'll explore four rarely discussed though common gender energy challenges:

- Female—responsibility, misreading potential, and guilt
- Male—grief
- Female—sadness
- Male—rage

Male Energy: An Elegant Simplicity

The energy and programming that come with having a male reproductive system aren't nearly as complicated or as challenging as the energies that come with having a female reproductive system. Male grounding seems to help a man avoid the polarities of passivity and aggression. Compared to female grounding, male grounding is quite simple to do and sustain.[3]

FOR MEN

EXERCISE 21: Creating a Male Grounding Cord

To male-ground, after creating your grounding cord, men imagine an extension from their prostate gland (the walnut-size gland surrounding the urethra) flowing into their grounding cord at the base of their spine. The connection can be about the diameter of a half-dollar to a silver dollar.

1. Sit comfortably straight in your chair, feet flat on the floor, legs and arms uncrossed.
2. With a sense of openness, relax, close your eyes, and breathe gently into your belly.
3. Bring your awareness into the center of your head.
4. Explode your old grounding cord and create a new one.
5. Then imagine a stream of energy, about an inch to an inch and a half in diameter, flowing from your prostate gland (the walnut-size gland surrounding the urethra) over to your grounding cord at the base of the spine.
6. Breathe and allow yourself to rest in your male-grounded energy for about 5 minutes.
7. Allow the day's stress to simply flow down your grounding cord, and allow Mother Earth to recycle the energies for you.
8. Thank your body for being willing to change.
9. Take a few refreshing breaths and when ready stand up, gently stretch, and reverse polarities.
10. You may find it useful to make some notes of your experience.

Brian, multimedia designer and videographer: "Male grounding takes me out of single-pointed focus. It's no longer 'my way or the highway'—I can consider other people's perspectives and other solutions to a problem more easily."

Female Energy: An Elegant Complexity

By all accounts, the women we know who practice female grounding report that it is simply a gift from heaven. Large numbers of women, if not most women, enjoy supporting and nurturing people, and not only their children. Female grounding keeps a woman's nurturing and support consistent with her boundaries and other people's boundaries. Her nurturing and support can then become more fun, more helpful, less taxing, and more satisfying.[4]

We're often asked, "I've had a hysterectomy; will female grounding still apply to me?" Absolutely, and in some important ways, maybe more so. The psychic anatomy of a woman's female reproductive system continues to actively participate in a woman's life even after a hysterectomy, unless she closes it down. We often see women dismiss and alienate their female creative energy after a hysterectomy when it is all the more important for a woman in this situation to keep her reproductive spaces clear, fresh, energized, and in current time.

"I have been the main caregiver for my son, who has been recovering for the past several years from a life-threatening illness. Female grounding replenishes my energy and regulates the stress and emotional intensity of the complex work involved in my spiritual journey. My son benefits as well because my female grounding permits him to find his own space and create his own path to recovery."—**Deborah, retired lawyer**

"I think of female grounding like vitamins, something you do every day." —**Trish, psychologist**

To female-ground you'll connect your female reproductive system—each ovary, the uterus, a psychic ball of female creative energy out in front of your body, and also the sciatic nerve—into your grounding cord.

You might imagine it like the confluence of six rivers—a stream of female grounding from each ovary (or ovary space if you have had a hysterectomy), a stream from the uterus, a stream from the ball of female creative energy out in front of your body, and a stream from each side of the sciatic nerve at the hip—flowing into your main grounding cord that commences at the base of your spine. From there it will ground you in a continuous flow to the Earth's loving center. (See Figure 3, "Female Grounding," page 74.)

Along with her reproductive system, a woman will find a ball of female creative energy about 4 inches out in front of her body, just in front of the uterus. A lot of women report that they find it to be like a fuzzy ball shape 4 to 8 inches in diameter. You can often feel it just by running your hand down in front of your body, sensing it as heat or coolness, or you might feel yourself kind of bump into an energy. It'll be subtle, but it's there. So, as part of your female grounding you'll add a stream of grounding energy from your female creative space into your grounding cord.

Why is the sciatic nerve part of female grounding? There is a great deal of psychic energy running through a female reproductive system that tends to heat up the sciatic nerve, and by grounding you can keep it cool and balanced.

The sciatic nerve is one of the largest nerves in the body. It connects to several places on both sides of the sacrum, the big butterfly bone near the base of your spine. It then runs down the back of both legs and tucks under the heel a little bit. Since there is a lot of female creative energy circulating throughout the entire hip area, by female-grounding into the sciatic nerve you not only cool it but you balance it and bring awareness and healing energies into your legs and the back side of your body.

Gloria: "With several female clients who are dancers with recurring leg and ankle injuries, I often see that they do not run energy all the way down their sciatic nerve into the area of chronic injury. When they attend to their female grounding, and kind of 'tuck in' their sciatic nerve under their heel, they own that portion of their leg, and report that they are more balanced and have fewer injuries."

Figure 3: Female Grounding

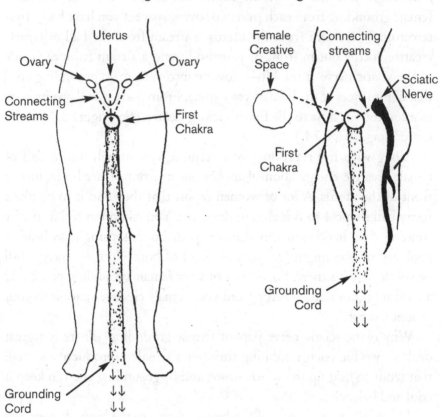

STEP 1: After creating a grounding cord from the base of your spine all the way down to the earth's neutral center, imagine a stream of energy flowing from your uterus and each ovary into your grounding cord.

STEP 2: Imagine a stream of energy flowing from your sciatic nerve (one stream from each side of your hips) into your grounding cord.

STEP 3: Imagine a stream of energy flowing from the female creative space (about four inches in front of your uterus) into your grounding cord.

In the following exercise we'll explore what it feels like to be female-grounded. Then, for comparison, we'll have you imagine two challenging situations—one where you are female-grounded, and one where you are not.

FOR WOMEN

EXERCISE 22: Creating a Female Grounding Cord

1. Sit comfortably straight in your chair, feet flat on the floor, legs and hands uncrossed.
2. With a sense of openness, relax, close your eyes, and breathe gently into your belly.
3. Bring your awareness into the center of your head.
4. Explode your old grounding cord and create a new one.
5. Imagine a small stream from each ovary, or ovary space, flowing to the base of your spine and into your main grounding cord.
6. Next, become aware of a ball of female creative energy about 4 inches out in front of your body, just in front of the uterus, and imagine a stream of grounding energy flowing from there to the base of your spine and into your main grounding cord.
7. Then imagine a small stream of grounding energy flowing from your uterus into your main grounding cord.
8. Next imagine small streams from your sciatic nerve (two streams, one from each side of your hips) flowing into your main grounding cord.
9. Breathe gently and deeply into your belly, and allow yourself to rest in your female-grounded energy for about 5 minutes.
10. And finally, allow the day's stress to simply flow down your grounding cord, and allow Mother Earth to recycle the energies for you.
11. Thank your body for being willing to change.
12. Take a few refreshing breaths and when ready stand up, gently stretch, and reverse polarities.
13. You may find it useful to make some notes of your experience.

Next, so that you can experience firsthand how challenging it is to remain female-grounded under certain circumstances, please choose someone who you think is engaged in foolish and damaging behavior to contemplate for the following meditation.

FOR WOMEN

EXERCISE 23: Intentionally Challenging Your Female Grounding

The following exercise is very powerful and for many women life-changing. As it can be somewhat intense, please pay attention to your body and emotions. Explore the exercise at a comfortable pace. If you find yourself excessively lit up, be gentle with yourself—take a break, breathe, find some playfulness, and explode some pictures before proceeding.

1. Sit comfortably straight in your chair, feet flat on the floor, legs and hands uncrossed.
2. With a sense of openness, relax, close your eyes, and breathe gently into your belly.
3. Bring your awareness into the center of your head.
4. Explode your old grounding cord and remain *un*grounded for the first part of this meditation.
5. Think of someone you know who you think is engaged in foolish and damaging behavior, and imagine a picture of them on a rose about 7 feet out in front of you.
6. Spend a few minutes contemplating the behaviors that concern you as you observe how your body feels, as well as your emotional responses.
7. When ready create a new female grounding cord—with streams of grounding energy flowing from each ovary, from the uterus, the sciatic nerve, and from the female creative space out in front of your body at the level of the uterus, all going into the main grounding cord at the base of your spine.
8. Let any energies that are not yours simply flow down your grounding cord.
9. Explode your picture of the person, and any pictures that lit up in your space, and then replenish your aura with golden cosmic energy.

10. Now, repeat the process: Imagine someone you know who you think is engaged in foolish and damaging behavior (it can be the same person or another) and create a picture of them about 7 feet out in front of your body.

11. While being nicely female-grounded, observe that picture and contemplate the behaviors that concern you for a few minutes. Observe and acknowledge how your body feels, and your emotional responses.

12. With a playful curiosity, monitor whether you are maintaining your female grounding, and if not, simply reestablish it.

13. Next, intentionally break your grounding, allowing yourself to become ungrounded.

14. Notice what happens to your energy and your emotions as you think of the person while being ungrounded.

15. Reestablish your female grounding and look at the situation again.

16. Finish the exercise by checking one final time to see that you are still female-grounded. Female grounding can be lost very quickly, therefore we suggest checking often in the initial stages of this important practice.

17. Explode the rose holding the picture of the person whose behavior concerns you and recycle your energy back into your crown.

18. Fill your body and aura with lots of neutral golden cosmic energy.

19. Thank your body for being willing to change.

20. Take a few refreshing breaths and when ready stand up, gently stretch, and reverse polarities.

21. You may find it useful to make some notes of your experience.

A lot of women emerge from the previous exercise with a knowing look on their face, shaking their head, feeling like they have gained great insight about themselves, their mothers, their aunts, their sisters, their girlfriends, or their daughters. If that was not your experience, please come back to the exercise another time.

Discovering and Appreciating the Beauty and Strength of Your Gender's Biological Energy

Please take a few moments with the respective male- or female-oriented meditations to deepen your understanding and appreciation of the natural beauty and strength of your own gender's biological energy and how it contributes to the creation of your aura.

Instructions for both men and women: To begin, you'll first observe and acknowledge your natural biological energy. Then see if you can sense your biological energy's frequency, as well as its natural impulse—whether it seems inclined to move quickly or slowly. Last, as you rest in the naturalness of your biological energy, see if you can sense how it contributes to the creation of your personal aura. Perceiving these energies may take practice, as they can be subtle. You may want to repeat the exercise several times over a period of days, weeks, or even months.

FOR WOMEN

EXERCISE 24: Acknowledging Your Exquisite Complexity

1. Sit comfortably straight in your chair, feet flat on the floor, legs and arms uncrossed.
2. With a sense of openness, relax, close your eyes, and breathe gently into your belly.
3. Bring your awareness into the center of your head.
4. Cut off your old grounding cord, put it in a rose, and explode it.
5. Female-ground.
6. Continue breathing gently and deeply into your belly, and spend a few minutes observing and appreciating your aura's natural complexity.
7. See if you can sense your body's energy frequency. If you hear energy, it will probably be a fairly high tone.
8. Also, take a few moments to observe the various energies of your female grounding. See if you can discern the different frequencies of your ovaries, uterus, sciatic nerve, and the space of female creative energy out in front of your uterus. The energy differences may be quite subtle.

9. See if you can sense your female creative energy's natural and spontaneous impulse. Does it seem inclined to move slowly or quickly?

10. As you rest in the naturalness of your biological energy, see if you can sense how it contributes to the creation of your personal aura.

11. Explode any pictures that may have lit up.

12. Replenish your body and aura with golden cosmic energy.

13. Bring up just the right amount of earth energy for your body and aura at this time.

14. Thank your body for being willing to change.

15. Take a few refreshing breaths and when ready stand up, gently stretch, and reverse polarities.

16. You may find it useful to make some notes of your experience.

FOR MEN

EXERCISE 25: Acknowledging Your Exquisite Simplicity

1. Sit comfortably straight in your chair, feet flat on the floor, legs and arms uncrossed.

2. With a sense of openness, relax, close your eyes, and breathe gently into your belly.

3. Bring your awareness into the center of your head.

4. Cut off your old grounding cord, put it in a rose, and explode it.

5. Male-ground.

6. Continue breathing gently and deeply into your belly, and spend a few minutes observing and appreciating your aura's natural male simplicity.

7. See if you can sense your body's energy frequency. If you hear energy, it will probably be a fairly low tone.

8. As you rest in the naturalness of your male biological energy, see if you can sense how it contributes to the creation of your personal aura.

9. Explode any pictures that may have lit up.

10. Replenish your body and aura with golden cosmic energy.

11. Bring up just the right amount of earth energy for your body and aura at this time.

12. Thank your body for being willing to change.
13. Take a few refreshing breaths and when ready stand up, gently stretch, and reverse polarities.
14. You may find it useful to make some notes of your experience.

Observing and Appreciating the Biological Energy of the Other Gender

Please take a few moments with the respective male- or female-oriented meditations to deepen your understanding and appreciation of the other gender's biological energy. Women will observe the uniqueness, natural beauty, and strength of a male's biological simplicity. Men will observe the uniqueness, natural beauty, and strength of a female's biological complexity.

Instructions for both men and women: For the following exercises please choose someone of the opposite gender whose natural biological energy you'd like to observe and compare to your own. To begin, you'll first observe and acknowledge your own biological energy. Then you'll create a rose to hold a picture of the person's energy you've chosen to observe. It may be subtle, but see if you can also sense your energy's natural impulse as you observe the other gender's energy. Remember, when you acknowledge your perceptions and experience, no matter how subtle, your practice will become more real and meaningful for you.

FOR WOMEN

EXERCISE 26: Acknowledging Your Female Complexity and Male Energy Simplicity

1. Sit comfortably straight in your chair, feet flat on the floor, legs and arms uncrossed.
2. With a sense of openness, relax, close your eyes, and breathe gently into your belly.
3. Bring your awareness into the center of your head.
4. Cut off your old grounding cord, put it in a rose, and explode it.
5. Female-ground.

6. Observe and acknowledge your aura's natural female creativity and complexity.
7. Next, create a rose and ask that a picture of the male whose energy you've chosen to observe go out onto your rose.
8. Once again check your grounding, paying attention to your boundaries so that your energy doesn't jump into his space. To increase your awareness of your natural and unconscious impulse, ask yourself, "Was my energy poised to jump into his space or fix him?" Be sure to acknowledge and appreciate the significance of your perception, whatever you find.
9. Observe the elegance and strength of his biological simplicity.
10. Notice, if you can, that his body is probably vibrating at a lower frequency than yours. (Many people vibrate their body towards or even at the frequency of the other gender.)
11. Compare and contrast your natural differences and similarities.
12. Explode any pictures, particularly any judgment pictures, that may light up in your aura.
13. Breathe your energy back from his aura (back through your crown).
14. Send his energy from the rose and anywhere in your aura back to him or his guides.
15. Explode the rose you created and recycle that energy back through your crown.
16. Allow any anxiety or excess energy to simply flow down your grounding cord, letting Mother Earth recycle the energies for you.
17. Replenish your body and aura with golden cosmic energy.
18. Bring up just the right amount of earth energy for your body and aura at this time.
19. Thank your body for being willing to change.
20. Take a few refreshing breaths and when ready stand up, gently stretch, and reverse polarities.
21. You may find it useful to make some notes of your experience.

FOR MEN

EXERCISE 27: Acknowledging Your Male Simplicity and Female Energy Complexity

1. Sit comfortably straight in your chair, feet flat on the floor, legs and arms uncrossed.
2. With a sense of openness, relax, close your eyes, and breathe gently into your belly.
3. Bring your awareness into the center of your head.
4. Cut off your old grounding cord, put it in a rose, and explode it.
5. Male-ground.
6. Observe and acknowledge your aura's natural male simplicity.
7. Next, create a rose and ask that a picture of the female whose energy you've chosen to observe go out onto your rose.
8. Explode any pictures, particularly judgment pictures, that may light up in your aura.
9. Observe the elegance and strength of her biological complexity.
10. Notice, if you can, that her body is probably vibrating at a higher frequency than yours. (Many people vibrate their body towards or even at the frequency of the other gender.)
11. Again observe the elegance and strength of your biological simplicity.
12. Compare and contrast your natural differences and similarities.
13. Breathe your energy back from her aura (back through your crown).
14. Send her energy from the rose and anywhere in your aura back to her or her guides.
15. Explode the rose you created and recycle your energy back through your crown.
16. Replenish your body and aura with golden cosmic energy.
17. Bring up just the right amount of earth energy for your body and aura at this time.
18. Allow any anxiety or excess energy to simply flow down your grounding cord, letting Mother Earth recycle the energies for you.
19. Thank your body for being willing to change.

20. Take a few refreshing breaths and when ready stand up, gently stretch, and reverse polarities.
21. You may find it useful to make some notes of your experience.

Two Drives: Responsibility and Supporting "Potential"

In support of a woman's capability for childbearing, she runs two drives that arise naturally out of her reproductive programming: 1) an instinctive programming to be responsible for others (especially her children), and 2) an instinctive programming to support people, but according to what her genetic programming tells her is their potential.

When a woman is female-grounded she can acknowledge and balance these two major drives with a flexible perspective and healthy boundaries. When she is not female-grounded, these instincts can manifest as a driving, sometimes crushing sense of responsibility. In the manner that we are using the term "female responsibility," it is an energy that pushes. It pushes the woman, it pushes others. So, not only does this stress her on all levels, but her fervent attention on others is often experienced by them as excessive, overbearing, and disrespectful.

"Do I want to help?" and "Why?"

To avoid being driven unconsciously and inappropriately to help (or fix) someone, it behooves a woman to ask herself a series of questions. The first is "Do I want to help?" If so, she can then ask the follow-up question, "Why?" because she may have answered yes because she wasn't sufficiently female-grounded. When a woman female-grounds, she creates the space to answer "Do I really want to help?" more authentically.

"Does he or she genuinely want my help?"

Asking the next question, "Does he or she genuinely want my help?" helps a woman take a more objective look at her own boundaries and to determine what help, if any, someone is open to receiving. Even if a person of interest has, in fact, a certain potential, he or she may not intend to achieve that potential, or maybe not at this time. It may not be his or her spiritual path. This is an important and subtle understanding.

Another level of complexity is inherently present: what a woman may perceive as someone's potential may not be his or her own authentic potential, but a reading of her own personal biological programming. Female grounding helps negotiate this pitfall.

The intensity and verve of female creative energy drive behavior, sometimes in ways that are not as adaptable as you would like them to be. The downside of a woman's sense of responsibility can be a crushing anxiety that a woman without female-grounding often feels—for example, whenever she senses that she won't be able to provide sufficient support to help her friend, husband, or child reach what she is imagining to be his or her full potential. Her imaginings arise out of a particular kind of psychic structure called *perfect pictures*. (See the section entitled "Perfect Pictures," Chapter 9, "Opening to Life As It Is: Resistance and Neutrality.") Both men and women can have perfect pictures, but a man's perfect pictures will not be driven by his biological instincts, whereas a woman's can be. Every woman is born with a particularly powerful set in her reproductive system.

A woman's ovaries carry a set of perfect pictures inherited from the women in her lineage. They are a product of her ethnic group's history. So, while every woman will have perfect pictures, each woman's pictures will vary. Her pictures also hold encoding for what a woman's soul intends for her to explore in a lifetime, including the advantages and weaknesses that will help her become a more kind and generous person. Vibrating at a white-light level, perfect pictures represent an unachievable perfection, beyond the human range.

We often work with women in despair over the fact that a loved one or friend is going in an unfortunate direction. We all, men and women alike, have difficulty seeing our loved ones and friends make unfortunate choices. But we find that in general, there's a kind of urgency, anxiety, and sense of necessity that a woman is more likely to have than a man is.

Usually we find that if a man feels a similar sense of urgency, he'll be operating out of different psychic energies (more likely his third chakra), and the urgency can be more about control than about support. When the urgency energy is not authentic for a man, his urgent impulse will most likely come from an energy in his space from a significant woman in his life: his mother, girlfriend, wife, friend, etc. When the urgency is authentic for a man, it will have a unique simplicity, an unfussiness. As a reminder, we all have a natural blend of male and female energies: We all have the capacity to be responsible, and we all have the capacity to be neutral and willing to allow people to make their own decisions, and both capacities are important. Additionally, we each have our gendered body that generates very different energies. By grounding appropriately, we can enjoy that difference while still utilizing our innate capacity for wise, generous decisions.

John: "In many readings I will see a woman going into responsibility. When I suggest she look at it, I often see her search only that part of her aura generated by her conscious self. Often the responsibility energy will have been generated automatically by her reproductive system rather than by her conscious attention."

When most of us, male or female, ask, "What do I think and feel?" we search or track only those parts of ourselves included in our ego. Various instinctual drives won't be attended to without a special effort.

When a woman asks, "What do I want to do?" she will often get an answer that is accurate from her belly button up—more from her intellect or personality level (the third through seventh chakras). Her answer won't take into consideration what her instinctive energy is doing in her reproductive system. So, we add a refinement to clarify which energy is driving a woman's reaction by suggesting that she ask two separate questions. The first is "What do I want to do about this?" Then, for a more biological focus, "What is my female reproductive system instinctually directing me to do?"

Let's take an example of a teen going off to college (we could just as easily use numerous scenarios where female grounding would be very helpful: a boyfriend who is always in need of rescue; a husband's layoff late in life as he begins a new career; an alcoholic sibling; an aging parent who continues to drive, etc.).

When a teen goes off to college it can be hard on both parents but often more challenging for a mother. She'll be excited that her teen will soon explore new levels of independence and embark on new adventures, so she'll work hard to stay out of his or her space. She'll be interested and will want to know everything, and she'll worry—it's a big world out there ... She'll want him or her to know she trusts him or her, but she'll remember her own college days ... And she'll try to give him or her all the space needed to mature.... But, as any mother knows, it's not easy.

Asking the question "What is my female reproductive system instinctually directing me to do?" refines your awareness. Even if you don't think you're jumping into your child's space, ask and observe your energy psychically: "What is my reproductive system doing here?" You'll often find that while you're trying not to jump into your child's space, your female creative energy is.[5]

Your teen is not going to make that distinction, and furthermore, your energy, no matter how lovingly intended, will not be easy for your teen to deal with. Instead of your energy feeling supportive and loving it may instead manifest as an increased uneasiness, and in some cases even panic. When you ask yourself, "What is my reproductive system doing?" it will help you do a better job of staying out of your teen's space while remaining engaged, supportive, and responsive. And you will model an important life skill: how to remain calm, resourceful, and flexible in the midst of dramatic change.

John: "When Lewis [Bostwick] and the psychics studying with him observed how quickly a woman's programming sent her into overdrive, the first thing they tried to do was to clear that programming out of a woman's space, so that she would be more able to freely evaluate when and how to help someone. But they found that clearing the reproductive programming threw a woman's hormonal balance off. They then developed female grounding, which allowed a woman to have her programming, to have her drives, to have her hormonal balance, and to be able to choose—from the center of her head—what she wanted to do. Female grounding keeps the pictures and programming but changes a woman's response to them from being absolute drivers to being only one source of information that would aid a woman, in her executive capacity, to decide what she wants and doesn't want to do."

It's probably obvious by now that, in addition to helping women make better choices, female grounding greatly relieves anxiety and stress, and allows life to be far more enjoyable. Her programming remains intact, and instead of being driven by her programming, she can learn to make decisions from the center of her own "I-ness."

IN SUMMARY, THE QUESTIONS A WOMAN CAN ASK TO AVOID BEING DRIVEN UNCONSCIOUSLY AND INAPPROPRIATELY:

"Do I want to help?" If yes, "Why?"

For appropriate boundaries and to determine what help someone is open to receiving:

"Does he or she genuinely want my help?"

If someone is open to receiving help, to clarify what manner of support is appropriate:

"What do I want to do to help?"

Then, for a more physical focus:

"What is my female reproductive system instinctually directing me to do?"

Or even more subtle: "What is the energy of my female reproductive system actually doing without my conscious awareness?"

Male Grief and Female Guilt

There can be a tendency to get serious about male grief and female guilt, so please play with these ideas lightly. The short answer to both male grief and female guilt is to male- or female-ground and give the other person space to explore his or her respective journey.

"I don't understand why I am so terribly sad!" If a woman finds herself feeling extremely sad and crying for no recognizable reason, with a depression that seems to come out of nowhere, it is a clue that she may be harboring an energy called *male grief.* Of course, both men and women can have biological predispositions to deep depressions, and, for a woman, such a predisposition will certainly contribute.[6] Here, we're referring to a specific male energy she would have unknowingly pulled into her space that can usually be traced to her lack of female grounding and a pattern of rescuing males.

Male grief is an energy produced in a male body that arises out of the natural process of separation from his mother at birth. It's an energy created by his body's shock and growing awareness that he's no longer surrounded by her female creative energy. For female babies, though birth is still a shock, the separation isn't as traumatic because they are born with their own female creative energy. All men have some form of male grief energy. The use of the term is somewhat confusing. We use it because the energy feels so overwhelmingly sad to a woman, and if a man fails to address it, he will feel sad and driven to seek a woman's rescue. But the purpose of the male grief energy itself is to move him to understand his own natural simplicity.

Ideally, the boy's body fairly quickly becomes accustomed to the new, simpler energy environment and the boy develops what we call *male clarity.* (See page 91.) Often, however, the karmic energy set up between the boy and his mother generates her "rescue" of him. She unconsciously senses his disorientation and psychically surrounds him in a warm field of her female creative energy. For some men this initial rescue experience creates a habitual pattern that becomes a powerful unconscious drive, causing them to spend their lives looking for women who'll wrap them in their female creative energy—attempting to rescue them.

We've all seen the dynamics played out repeatedly in codependent relationships—often involving substance abuse and emotional addictive behaviors. As dysfunctional as the trap may be, there is always a payoff; unfortunately the payoff perpetuates the dysfunction as enmeshment.

John: "Some men unknowingly show a woman a psychic picture, 'Woe is me,' and if the woman is not female-grounded she may go rushing in to save him by taking on his pain herself."

The love song "As Long As He Needs Me" from the 1960s musical *Oliver* is a perfect example of the male grief and the female rescue syndrome. It may be a natural and immediate response for some women and young girls to rescue, and even though it may seem to be a noble attempt to nurture, here's why it doesn't work. When she consciously or unconsciously tries to rescue a male from his male grief, his male grief energy floods into her space. Remember, male grief is a male body energy; it is biologically natural to men only. But male grief in a female's space can be excruciating for her—so lonely, so sad, and so alienated. To a woman, being a man bereft of female creative energy can feel like the world's worst tragedy. Maybe that's a little over-stated, but if so, not by much.

Let's break that out a little more. He may feel better temporarily, but, by a female taking on his pain, he has lost an important opportunity to grow and to acknowledge and appreciate his natural path. She'll feel terrible with his pain in her space, and she'll have lost an opportunity to create healthy boundaries, as well as the opportunity to value his spiritual journey. They become enmeshed, and her intended generosity perpetuates codependence, which often has its own addictiveness.

It is important to remember that not everyone is ready and willing to heal, and that choice not to heal can be an authentic part of his or her journey—exasperating for their loved ones but authentic for the person nonetheless. For instance, someone may choose to explore alcoholism for several lifetimes until all avenues of interest are exhausted. It is also common for someone to surround him- or herself with the same people for several or many lifetimes, where as a group they work through certain issues of relationship and karma. That doesn't mean that the karmic group can only move in unison. When someone decides that he or she wants to break out of the pattern and grow in a different way, he or she will gather the meaning from the experience and cease creating codependent relationships.

This is not a conscious process; a woman is not going to say, "Being born male is the worst thing that could ever happen." It's just that male grief in a female aura looks and feels like a huge void—divorced from the energy necessary and vital to her body as a woman. So her body will try to process it to find an answer for that lack. No matter how much a woman would like to solve a male's pain of not having resolved and learned from his male grief, she cannot be an authentic solution to that male grief. However, when she is female-grounded she will be more able to help him find his own answers, if she chooses to.

Male grief can sit in a woman's space without her recognizing it. It would be a sustained background of pain and sadness that she assumes is natural. As a woman you'll be surprised at how often you'll find your father's, boyfriend's, husband's, or brother's male grief in your space. It's always empowering to remember your amusement and find and clear the matching energy with which you invited his male grief into your space.

FOR WOMEN:

EXERCISE 28: Female Grounding for Male Grief in a Woman's Space

For the following exercise please choose a male whose male grief you feel you may have pulled into your aura. If you cannot think of any male in particular, simply work with a male that you are close to, and repeat it with two or three other males you know. Then compare and contrast your experience of each. You may be surprised by what you find.

1. Sit comfortably straight in your chair, feet flat on the floor, legs and arms uncrossed.
2. With a sense of openness, relax, close your eyes, and breathe gently into your belly.
3. Bring your awareness into the center of your head.
4. Cut off your old grounding cord, put it in a rose, and explode it.
5. Create a new female grounding cord.
6. Observe and acknowledge your aura's natural female creativity and complexity.
7. Create a rose for the male relationship and let a picture of him go out on your rose.
8. Acknowledge the sacredness of the male journey.
9. Breathe your energy out of the male's space.
10. Respectfully send his energy back to him or his guides.

11. With self-compassion, set your intent to cultivate better boundaries in the future.
12. Cut off your old grounding cord, put it in a rose, and explode it. (Many women will have lost their female grounding by now. At this point in the exercise some women will be able to affirm that they maintained their female grounding, while others will be surprised to find that they have already lost it again. Exercises such as this build discernment of these subtle energies.)
13. Create a new female grounding cord.
14. Allow any excess energy to simply flow down your grounding cord, letting Mother Earth recycle the energies for you.
15. Replenish your body and aura with golden cosmic energy.
16. Bring up just the right amount of earth energy for your body and aura at this time.
17. Thank your body for being willing to change.
18. Take a few refreshing breaths and when ready stand up, gently stretch, and reverse polarities.
19. You may find it useful to make some notes of your experience.

Male Clarity

A male's answer to his male grief is *male clarity*, the awareness that he does not need and cannot use female creative energy to be complete. He can come to this awareness at any point, even as a baby. Without any conscious thinking process, he can intuitively know, "It's true; my body does not produce female creative energy. I'm not naturally surrounded by female creative energy, and while that initially seemed like a problem, it isn't a problem. This is my way." When a man is in resistance to this awareness he's caught in male grief. Embracing his own energy's natural simplicity brings male clarity.

FOR MEN:

EXERCISE 29: Cultivating Male Clarity

1. Sit comfortably straight in your chair, feet flat on the floor, legs and arms uncrossed.

2. With a sense of openness, relax, close your eyes, and breathe gently into your belly.
3. Bring your awareness into the center of your head.
4. Cut off your old grounding cord, put it in a rose, and explode it.
5. Create a new male grounding cord.
6. Observe your aura, and as you acknowledge your natural simplicity, notice that your aura does not naturally contain female creative energy, or female complexity.
7. Affirm to yourself, "I acknowledge and embrace my biological simplicity."
8. Allow any excess energy to simply flow down your grounding cord, letting Mother Earth recycle the energies for you.
9. Replenish your body and aura with golden cosmic energy.
10. Bring up just the right amount of earth energy for your body and aura at this time.
11. Thank your body for being willing to change.
12. Take a few refreshing breaths and when ready stand up, gently stretch, and reverse polarities.
13. You may find it useful to make some notes of your experience.

Female Guilt

Female guilt is a biological energy, a body programming that creates a driving and unique kind of guilt or pain that a female experiences when she's unable to meet her instinctual expectation of responsibility. Remember, a woman's reproductive system is naturally programmed to be responsible for people, especially her children, and is also set up to evaluate people's potential according to her genetic programming.

Female guilt energy has strong emotional ramifications. If a woman is not female-grounded she may go into "get it done" or survival mode. That guilt is what pushes responsibility into overdrive. It can be a difficult energy for others, male or female, to contend with, and paradoxically, that intensity is usually driven by the best of intentions: to help.

Gloria: "Long before I learned this system I worked for ten years as the only female photographer in an all-male media productions department. I laugh now when I remember how the men in my department would jump ship whenever I'd run female guilt energy."

FOR WOMEN:

EXERCISE 30: Female Guilt

For the following exercise please choose someone, a male or a female, in whose space you feel you may have unknowingly put your female guilt. If you cannot think of anyone in particular, simply work with someone that you are close to.

1. Sit comfortably straight in your chair, feet flat on the floor, legs and arms uncrossed.
2. With a sense of openness, relax, close your eyes, and breathe gently into your belly.
3. Bring your awareness into the center of your head.
4. Cut off your old grounding cord, put it in a rose, and explode it.
5. Create a new female grounding cord.
6. Acknowledge your natural complexity.
7. Create a rose and allow a picture of the person to go out on the rose.
8. Breathe your female guilt energy out of the other's space.
9. Respectfully send his or her matching energy back to him or her, or his or her guide.
10. With self-compassion, set your intent to cultivate better boundaries in the future.
11. Allow any anxiety or excess energy to simply flow down your grounding cord, letting Mother Earth recycle the energies for you.
12. Cut off your old grounding cord, put it in a rose and explode it, and create a new female grounding cord.
13. Replenish your body and aura with golden cosmic energy.
14. Bring up just the right amount of earth energy for your body and aura at this time.

15. Thank your body for being willing to change.
16. Take a few refreshing breaths and when ready stand up, gently stretch, and reverse polarities.
17. You may find it useful to make some notes of your experience.

Male Rage

In the same way that a woman's body cannot run or understand the biological energy of male grief, men cannot process or understand female responsibility in their body. Sorry, guys—even when a man is grounded, it might not be easy to remain grounded in the midst of the intensity of female responsibility and guilt, especially if there is already some enmeshment.

While a woman's experience of male grief can be a feeling of tragic alienation, a man's experience of female guilt can be an overwhelming feeling of chaos—a chaos that seems to be surreptitiously demanding something of him that he'll never satisfy. This brings us to the point: female guilt in a man's space very often results in him becoming angry, even enraged.[7] Of course, if you are male, it's still your responsibility to monitor your emotions and then respond skillfully. Stopping to take some deep breaths, grounding, and pulling your energy out of her space so it becomes easier to send hers back are all good ideas. (Chapter 9 and several chapters in Part Three address how to handle difficult emotions.)

Please keep in mind that these are unconscious energies, unseen and unintentional drivers of many of life's dramas, and unfortunately the downfall of many relationships. When the man recognizes the situation, even if it is a week later, he can ground, find a little humor, pull his energy out of the woman's space, and send her energy back to her.

When a woman recognizes the situation, even if it is a week later, she can female-ground, find a little humor, pull her energy out of the man's space, and send his energy back to him. Apologizing is probably a good idea for both sexes. Even if the situation was a disaster, recognition of the underlying energies will open the space for more authentic communication next time. Showing respect and creating healthy boundaries never goes out of style.

Female responsibility energy doesn't always have to be at a high intensity for it to jump into a male's space, or for a man to pull it into his space. It can happen during simple, casual conversation. From her perspective, she may simply be problem solving—talking, sharing, thinking out loud, trying to figure out how to help a child who is having trouble at school, or how to balance her budget, or how to communicate better with her coworkers. For the woman, she is just talking through her thought process, when all of a sudden, the man flies into a rage.

With a little practice a man can begin to catch more quickly when he is lit up by a woman's female guilt, eventually even in the moment. By cultivating amusement and curiosity he can wade through the situation more easily when he notices himself becoming antsy or even angry. "Oh, I bet that's female guilt, that's what's happening here. I don't like the way I feel. How interesting. She may or may *not* be telling me to do something. But even if she is, I don't have to run that energy through my body. My body doesn't know how to deal with it. I can ground, pull my energy back, and give her energy back to her. It's amazing how much she cares about this issue. Still, I don't have to get caught up in the energy. If I separate our energies I might even find that I can continue listening."

If you recognize the pattern, it will be helpful to contemplate the uniqueness of both male simplicity and female complexity, valuing each for its contribution to the richness of your life.

FOR MEN:

EXERCISE 31: Male Rage

Men, for the next meditation please contemplate a woman with whom you feel you might share some enmeshment around female guilt energy.

1. Sit comfortably straight in your chair, feet flat on the floor, legs and arms uncrossed.
2. With a sense of openness, relax, close your eyes, and breathe gently into your belly.
3. Bring your awareness into the center of your head.
4. Cut off your old grounding cord, put it in a rose, and explode it.

5. Create a new male grounding cord.
6. Observe your energy to see if you have pulled a woman's female guilt into your space.
7. If so, find some amusement, and congratulate yourself on the significance of your perception.
8. With a respectful acknowledgment, breathe your energy back from the woman's space, and send her energy back to her or her guides.
9. Explode anger pictures until you feel clearer.
10. Allow any anxiety or excess energy to simply flow down your grounding cord, letting the earth recycle the energies for you.
11. Fill your body and aura with golden cosmic energy.
12. Thank your body for being willing to change.
13. Take a few refreshing breaths and when ready stand up, gently stretch, and reverse polarities.
14. You may find it useful to make some notes of your experience.

A Reminder: Explore these Ideas with a Playful Curiosity

About this time in our classes we'll look out to see a significant number of men and women wide-eyed, or holding their breath, or ready to bolt—with lots of pictures lit up in their aura.

Are you lit up? Holding your breath? If not, that's fine. It may mean that this material doesn't seem to be relevant to your relationships; or perhaps you do recognize its relevance, and you're okay with it, finding it useful and interesting. Or perhaps you can't see its relevance yet. Everyone's experience will be unique, as is each person's spiritual journey.

If you are lit up, good. It means you are finding the pockets where these ideas resonate, or *don't* resonate; where you agree or disagree.

In the beginning it will probably be easier to see these issues in others—perhaps your mother, or aunt, best friend, or brother, etc. Acknowledge your perceptions, and if you recognize that some of this is beginning to sound true for you also, you're in good company. Congratulate yourself. Ground, explode some pictures, and find your humor. Recognizing your own issues can often take time and a little courage.

It is wonderful when friends or couples explore these concepts together and develop the deep and compassionate skills of genuine communication. We have seen many marriages pulled from the ashes by the partners' understanding of these energies. Most of the time, however, you will not have the luxury of being on the same spiritual journey as your partner. You may not have the permission to say, "You know, I think we're in each other's space." Most of the time your only option will be to engage the challenging energies yourself—investing in a self-reflective participation—and therein lies true freedom.

Recap

Male grief for a woman (female grounding): When a woman finds herself responding to male grief and going into rescue mode for a male, she can practice acknowledging her natural complexity and her driving wish to help. Then she can find her playfulness, female-ground, begin exploding pictures, breathe her energy back out of the male's space, respectfully send his energy back to him or his guides, set her intent to cultivate better boundaries in the future with compassion for herself, and recognize the sacredness of the male journey.

Male grief for a man: When a man recognizes himself operating out of his male grief, he can acknowledge his energy's natural simplicity and the tendency for some females in his life to try to rescue him from his pain. Then he can find some playfulness, male-ground, breathe his energy back out of the woman's space, respectfully send the woman's energy back to her, explode any "rescue me" pictures he may inadvertently have shown others, value his unique journey as a male, and move to male clarity.

Female guilt: When a woman finds herself going into female guilt she can practice acknowledging her natural complexity and the sacred journey of others. Then she can find her playfulness, female-ground, breathe her energy back out of the other's space, appreciate his or her free will and unique journey, and with compassion for herself relax and set the intent to cultivate better boundaries in the future.

Male rage: When a man finds himself getting enraged he can check to see if he has pulled a woman's female guilt into his space. If so, he can find some amusement, male-ground, breathe his energy back out of her space, acknowledge her responsibility energy, respectfully send her energy back to her or her guides, set the intent to cultivate better boundaries in the future, and practice understanding the difference between male simplicity and female complexity.

A FEW EXAMPLES OF NATURAL FEMALE AND MALE GROUNDING

We list here a few high-profile women who, without technique, often demonstrate natural female grounding: Barbara Walters, Margaret Thatcher, Hillary Clinton, Meryl Streep, Michelle Obama, Margaret Meade, Phylicia Rashad, Julie Andrews, Madeleine Albright, and Halle Berry.

And a few high-profile men who, without technique, demonstrate natural male grounding: Clint Eastwood, Walter Cronkite, Brad Pitt, Ronald Reagan, Rafael Nadal, Anderson Cooper, Morgan Freeman, Paul Newman, Ted Turner, and Barack Obama.

CHAPTER 7

The Seven Major Western Chakras:
Psychic Centers of Awareness and Healing

There are powerful energy centers in the aura called *chakras,* which, when you meditate on them, enormously amplify the energy and psychic perception that you have access to. Meditating on the chakras increases your power to heal and transform yourself and your relationships. "Chakra" is Sanskrit for wheel, disc, or cyclone, referring to how these vital and dynamic energy centers appear to psychic perception as spinning vortices of light and energy.

Through the study of and meditation on the chakras, you can begin to evaluate and understand your energy precisely. Initially, your perception of chakras may be subtle. Through specific meditations you can learn to develop your perception and enhance your ability to recognize a wide variety of energies in your aura that influence your life and relationships every day—whether or not you have been conscious of them. You'll be able to recognize and acknowledge which of your energies are in current time and flow, and which of your energies are not in current time, thus obstructing your natural flow. As your abilities grow you will not only come to understand what those energies do, but equally important, you'll understand your role as collaborator in creating your life: how you co-create what works well for you, and how you co-create what does not work well for you.

Just beyond the range of physical sight exist thousands of tiny energy systems in the aura called *nadis.* Most nadis are within the scope of the body, and some extend beyond. The chakras form where major nadis or energy lines intersect. Though there are hundreds, even thousands of chakras, for the purposes of our exploration we will work with seven major chakras aligned along the spine, as well as with the increasingly important chakras in the hands and feet. As everyday life becomes the center of humans' spiritual journey, the hand and feet chakras, which facilitate movement and social interaction, become more central to our journey.

Chakras are actually multidimensional and are only approximately located at a particular point. Any particular form that the chakra takes depends on your focus and your attention. For example, when you meditate from a Hindu yoga orientation, you will find the chakras inside the spinal cord (the *sushumna*). The chakras will be horizontal to the floor when you are standing and your spine is erect.

You might understand the chakra system as being both discovered and developed. Chakras are discovered in the sense that they pre-exist with a natural form and function prior to your noticing them. They are developed in the sense that your meditation affects the scope, size, and even the placement of each chakra. In fact, since there are numerous chakras, for some major chakras there are choices. For example, if you meditate on the chakra commonly called the third chakra at the belly button, then an alternative placement for the third chakra just a few inches higher becomes a secondary chakra. Meditate on the higher placement, and the belly button chakra becomes the secondary chakra. Each choice has slightly different outcomes. The energies and abilities that result from meditation on the belly button chakra will be similar but not the same as meditation on the higher version of the third chakra.

We'll be working with the chakras in a particular set of placements that is especially effective for engaging the personality and the psychological aspect of the chakras. Many of the functions of a particular chakra are connected to an associated gland and hence to a specific physical location in the body. However, the chakras are not in the same energy frequency range as the physical body, and consequently their location vis-à-vis the physical body is only close, not exact. Even so, turning your attention to specific physical locations will help you find each chakra.

We will refer to the seven major chakras by number: the first chakra, the second chakra, the third chakra, and so forth, through the seventh.

It will be helpful for you to practice honing in on each chakra's energy as we discuss the chakra placement. "(See Figure 4, "The Seven Major Western Chakras," below.)"

Figure 4: The Seven Major Western Chakras

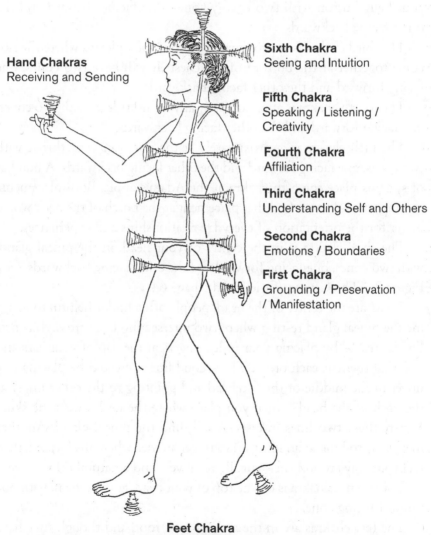

Crown Chakra
Knowingness and Connection with Your Path

Hand Chakras
Receiving and Sending

Sixth Chakra
Seeing and Intuition

Fifth Chakra
Speaking / Listening /
Creativity

Fourth Chakra
Affiliation

Third Chakra
Understanding Self and Others

Second Chakra
Emotions / Boundaries

First Chakra
Grounding / Preservation
/ Manifestation

Feet Chakra
Grounding and Mobility

Chakra Placement

The first chakra is approximately at the base of your spine. Its exact configuration is more complex than we will address in this book, so for the general purposes of clearing we will imagine it as having two energy cones, one facing forward and the other facing backwards.[1]

The second chakra is approximately two to three finger widths below your belly button with two energy cones, one facing forward and the other facing backwards.

The third chakra is approximately at your solar plexus, where the ribs come together at the bottom of the chest. It will have two cones, one facing forward and the other facing backwards.

The fourth chakra is approximately at your heart level with two cones, one facing forward and the other facing backwards.

The fifth chakra is approximately at the notch in your throat with two cones, one facing forward and the other facing backwards. A number of systems place the fifth chakra at the Adam's apple. Both placements are important, but we find that placement at the notch of the neck works better for the orientation of everyday relationships and experiences.

The sixth chakra is in the center of your head, in the pineal gland, with two cones, one facing forward and the other facing backwards. (See Figure 2, "The Center of the Head," page 64.)

To locate the center of the head, people often find it helpful to imagine the pineal gland resting where two intersecting lines cross. The first line is created by placing your index fingers at the top of your ears and pointing them at each other. The second line is created by placing one finger in the middle of the forehead and pointing to the other finger at the back of the head, which you place where the neck meets the skull. Where these two lines intersect you'll find the pineal gland. Another method is to look at an illustration to get an idea where it's located, then feel your way around energetically until you find a natural calm space.

The seventh chakra is on the top of your head, at the crown, with one upward-facing cone.

The feet chakras are in the arch of each foot, and though they have energetic cones facing in opposite directions, for our purposes you will work with the downward-facing cone.

The hand chakras are approximately in the center of your palms, and they too have cones facing in opposite directions, but for our purposes you will work with the cone facing outward from each palm.

Most Western orientations of the chakra system place the chakras similarly to how you will engage them in psychic psychology. For example, our orientation is similar though not exactly as depicted in author and healer Barbara Brennan's encyclopedic book *Hands of Light: A Guide to Healing the Human Energy Field.*[2] Her extraordinary book with superb illustrations and descriptions of the chakras as well as other important aspects of the psychic world is vital to any serious metaphysical library. Since you will explore and work with specific functional, emotional, or psychological aspects of the chakras, we also highly encourage you to read the comprehensive works of chakra scholar Anodea Judith, PhD. Specific to our exploration are *Eastern Body Western Mind: Psychology and the Chakra System* and *Wheels of Life: A User's Guide to the Chakra System.* Anodea Judith's books also cover the more mystical aspects of the chakras that you may encounter, as does Harish Johari's classic book based on a purely Hindu perspective, *Chakras: Energy Centers of Transformation.*

John: "I find from time to time that I will change somewhat how I work with the chakra system. When Gloria and I wrote our first book, Basic Psychic Development: A User's Guide to Auras, Chakras & Clairvoyance, *for example, we placed the first chakra facing both forward and back. Gloria continues to work with the first chakra in that manner for emotional/astral work, and for the time being, at least, I work with the first chakra as simply facing backwards, and not also facing forward. That has to do with some of the etheric and other energies I am exploring at this time."*

In our meditation retreats we often explore several energy ranges, meditating on both the Hindu chakras and the Western chakras, sometimes in the same exercise. Your personal orientation and objective will determine a natural perspective for you. Your developing psychic perceptions will guide you to a relevant focus of meditation as it relates to your personal spiritual journey.

Chakra Functions

First Chakra: Grounding, Preservation, and Manifestation

Please take a few moments to become more familiar with the energy of your first chakra.... Focus your awareness on the first-chakra energy at the base of your spine.... Then allow your awareness to relax and slowly expand to also include the backward-facing funnel-shaped energy emerging from that space.... With a sense of playfulness and discovery affirm to yourself, "My first chakra, my grounding, my foundation...." Ground and breathe gently into that space for a few moments....

At the base of the spine is the principal chakra of grounding and materialization, your foundation. You naturally engaged this energy as you practiced male and female grounding in the previous chapter. It is often called the survival chakra because it supports the functions necessary for your existence—food, shelter, health. The first-chakra energy must be congruent and engaged for your dreams and desires to become physically manifested. For instance, to manifest health or wealth, some portion of your desire for health or manifestation will need to be aligned and grounded enough to vibrate at the frequency range of the first chakra. If it isn't, the desire will continue to remain merely an idea or wish. You might imagine your relationship with your first chakra as similar to a house and its foundation.

First-chakra developmental nuances and balances you will explore:
    Foundation
    Grounding
    Manifestation
    Health
    Shoulds, have tos, and oughts

Second Chakra: Emotions, Boundaries, and Creativity

Please take a few moments to become more familiar with the energy of your second chakra.... About two to three finger widths below your belly button, focus your awareness on the second chakra energy in your spinal column.... Then allow your awareness to relax and slowly expand to include the two funnel-shaped channels of energy emerging from that space—one facing forward, one facing backwards.... With a sense of play-fulness and discovery affirm to yourself, "My second chakra, my creative energies, my boundaries, my emotions...." Ground, and breathe gently into that space for a few moments.

The distinctive complexities of the second chakra generate the first developmental challenge to balanced, integrated psychic awareness at the personality level: the challenges of avoiding energetic enmeshment by having clear boundaries. You will find the second chakra two to three fingers widths below the belly button. It is the energy source of a complex dance of emotions, desire, sexuality, creativity. Using the second chakra, you unconsciously pull other people's energy directly into your aura to experience it—whether you like them or not, whether you know them or not. You can literally feel someone else's energy or emotion, particularly pain. Because the second chakra works by opening up to and feeling energies other than your own, it can render your separate identity fuzzy.

The second chakra is the chakra of sexual relations, the natural, beautiful, and healthy exchange of energies. So, when having sex, open your second chakra and enjoy. We encourage people to reset their boundaries within a few hours following sexual relations.

Many professional clairvoyants and healers intentionally or unintentionally work by bringing the energy they are trying to read inside their aura. Though it is true that you can access a lot of information this way, the down side is that the pain, or the question, or the disease is brought right into the body. If you are not careful to clear those energies out of your system they can impact your state of mind, and even your health. This is one reason a lot of psychics and healers exhaust themselves and sometimes actually burn out.

As you learn to use the tools like grounding, clearing energy that isn't yours, and exploding pictures, you will be more in touch with your desires, sexuality, and creativity. You will even, where appropriate, feel energy that isn't yours without losing track of what is you and what is not. There is nothing wrong with the energy of the second chakra. These energies are vital, dynamic, and creative, but they take practice and skill to use to best effect. Remember, of course, that an energy cannot come into your space without your inviting it. If group interactions tire you, explore your matching energy that is the invitation for someone to jump into your space. Learn to close your second chakra down somewhat when in a shopping mall, a hospital, or at a football game, etc. But if you are out in nature—in the woods, at the ocean, in the desert—by all means open your second chakra and drink in the magnificence. Let nature replenish you; let its vitality flow through you as a healing.

Second-chakra developmental nuances and balances you will explore:
Discernment
Grounding, with special attention to female grounding
Boundary enmeshments
Monitoring energy—Jumping into another's space
Intensity not meaning truth
Shoulds, have tos, and oughts
Emotions
Desire
Male grief
Female responsibility

Third Chakra: Success in Everyday Life, Understanding Self and Others

Please take a few moments to become more familiar with the energy of your third chakra. . . . At the level of your solar plexus—just below where the ribs come together—focus your awareness on the third-chakra energy in your spinal column. . . . Then allow your awareness to relax and slowly expand to include the two funnel-shaped channels of energy that emerge from that space—one facing forward, one facing backwards. . . . With a sense of playfulness and discovery affirm to yourself, "My third chakra, my understanding of myself and others. . . ." Ground, and breathe gently into that space for a few moments.

Like a wise navigator, a balanced third chakra leads to a realistic sense of who you are. Use it well and you will appropriately value and understand yourself and others, even those with whom you disagree. Whereas with the second chakra you experience boundaries, or lack thereof, with the third chakra you experience the ability to honor the boundaries of others, as well as establish healthy boundaries for yourself. Your third chakra is imbued with your sense of "I," your natural, spontaneously arising sense of being a separate individual. That is why it is often called the chakra of ego and personal will.

When your energy in the third chakra is excessively egocentric it can lead into a delusional space that the universe ought to bend to your rules; that you ought to be "Czar of the Universe."[3] You'll see this in relationships where there is no flexibility, no room for collaboration or genuine communication. On the other hand, if your energy in the third chakra is excessively self-deprecating or you respond as a victim, the third chakra and the third layer of the aura will close down and collapse, leaving you feeling even more powerless, lost, and diminished. Obviously relationships built on either type of imbalance are destined for trouble. A balanced third chakra gives you a good understanding of who you are, and of what another person wants and who he or she is. It thereby gives you the ability to take well-thought-out action based upon that balanced awareness. You will know how to pursue your own interests without ignoring or violating the other person's interests.

Another vital function of the third chakra is that it supports specific energetic mechanics for the aura. It distributes vital etheric and astral energies throughout the body and aura, similar to how the heart pumps blood. You took advantage of this distributing function in an earlier exercise when you brought the earth energy up to the solar plexus and allowed the third chakra to distribute the energy throughout the aura. In the beginning of your growth in psychic perception, the psychological significance of this distributing function of the third chakra may not be obvious.

As you grow in your ability to monitor your aura you will begin to notice how your third chakra responds to your emotions and life situations. The third chakra sets the boundaries of your aura in space and energizes you to take action. You will become more adept at monitoring and balancing the size of your aura and finding skillful responses to whatever happens.

Third-chakra developmental nuances and balances you will explore:
  Power and loss of power
  Shoulds, have tos, and oughts
  Understanding yourself
  Understanding and respecting others
  Appropriate boundaries to your aura

Fourth Chakra: The Heart Chakra—Love and Affiliation

Please take a few moments to become more familiar with the energy of your fourth chakra. At the level of the heart focus your awareness on the fourth-chakra energy in your spinal column.... Then allow your awareness to relax and slowly expand to include the two funnel-shaped channels of energy emerging from that space—one facing forward, one facing backwards.... With a sense of playfulness and discovery affirm to yourself, "My heart chakra, my self love, my relationships...." Ground, and breathe gently into that space for a few moments.

Universally known as the heart chakra, the fourth chakra is where your soul flows into your body and engages your life through your personality. It is the center of love, compassion, and community. Its balance relies on the appropriate functioning and engagement of the lower three chakras. As you develop a level of balance and nuance you come to see the fourth chakra in terms of affiliation: what the psychologist Erik Erikson called *industriousness*—the ability to engage in collaborative pursuits.

Most people understand the fourth chakra to be about love. Unfortunately, people often engage love and this chakra unskillfully because they have not balanced the lower three chakras. If you are not paying attention you may pull survival issues up from the first chakra, boundary issues from the second, and control issues from the third, and pump that lower-chakra energy through the heart chakra. This gives lower-chakra energies a coloration of heart-chakra energy, but without the balanced clarity of skillful heart-chakra energy. Using these lower-chakra energies rather than a true fourth-chakra energy can cause you to mistake lust for love, lose yourself in an un-self-aware desire to "save the world," or to generate a forced calm, when underneath that calm there is an obsessive energy—either an excessive narcissism or repression of all individuality. Finding a balanced, nuanced energy in the heart chakra, the kind of balance that's required for true love and natural playfulness, is another developmental goal of this system. This balance requires letting go of shoulds, have tos, and oughts, and becoming skilled communicators—skills we address in Part Three.

Heart-chakra developmental nuances and balances you will explore:
Authenticity
Love
Collaboration

Fifth Chakra: Communication, Listening, Inner Identity, and Telepathy

Please take a few moments to become more familiar with the energy of your fifth chakra.... At the level of the notch of your throat, focus your awareness on the fifth-chakra energy in your spinal column.... Then allow your awareness to expand slowly to also include the two funnel-shaped channels of energy emerging from that space—one facing forward, one facing backwards.... With a sense of playfulness and discovery affirm to yourself, "My fifth chakra, my voice, my inner identity...." Ground, and breathe gently into that space for a few moments.

You develop your inner identity—your eternal growing self—by cultivating your creative self-expression in your everyday relationships. Verbal communication and telepathy with others, including your guides, arise from your fifth-chakra complex. A well-balanced fifth chakra facilitates an authentic self-awareness, clear and skillful communication, and the essential ability to listen deeply.

Fifth-chakra developmental nuances and balances you will explore:
Communicating clearly
Listening skillfully
Owning your telepathic channels
Identity

Sixth Chakra: Beliefs, Clairvoyance, Center of the Head, and Neutrality

Please take a few moments to become a little more familiar with the energy of your sixth chakra. Focus your awareness in the center of your head, in the pineal gland.... Then allow your awareness to relax and slowly expand to include the two funnel-shaped channels of energy emerging from the center of the head—one facing forward, one facing backwards.... With a sense of playfulness and discovery affirm to yourself, "My sixth chakra, my beliefs, my intuition...." Ground, and breathe gently into that space for a few moments.

Your beliefs, abstract intelligence,[4] world view, intuition, imagination, vision, clairvoyance, ability to be in current time, and neutrality all flow from and through your sixth chakra. One of the central developmental goals of this system is the gentle state of neutrality, which is an emotional openness to experience. Neutrality allows you to release resistance and engage life as it is, without judgment. Neutrality arises in the sixth chakra in the center of the head—the space of the pineal gland and the sphere of spiritual energy surrounding and just behind the pineal gland. Being in the center of the head allows you to be in current time, a profoundly valuable and resourceful state.

Many systems call the center of the head the seat of the soul. Few of us naturally utilize the neutrality or seniority to be found in the center of the head. Enmeshment, judgment, power struggles, and other people's energies that you hold in your space stand in your way. Even so, with relatively little practice you can develop some neutrality through psychic techniques. (Working with your beliefs is addressed in Part Three.) As you do so, you will find changes in your perspective and stress level, and an emerging sense of playfulness.

With neutrality you create the maximum possibility of engaging life. You create the maximum possibility of seeking change in an authentic, balanced, mature, graceful, kind, and generous way. You create the maximum possibility of engaging in true intimacy, an intimacy in which you know who you are and you know who the other is, and from which you communicate with clear boundaries rather than through enmeshment.

Sixth-chakra developmental nuances and balances you will explore:
Neutrality
Center of the head/Current time
Flow
Clairvoyance
Intuition

Seventh Chakra: Knowingness, Seniority, and Connection with Your Path

Please take a few moments to become more familiar with the energy of your seventh chakra. Focus your awareness on the top of your head where a crown would sit. Then allow your awareness to relax and slowly expand to include an upward-facing, funnel-shaped channel of energy emerging from your crown.... With a sense of playfulness and discovery affirm to yourself, "My crown, my knowingness...." Ground, and breathe gently into that space for a few moments.

You engage spirit, connect with your path, and experience your knowingness through your crown chakra. Here you can know the entire cycle of being: the gift of creation, the gift of preservation, and the gift of destruction—what Hindu tradition calls the Shiva trinity. All of us naturally create our next moment by the dismantling (releasing) of the preceding moment. In a collaboration of the sixth and seventh chakras, a natural instantaneous process takes place beneath your conscious awareness where you simply create and destroy pictures when you are in flow.

Learning to own your crown and be senior to your experience are valuable skills to cultivate in your relationships. The frequency that you run in your crown chakra sets the tone for how you engage your relationships and the world. (See Chapter 9, "Opening to Life As It Is: Resistance and Neutrality.") The channeling of a guide and running white light skillfully are also crown chakra processes. While we do discuss the technical process for safe and conscious channeling in classes directly addressing channeling, it's outside the scope of this book.

Seventh-chakra developmental nuances and balances you will explore:
Owning the crown
Being senior to experience
Not jumping into other people's crowns
Engaging spirit

Feet Chakras: Grounded Mobility

Please take a few moments to become more familiar with the energy of your feet chakras.... Focus your awareness in the arch of each foot. Then allow your awareness to relax and slowly expand to include a downward-facing, funnel-shaped energy emerging from that space.... With a sense of playfulness and discovery affirm to yourself, "My feet chakras, my ability to move more playfully through the world...." Ground, and breathe gently into that space for a few moments.

In addition to the seven major chakras, you have the profoundly important chakras in the hands and feet. The feet chakras allow you to run powerful earth energies and facilitate your ability to ground flexibly. Running energy through the legs also provides healing to the numerous secondary chakras in the feet and legs. Clearing the feet chakras is highly recommended for all diseases, and particularly helpful in healing diabetes.

Earlier you practiced bringing earth energy up the legs and into the aura through your feet chakras.

Feet chakras developmental nuances and balances you will explore:
Grounding
Mobility
Flexibility
Flow

Hand Chakras: Healing and Communication

Please take a few moments to become more familiar with the energy of your hand chakras. Focus your awareness in the palm of each hand. Then allow your awareness to relax and slowly expand to include an outward-facing, funnel-shaped channel of energy emerging from your palm.... With a sense of playfulness and discovery say to yourself, "My hand chakras, my giving to the world." Ground, and breathe gently into that space for a few moments.

The hand chakras are very important to your creativity, health, and communication and are instrumental for projecting healing. It is particularly crucial for healers to keep their hand chakras clear and flowing. In this book, we don't discuss bringing energy in through the hand chakras, but rather focus on clearing the hand chakras and bringing them into current time. Basic healing through the hands is covered in the first book we wrote together, *Basic Psychic Development: A User's Guide to Auras, Chakras & Clairvoyance*, in Chapter Nine, "Communicating with Your Healing Guide."

Hand-chakra developmental nuances and balances you will explore:
Clarity
Flow

Though all the major chakras have to have some level of function for you to exist as a human being, with skillful meditation you can increase the functioning of a particular chakra almost without limit. You can hone and improve the focus of a particular chakra so that it performs more effortlessly in both creating your reality and helping you to experience and evaluate your reality.

With skillful meditation all the functions, skills, and powers that are imbedded in each chakra can be brought to life. For instance, part of the function of a body is to heal itself. Different aspects of that functionality, knowledge, and ability are contained in different chakras. Even without intellectually understanding that knowledge or ability, by meditating on the chakras your skill in healing yourself and others will grow simply, gracefully, and naturally. Intellectual understanding can then add to your ability to use those healing functions.

Opening and Empowering the Chakras

The next practice is a favorite for many. With it, you will develop a growing set of skills—opening, clearing, and setting your chakras. These skills will deepen your ability to engage your relationships with more openness, capability, and grace. For instance, setting your chakras at particular levels of openness will help you be more compassionate and resourceful with someone who is in emotional or physical distress. All seven major chakras (and many minor ones) will come into play in conversation. When you communicate with someone in emotional or physical distress and close your second chakra to a fairly low level, your boundaries will be clearer. As your skills grow, you will have a healthier aura, better communication habits, the capacity to monitor your aura in the moment, and greater ability to clear your energy after the fact.

For the next exercise you'll simply create a mental image of opening the chakras, running neutral energy though them, and then setting their openness. A useful metaphor for opening a chakra is to imagine the chakra face as similar to the aperture of a camera lens, which can be opened and closed. Let 100% open mean the widest a particular chakra can open *comfortably*. Why comfortably? If you are not careful or playful enough you can hyper-extend a chakra. In the energy range of the personal aura there's a natural and appropriate upper limit as to how open a chakra will be. That natural and appropriate upper limit is what we'll call 100%.

After you open the chakra as far as it will comfortably open, you'll imagine running a healing, clearing, neutral energy through it. For the next meditation you'll use a simple, natural approach—earth energy for the lower three chakras and golden cosmic energy for the upper four chakras.[5] As you become practiced we encourage you to experiment by using other colors also.

So, you'll open each chakra one at a time, as wide as it will open comfortably. Then run neutral green earth energy or golden cosmic energy though it to clear it. Once you've cleared it, then you'll close it back down to the suggested percentage (see below). Please note, percentages are suggestions and there are no hard and fast rules; there's no one right percentage for a chakra all the time.

Again, as is the case most of the time, your choices will depend upon your purposes in the moment. For example, when playing football you would want your first chakra fully open simply because football is a survival-oriented game. Having it wide open would help you be in touch with your reflexes and the adrenaline bursts needed for the game. When driving down a snowy and dangerous hill, you would do best to have your first chakra quite wide open because you would naturally be running a lot of survival energy, and you'd want your full attention directed towards making sure that you drove skillfully and safely. However, most of the time when you're driving you won't be in survival mode, so your first chakra will probably be set at about 25%.

One would hope that you're not in survival mode while meditating, so you can afford to close your first chakra down quite a lot. It is interesting to note that some meditation systems will essentially turn their first chakra off, facilitating a more transcendental state, which intentionally moves the meditator out of touch with his or her body. Those transcendental spaces are wonderful to experience but not practical for keeping the body and personality engaged in everyday life.

With experience it will be easy for you to determine how you'd like to set your chakras for your meditations. For training purposes in the next meditation we recommend the following percentages:

First chakra: 10%
Second chakra: 10%
Third chakra: 50% for women and 35% for men
> *We suggest that a woman leave her third chakra more open than a man's because a woman's body is set to run more energy than a man's, other things being equal.*
Fourth chakra: 50%
Fifth chakra: 50%
Sixth chakra: Leave the sixth as open as is comfortable
Seventh chakra: 50%
Hands and feet: 50%

Opening up to your deeper perceptions and clairvoyance is an art of energetic multitasking. To deepen your familiarity with the chakra locations and primary functions, we encourage flexing your perception by simultaneously contemplating the unique aspects of each chakra as you bring in the neutral energy. In the beginning spend about one minute per chakra. As you become more experienced and you have time, you can increase the time you spend exploring each chakra to five minutes.

Some or most of the chakra energies may seem quite elusive at first, so remember that acknowledging your experience, no matter how subtle, will help build and vivify your perception. If these energies still seem somewhat new, you may be surprised to know that your responses to everyday life are regulated by the responses of the chakras every bit as much as they are regulated by hormones coursing through your body. You have already experienced the chakras. For example, a constricting of the throat and inability to express yourself clearly when stressed is a fifth-chakra response; a gut feeling when you "know" something is often a second-chakra (sympathetic) response; and perhaps the most recognizable—a burst of joy from the heart when happy—is more accurately a heart-chakra response, not a physical heart response. Of course there are layers of complexity and subtlety to each of these examples. Your personality engages the world through your chakras and aura.

Please clear and replenish chakras one through three and the feet chakras with neutral green earth energy. For chakras four though seven and your hand chakras, please use golden cosmic energy.

EXERCISE 32: Opening and Empowering the Seven Major Chakras

1. Sit comfortably straight in your chair; breathe gently and deeply into your belly.
2. With a sense of adventure bring your awareness into the center of your head.
3. Cut off your old grounding cord, put it in a rose, and explode it.
4. Create your male or female grounding cord.

FEET CHAKRAS: THE ARCH OF EACH FOOT–GROUNDED MOBILITY

5. From the center of your head, imagine opening your feet chakras as far as they will open comfortably.
6. Invite neutral green earth energy to flow effortlessly up from the center of the Earth and stream through each of your feet chakras, giving them a gentle, thorough clearing.

7. From the center of your head, playfully close your feet chakras down to about 50%.

FIRST CHAKRA: BASE OF THE SPINE—GROUNDING, PRESERVATION, AND MANIFESTATION

8. From the center of your head gently and playfully open your first chakra as far as it will open comfortably.
9. Invite neutral green earth energy to flow effortlessly up from the center of the Earth, up through your feet chakras, ankles, shins, knees, and thighs, up the front of your body and into your first chakra, giving it a gentle, thorough clearing.
10. From the center of your head playfully close your first chakra , down to about 10%.

SECOND CHAKRA: TWO FINGER WIDTHS BELOW THE BELLY BUTTON—EMOTIONS, BOUNDARIES, AND CREATIVITY

11. From the center of your head gently open your second chakra as far as it will open comfortably.
12. Invite neutral green earth energy to flow effortlessly up from the center of the Earth, up through your feet chakras, ankles, shins, knees, and thighs, up the front of your body and into your second chakra, giving it a gentle, thorough clearing.
13. From the center of your head playfully close your second chakra down to about 10%.

THIRD CHAKRA: SOLAR PLEXUS—SUCCESS IN EVERYDAY LIFE, UNDERSTANDING SELF AND OTHERS

14. From the center of your head gently and playfully open your third chakra as far as it will open comfortably.
15. Invite neutral green earth energy to flow effortlessly up from the center of the Earth, up through your feet chakras, ankles, shins, knees, and thighs, up the front of your body and into your third chakra, giving it a gentle, thorough clearing.
16. From the center of your head playfully close your third chakra down to about 50% for women and about 35% for men.

FOURTH CHAKRA: HEART PLEXUS–LOVE AND AFFILIATION

17. From the center of your head playfully open your fourth chakra as far as it will open comfortably.
18. Invite neutral golden cosmic energy, from well above your crown, to stream down through your crown, the back of your neck, down your back, and into your heart chakra, giving it a gentle, thorough clearing.
19. From the center of your head playfully close your fourth chakra down to about 50%.

FIFTH CHAKRA: NOTCH OF THE THROAT–COMMUNICATION, LISTENING, INNER IDENTITY, AND TELEPATHY

20. From the center of your head playfully open your fifth chakra as far as it will open comfortably.
21. Invite neutral golden cosmic energy, from well above your crown, to stream down through your crown, the back of your neck, and into your throat chakra, giving it a gentle, thorough clearing.
22. From the center of your head playfully close your throat chakra down to about 50%.

SIXTH CHAKRA: CENTER OF THE HEAD–BELIEFS, CLAIRVOYANCE, AND NEUTRALITY

23. From the center of your head gently open your sixth chakra as far as it will open comfortably.
24. Invite neutral golden cosmic energy, from well above your crown, to stream down through your crown and into the back of your sixth chakra, giving it a gentle, thorough clearing.
25. From the center of your head playfully leave your sixth chakra as open as you can comfortably.

SEVENTH CHAKRA: CROWN–KNOWINGNESS, SENIORITY, AND CONNECTION WITH YOUR PATH

26. From the center of your head gently open your seventh chakra as far as it will open comfortably.

27. Invite golden cosmic energy, from well above your crown, to stream down into your crown chakra, giving it a gentle, thorough clearing.
28. From the center of your head playfully close your crown chakra down to about 50%.

HAND CHAKRAS: PALM OF EACH HAND–HEALING AND COMMUNICATION

29. From the center of your head gently open your hand chakras as far as they will open comfortably.
30. Invite neutral golden cosmic energy, from well above your crown, to stream down through your crown, the back of your neck, down your shoulders and arms, into your hand chakras, giving them a gentle, thorough clearing.
31. From the center of your head playfully close your hand chakras down to about 50%.

FINISHING YOUR MEDITATION

32. Release any excess earth or cosmic energy straight down your grounding cord.
33. Cut off your old grounding cord, put it in a rose, and explode it.
34. Create a new male or female grounding cord.
35. Replenish your body and aura with lots of golden sun energy.
36. Bring up just the right amount of earth energy for your body and aura at this time.
37. Thank your body for being willing to change and grow.
38. When ready stand up, stretch, and reverse polarities.
39. You may find it useful to make some notes of your experience.

How long will your chakras remain exactly as you set them? Probably not for long, because chakras are dynamic and constantly respond to your world and relationships. What you begin to accomplish with the meditation is a marked increase in your awareness of your chakras and an emerging balance and flexibility to empower your chakras to respond to your world more effectively and playfully.

Your body, emotions, and thoughts will set your chakras effectively most of the time. But in your daily life, you will encounter pictures or energies that trigger an unskillful and unexpected response. For example, even strong tennis players may lose focus or drive. Usually, but not always, they lose it as a consequence of their third chakra collapsing, which results in a severe drop in energy—either of vitality or will, or both. Through their sports training, experienced players tend to recover more quickly from their loss of focus or drive, and get back in the game. That recovery can be seen clairvoyantly as the tennis players own and reset their third chakra. If, for any reason, you were to experience a similar drop in energy, you could do a brief clearing of your aura, open your third chakra back up, and replenish your aura to facilitate a quicker recovery. Learning to recognize such an event and reset a chakra, or chakras, will allow you to regain your balance or composure or energy much more quickly.

Just how long your chakras remain balanced and flexible following this meditation will depend on a number of things, predominantly your energetic habits. As you'll often hear us remind you throughout the book, acknowledge your awareness; what you can observe, you can heal. With a sense of discovery simply observe how you perceive the effects right after the meditation, and notice how you perceive the effects in a few hours, and again in a day or two. Your particular balance will depend on your experience and your current patterns. Without judging yourself, pay attention to your particular response and experience. With a sense of adventure build your awareness of your energetic habits and patterns, as they are the entry to your deeper healing. Like strengthening a weak muscle, it may take a little time and patience, but it's always worth the effort.

Mantra Meditation

Another favorite meditation for connecting to the energy of the chakras is to repeat a mantra, a sacred sound specific to each chakra, and simply rest in the chakra's sublime energy.[6]

First chakra: Lam
Second chakra: Vam
(*The "v" is pronounced halfway between a "v" sound and a "w" sound.*)

Third chakra: Ram
Fourth chakra: Yam
Fifth chakra: Ham
Sixth chakra: Om
Seventh: Has no mantra

We suggest that beginners meditate for one minute on each chakra initially, and increase the time in subsequent meditations.

EXERCISE 33: Mantra Meditation for Each Chakra

1. Sit comfortably straight in your chair; breathe gently and deeply into your belly.
2. Allow your awareness to rest playfully in the center of your head.
3. Cut off your old grounding cord, put it in a rose, and explode it.
4. Create your male or female grounding cord.
5. Be open to changing and growing.

FIRST CHAKRA: "LAM"

6. From the center of your head repeat the mantra "Lam" silently to yourself, allowing the energy of the mantra to help you find your first-chakra vibration.
7. Rest in your first-chakra energy for 1 to 5 minutes.

SECOND CHAKRA: "VAM"

8. From the center of your head repeat the mantra "Vam" silently to yourself, allowing the energy of the mantra to help you find your second-chakra vibration.
9. Rest in your second-chakra energy for 1 to 5 minutes.

THIRD CHAKRA: "RAM"

10. From the center of your head repeat the mantra "Ram" silently to yourself, allowing the energy of the mantra to help you find your solar plexus-chakra vibration.
11. Rest in your third-chakra energy for 1 to 5 minutes.

FOURTH CHAKRA: "YAM"

12. From the center of your head repeat the mantra "Yam" silently to yourself, allowing the energy of the mantra to help you find your heart-chakra vibration.
13. Rest in your heart-chakra energy for 1 to 5 minutes.

FIFTH CHAKRA: "HAM"

14. From the center of your head repeat the mantra "Ham" silently to yourself, allowing the energy of the mantra to help you find your throat-chakra vibration.
15. Rest in your throat-chakra energy for 1 to 5 minutes.

SIXTH CHAKRA: "OM"

16. From the center of your head repeat the mantra "Om" silently to yourself, allowing the energy of the mantra to help you find your sixth-chakra vibration.
17. Rest in your sixth-chakra energy for 1 to 5 minutes.

FINISHING YOUR MEDITATION

18. Release any excess energy straight down your grounding cord.
19. Cut off your old grounding cord, put it in a rose, and explode it.
20. Create a new male or female grounding cord.
21. Replenish your body and aura with golden sun energy.
22. Bring up just the right amount of earth energy for your body and aura at this time.
23. Thank your body for being willing to change and grow.
24. When ready stand up, stretch, and reverse polarities.
25. You may find it useful to make some notes of your experience.

CHAPTER 8

Tools for Large-Scale Changes

There are three parts to the core techniques for developing and using your psychic awareness for life skills and relationships. You've covered most of the first two. Now is a good time to spend a few paragraphs on how what you've learned relates to what is coming.

In Chapters 2 and 3 you learned the two legs on which this system moves—the two questions: Is it my energy, and if so, is it in current time, open to new experience? Every technique we use for the personal aura builds on these foundational questions.

In Chapters 3 and 4 you learned most of the operating system of the aura. Grounding, running energy, and the center of the head help you coordinate various frequency ranges that must interact congruently for your flowing engagement with everyday life. Then, meditating on the chakras amplifies your abilities and energy, while healing and clearing your aura. Of course, each part interacts with all the others. Meditating on your chakras also stabilizes your aura and the interaction of dense physically oriented energies, the personal aura, and the soul; while grounding, running energy, and the center of the head amplify your energy and perception; and finally, the foundation of the whole system, utilizing the basic awareness of whose energy and current time (exploding pictures) are vital to every psychic perception and practice we are cultivating in this part. Understanding the primary use of each technique helps you imagine and utilize the whole system ever more skillfully, and will allow you to improvise your own ways of using the system as you gain basic competency. The techniques we discuss in this chapter will add to your psychic skills.

The techniques of this chapter allow you to perform large-scale clearings rapidly. The first technique, creating and destroying roses, allows you to explode more than one picture at a time and explode pictures continuously. The second and third clearing techniques, vacuuming energy and removing cords, both address energies that aren't yours. Vacuuming energy allows you to clear large amounts of energies that aren't yours at one time. Removing cords allows you to stop the future flow of one particular, important source of energy in your space that isn't yours. Cords are long-standing currents of one person's energy into another person's space. By removing cords, you transform the underlying energy relationship so that you are no longer taking in continuous streams of energy or putting them into another person's aura.

There is a second reason your clearings gain power with these new techniques. You will be applying the techniques to specific parts of the aura. By utilizing the techniques specifically at the chakras in this chapter, and later throughout the aura, the techniques hone in on obstructions. Eventually you begin to perceive the aura more and more holistically, and you will go directly to obstructions. You won't have to just guess what event you might be resisting, or with whom you might be enmeshed; you will first start to notice in your clearing meditations, and later in the process of everyday life, exactly what you are resisting or enmeshed with, and you will begin to clear your obstructions at the time of the event or soon after. You will be more and more effective and open in the moment to life as it is.

Creating and Destroying Roses

The objective of exploding pictures is not only to break up the frozen energy but to integrate and assimilate the underlying experience, consciously or unconsciously, so that you move out of resistance. To further that objective you'll next explore a fast-moving method for clearing lots of pictures called *creating and destroying roses*. You may release ten, a hundred, or even a thousand pictures in a sitting. Again you may see pictures, you may not. It really won't matter for your purposes here. What matters is your sense of openness.

To create and destroy roses you first imagine a picture-blowing rose out in front of your aura at the level of the chakra you would like to clear. Then allow it to begin to attract any pictures from within or near the chakra that you are ready to explode—from any time, any place. The rose usually fills very quickly. Simply intend that it explode when "full." Also intend that another picture-blowing rose will immediately take its place. Continue the process: fill and explode, fill and explode, and so forth. Intend that as you create roses there will be a magnetic connection between the roses and the pictures next in line to be exploded. Again, let it be easy and fun.

This technique is one of many that you could choose to create and destroy roses, but practicing in this manner will help you gain a comfortable proficiency with the process. A couple of other favorites: surround your body at a particular chakra level with a ring of roses, then explode rings of roses continuously; or imagine that your entire aura is surrounded by roses which magically explode when full, like fireworks. Play with whatever technique is the most enjoyable for you.

EXERCISE 34: Second Chakra—Creating and Destroying Roses

For the next meditation you will create and destroy roses for your second chakra—your chakra of emotions, sexual creative energies, and boundaries. We could have chosen any chakra for this exercise, but because of its energy range the second chakra often holds lots of pictures for all of us.

To begin you'll first find the energy of your second chakra, two to three finger widths below the belly button. Then bring neutral green earth energy up through your feet chakras, up through your legs and into your second chakra, where you will allow the earth energy to help you open it as wide as it will comfortably open.

Then you'll imagine a picture-blowing rose out in front of you at the level of the second chakra and allow it to attract any pictures from within or near your second chakra that you are ready to explode—from any time, any place.

You'll then replenish your second chakra with neutral green earth energy and close it down to about 20%. Again, you could close it down to other percentages depending on your particular circumstances. The comparatively low percentage of 20% is a good all-purpose percentage for the second chakra.

1. Sit comfortably straight in your chair; breathe gently and deeply into your belly.
2. With a sense of adventure bring your awareness into the center of your head.
3. Cut off your old grounding cord, put it in a rose, and explode it.
4. Male- or female-ground.
5. From the center of your head find the energy of your second chakra, at about two to three finger widths below your belly button.
6. Observe as fresh green earth energy streams up from the very center of the Earth, up through your feet chakras, ankles, shins, knees, thighs; up the front of your body into your second chakra.
7. Let your second chakra open as wide as you can comfortably.
8. Allow that earth energy to stream around and through the second chakra and the area around the second chakra to a radius of about 4 inches.
9. Create and destroy roses out in front of your second chakra, exploding any and all pictures that you are ready to explode.
10. Replenish your second chakra and the surrounding area with fresh neutral earth energy.
11. Then close your second chakra down to about 20%.
12. Take a moment to acknowledge the healing you've given your second chakra.
13. Replenish your body and aura with fresh golden cosmic energy.
14. Bring up just the right amount of earth energy for your body and aura at this time.
15. Thank your body for being willing to change and grow.
16. Take a few refreshing breaths and when ready stand up, gently stretch, and reverse polarities.
17. You may find it useful to make some notes of your experience.

In Front and Behind, Above and Below, and Side to Side: If you were to only create and destroy roses in front, you might miss the pictures that are in the back or to the sides or above and below. So, as you begin to feel comfortable with the process, we suggest you begin to create and destroy roses all around a chakra—in front, behind, above, below, and side to side for any and all pictures anywhere in that area.

Vacuuming Energy

One of the most effective and enjoyable tools for clearing other peoples' energy out of your aura is the *rose vacuum cleaner*. Playfully imagine a rose out in front of your aura and allow its stem to drop all the way down to the center of the earth and become its own grounding cord. In your imagination empower your rose with the ability to gently vacuum other people's energies out of your aura, and then let those energies flow down your rose's grounding cord to the center of the Earth. Simply allow Mother Earth to recycle those energies for you without your conscious attention. Remember, you will be using your rose's grounding cord to release the energies and not your body's grounding cord with this technique.

You can, of course, choose a different metaphor to play with. Some people like to imagine an actual vacuum cleaner. Create and play with whatever works well for you. Let it be gentle, easy, and fun.

EXERCISE 35: Fourth Chakra—Vacuuming Energies

For this exercise you'll bring in golden cosmic energy. After you find the energy of your fourth chakra, invite a stream of golden cosmic energy from well above your crown down through your crown, the back of your head, into your fourth chakra, and out into the area around the fourth chakra to a radius of about 4 inches.

1. Sit comfortably straight in your chair; breathe gently and deeply into your belly.
2. With a playful curiosity allow your awareness to rest in the center of your head.

3. Cut off your old grounding cord, put it in a rose, and explode it.
4. Male- or female-ground.
5. From the center of your head find the energy of your fourth chakra, in the center of your sternum.
6. Invite a stream of golden cosmic energy from well above your crown down through your crown, the back of your head, into your fourth chakra, and the area around the fourth chakra to a radius of about 4 inches.
7. Allow your fourth chakra to open up as far as you can comfortably.
8. Create a rose vacuum cleaner in front of your fourth chakra then vacuum the chakra and about a 4-inch radius around it. Vacuum out any energy that is not yours that you're ready to release.
9. When through, bring down a generous stream of golden cosmic energy from well above your crown, down through your crown, head, and back, replenishing that entire fourth chakra and surrounding area.
10. Close your fourth chakra down to about 50%.
11. Take a moment to acknowledge the healing of your fourth chakra.
12. Replenish your entire body and aura with lots of golden cosmic energy.
13. Bring up from the center of the Earth just the right amount of earth energy for your body and aura at this time.
14. Take a few refreshing breaths and when ready stand up, gently stretch, and reverse polarities.
15. You may find it useful to make some notes of your experience.

Grounding an Energy Out of Your Body and Aura with Your Grounding Cord

Vacuuming energies is a powerful tool, especially for clearing energies in specific parts of the aura. But you can also clear large portions of your aura or even your entire aura of an energy by *grounding it out*—that is, let any excess energy that is not authentically yours simply fall down your grounding cord. Mother Earth will recycle it back to its origins. But keep in mind, this technique will move lots of energy very quickly, so it will be important for you to replenish your aura with fresh neutral energy.

EXERCISE 36: Full Aura Clearing Using Your Grounding Cord

1. Sit comfortably straight in your chair; breathe gently and deeply into your belly.
2. With a playful curiosity bring your awareness into the center of your head.
3. Cut off your old grounding cord, put it in a rose, and explode it.
4. Male- or female-ground.
5. From the center of your head intend that any excess energy or other people's energy that you are ready to release flow out of your body and aura and down your grounding cord to the Earth's center.
6. Allow Mother Earth to recycle those energies for you.
7. Replenish your entire body and aura with lots of golden cosmic energy.
8. Bring up from the center of the Earth just the right amount of earth energy for your body and aura at this time.
9. Take a few refreshing breaths and when ready stand up, gently stretch, and reverse polarities.
10. You may find it useful to make some notes of your experience.

Cords: Limitations on Communication and Autonomy

A cord is an energetic structure between two people or entities that streams energy and information back and forth between their auras. In the same way that everyone has energy in their space from others and everyone has pictures, everyone will also have cords.

Cords require some type of collaboration between people to be sustained—perhaps a mutual concern, resistance, or judgment. It can involve the intent to help or the intent to control, and very often love or hatred. While cords may seem innocuous or even desirable at first, they are usually programmed for some level of restriction. Cords focus growth and communication in various ways, restricting the relationship to a limited energy range that is set for the purpose and in the time period in which the cords were originally created. They can originate in this lifetime and can even remain active from and into other lifetimes. We feel that as an individual becomes aware of a cord in his or her aura, even when the original purpose was a worthy one (it often isn't), it is most likely time to reevaluate the cord and release it to bring the associated relationship and issues into current time.

Though cords represent a collaboration of some sort, made for reasons you may never know, cords are held in place by your beliefs and by your pictures. To release a cord it is most effective to also explode the accompanying pictures. You don't have to identify the limiting belief to release the pictures. Intend to explode "any and all pictures that the cords come in on." Clearing the underlying pictures brings your energy that had been stuck in the repetitive pattern of the picture into current time. You therefore don't have to think through or even consciously address the events you had been resisting. The clearing of your resistance, then, addresses the underlying limiting beliefs and agreements with which you originally created the cord.

Just like clearing energy that is not yours, clearing cords is not a rejection of others. It's an opportunity to acknowledge your own and others' autonomy, as well as your and others' unique spiritual journey. By releasing cords you change yourself, which doesn't require that others change. The beauty of taking unconditional responsibility is that your personal growth is never dependent on others changing. You can continue to have energy communication with the other if that's what you want. It will just be more free and in current time regardless of whether the other changes or not.

You will likely find that you have cords with your family, sweetheart, and friends, and most certainly with any relationship in which you feel there are "strings attached." It is also not unusual to find cords between you and your guides, and even between you and your animals. At times you may know exactly who you have cords with, and at times you may not. Being able to perceive cords, or to know exactly who they are with or even from what time period they originate, is not necessary in order for you to release them and come into current time with the relationship they represent. If you don't perceive cords, in the same way that you might work with energy or pictures, simply intend to release any and all cords that you are ready to let go of. Your unconscious will oblige. Other things being equal, seeing pictures, cords, and energy gives you more options and accuracy; but no matter how psychic you become, there will always be psychic structures you don't perceive but which you can change appropriately nevertheless.

Two common ways to recognize that you are dealing with a cord are 1) an excess energy in your aura, and 2) emotional or physical pain. Also, if after you've finished a clearing meditation you find that the energy you cleared returns in thirty minutes or a day later, you can safely assume that you have cords with someone. Certain kinds of pains, especially headaches, are caused by cords. Though physical pain is often the consequence of a cord, neither of us can recall finding a cord in ourselves or in a client's aura put there with the conscious intent to cause pain. The placing of cords is, with very few exceptions, an unconscious process.

When people first learn about cords they often become serious about them.[1] A cord represents your agreement with someone to have each other's energy engaged in your lives in some manner. Remember, in the logic of psychic reality, resistance is a kind of agreement, a kind of collaboration. (See Chapter 9, "Opening to Life As It Is: Resistance and Neutrality.") Even though cords are a collaboration, removing cords with someone does not require his or her permission. It simply requires that you take responsibility for your side of the equation, i.e., your limiting beliefs that sustain the cords. If the other person is depending on the cord, you may want to ask their or your guides to make alternate arrangements. (You don't have to see them to ask.) You never need another's permission to heal your own aura.

Cords will have a definite shape and form created by the current of energy streaming between the two people. Their characteristics—color, tone, texture, sound, or feel—will reflect the nature of the relationship you have with the person with whom you have created the cord. For example, a natural cord between a mother and her newborn will usually seem pliable, nurturing, and feel warm to the touch; whereas a cord from a jealous lover will usually seem rigid, demanding, and feel excessively cold or hot to the touch.

Although you may find cords in any part of your aura, you will tend to find the most important cords connected into the seven major chakras, or into the hands or feet. It is not unusual to also find "fear of moving forward" cords in and around the feet chakras and ankles.

Those of you who are more kinesthetic might feel the cords. They might seem cool or warm, or rough or smooth, have an energetic or emotional charge, or simply be neutral. Those of you more naturally clairvoyant may see the cords as different sizes and colors; some may be pretty, and some may be ugly. The shapes may vary quite a bit, sometimes appearing as tiny as a thread or as big as a tree trunk; soft and pliable like an umbilical cord or rigid and stiff like a wire; or sometimes like a tangle of spaghetti. Often when you touch or see a cord you may get a strong impression of the person with whom you have created the cord, but again it's not necessary that you know.

For technical reasons that we discuss in the "Seniority" section in Chapter 9, a cord will connect into a chakra at a slightly higher frequency than the chakra itself. Those of you who are clairaudient (that is, you hear energy) may sense the cords as different frequencies and tones. To help you find cords more easily, begin by finding the chakra's specific vibration, then like a jazz musician go a little sharp on that note, the tiniest bit higher, and you will probably find some cords. It's the same for feeling or seeing: just look the tiniest bit higher in frequency.

If you do not perceive the cords at all, just intend to release any cords you are ready to release. Acknowledge your perceptions no matter how dramatic or subtle because acknowledging your perceptions creates the space for your perception to grow.

Many cords are created with the best of intentions such as between a parent and a child, sweethearts, husbands and wives, teachers and students, doctors and patients, healers and clients. Even cords such as those created out of jealousy often arise though someone's underlying wish to be loved. Many cords, like leaves on a tree ending their season, simply drop away. But occasionally people find a cord that they had created with such great seriousness that it can last a long time, even across lifetimes.

You might imagine how a cord created by the vow "I will love you, and only you, for all eternity" can wreak havoc over time. Such cords represent one example of *contracts*, which we address in the endnotes of this chapter.[2] Most cords, such as the ones you'll engage in the following exercise, can be addressed easily by releasing them and exploding pictures, and by bringing the underlying beliefs and relationship into current time.

Cords often result in stagnation and resentment. You can probably imagine the distress created by two very commonly corded relationships. The first example, stagnation, can be caused by a cord between someone and an authority figure from lifetimes ago, which may still be active in your crown chakra. The edicts of the seventeenth century are hardly going to be relevant to your modern life. Releasing cords with such an authority figure allows each person to be his or her own authority. And the inverse, releasing any cords where you acted as a domineering figure, would also be an excellent healing. Most of us have played both sides of that polarity on our spiritual journey.

The second example, resentment, is often the result of a parent overprotecting his or her child. Releasing or updating your cords with your children is the gift of letting them grow up. "Cutting the apron strings" is a great way to respect your child's boundaries, as well as to free up your own vitality. Parents often report that learning how to give their children their space has been the best thing to ever happen to their relationship. It doesn't make the relationship perfect, but giving the child their own spiritual space does foster more respect and open communication.

Other systems work with cords in various ways, depending on their purposes. For instance, in some systems cords are intentionally created, such as in many Buddhist initiations that involve a cord between the Lama and the student, which is authentic to some people's spiritual path. Barbara Brennan, best known for her pioneering and encyclopedic book on the aura and healing, *Hands of Light*, suggests that when a healer perceives a cord running from the client to someone, the healer not remove the cord but heal it by straightening and generally clarifying the flow.[3]

There are no boundaries breached by removing cords that are in your own personal space. Your body and aura are your frontiers to explore and heal. But we can make a strong argument in favor of Barbara Brennan's approach, because in her role as healer, she might choose to let the relationship play out in a different way than we might. Different systems will have their own approach to cords, according to their intent and the energy range in which they work.

A Few Important Exceptions

We often joke that the only good cord is a grounding cord, but there are a few important exceptions we recognize such as with newborns and occasionally as caretaker for the ill or dying. A newborn baby will often require cords from his or her mother and father through early infancy. As a parent you can meditate to find the cords with your baby, but before removing any, ask yourself, "What is this cord accomplishing? Is there any part of the energy running down this cord that isn't needed anymore?" If so, you can reduce the size of the cord to what seems proper and appropriate at that time, and eventually release it after it has served its purpose. Cords are fine with your baby, unless your baby is eighteen. At some point, well before your baby is eighteen, it will strengthen your relationship to remove your cords.

There are special circumstances when it would be appropriate for you as a caretaker to have a small cord to someone who is ill or dying for a limited amount of time. In such cases you'd want to be careful not to overstep bounds and impose your will, and to simply provide support in those transitional moments. After the cord has served its purpose it is important to release it so that it doesn't cause a drain on your vitality, or inadvertently hold the beneficiary back from his or her next appropriate step.

Three Methods for Removing Cords

For most people, the method for removing cords that is easiest to learn is to imagine that you have a pair of psychic hands and move them all around the chakra: in front, behind, above, below, and to each side of it—feeling, imagining, allowing—removing any cords you encounter. The second method is to see or imagine the cord and just intend that it dissipate or dissolve. The third method is to see or imagine the cord, breathe your energy out of the cord, and let it drop away. A cord cannot exist in your space without your energy holding it. So breathe your energy back out of the cord or visualize your energy flowing out of the cord and into your free-flowing aura space. Then explode the pictures that set the cord up, and let it go.

As you release cords, the other person will often release them simultaneously. Please be careful not to accidentally force cords out of another person's aura. Cords tend to be a very palpable energy, so forcing a cord out of another's space might cause him or her to get a headache or to suddenly feel off balance. Pull the cord out of your aura, breathe your energy out of the cord, or just intend that it clear out of your aura. At an unconscious level, the person with whom you shared the cord can then decide how to proceed in his or her own time.

Occasionally you will find that after you've removed a cord it'll move outside your aura only to hang there, floating. Should you become aware of that happening, congratulate yourself for that awareness, then playfully explode more pictures, breathe more of your energy back, and check to see if you are, in fact, ready to come into current time with that relationship. Sometimes it's hard to let go even when you know it is the healthy thing to do.

EXERCISE 37: Third Chakra—Removing Cords

In the following exercise you will clear cords from in and around your third chakra using golden cosmic energy. Found at the solar-plexus level, your third chakra is the energy range with which you engage your personal power and understanding of yourself and others.

A quick recap of the process: After you male- or female-ground, you'll find the energy of the third chakra, and ask or intend that any cords that you are ready to release light up—from any time, any space, any relationship with which you want to cultivate more authenticity and freedom. Imagine that you have psychic hands that gently pull or cut the cords as you encounter them. You'll find them at a frequency that is ever so slightly higher than the frequency of the chakra. Explode any relevant pictures that are lit up by the process and intend to breathe your energy back into current time, and let the cords fall away.

1. Sit comfortably straight in your chair; breathe gently and deeply into your belly.
2. With a playful curiosity bring your awareness into the center of your head.
3. Cut off your old grounding cord, put it in a rose, and explode it.
4. Playfully create your male or female grounding cord.
5. From the center of your head, please become aware of the energy of your third chakra in the solar-plexus area a little below where the ribs come together, at the bottom of the sternum.
6. Imagine golden cosmic energy streaming down from well above your crown, down through the back of your crown and head, down the back of your neck and chest, and into your third-chakra area.
7. Allow it to flow in and around and through the third chakra and out into the entire area surrounding the third chakra, to a radius of about 4 inches.
8. Imagine that your psychic hands can go fully around the third chakra—above, below, in front, behind, and side to side—and gently remove any cords you are ready to let go of.
9. Create and destroy roses so that the pictures holding the cords in place explode.
10. Playfully breathe your energy out of the cord(s).
11. From the center of your head, bring in lots of golden suns to fill your third chakra and your aura, allowing any excess energy to flow down your grounding cord.
12. From the center of the Earth bring up just the right amount of fresh earth energy for your body at this time.
13. To help you integrate the clearing, cut off your old grounding cord, put it in a rose, and explode it.
14. Playfully create a new male or female grounding cord.
15. When ready stand up, stretch, and reverse polarities.
16. You may find it useful to make some notes of your experience.

The Power and Freedom of Healthy Boundaries

Following this exercise we hear lots of "Ah-ha!"s as the power and freedom that comes with releasing cords begin to make everyday practical sense.

The change you feel in your aura from removing cords can often be more dramatic than either clearing pictures or other people's energy. But even if you do not sense cords yet, by intending to clear them you will have initiated deep unconscious changes at all levels of relationship. To continue to integrate this healing, it will be quite helpful to update your grounding several times over the next few hours. Also, if you are inclined, journaling helps you assimilate your experience.

Though it is not necessary to your healing for you to know with whom or why you created a cord, it can be enlightening. Upon such discovery we often hear people lament, "What was I thinking?!" We offer a gentle reminder to be compassionate with yourself. In such cases you will have revisited a moment in time when you were not as ready, aware, or capable as you are today.

Again, it's easy to get serious about someone being in your space with a cord. But it helps build a healthy humility to remember that you are, or were, in his or her space on the other end of the cord. We're not suggesting that you won't also feel frustrated and impatient. We're just suggesting that you understand that however much energy awareness you have, there will always be aspects of your energy you want to improve, sometimes a lot.

There's no such thing as a negative emotion, just unskillful ways of handling emotions. There's nothing wrong with getting angry that someone is in your space. But it would be unskillful to wallow in self-pity and a sense of victimization; or to aggressively demand that he or she change their behavior. Take unconditional responsibility and, with patience, give yourself the necessary space and time it takes to change your own patterns. Acknowledge the inevitable emotions along the way.

For your next exercise, you will use all three of the core clearing tools for large-scale changes. For practice you can use any chakra; we'll use the fifth chakra in the following exercise.

EXERCISE 38: Fifth Chakra—Exploding Roses, Vacuuming Energy, and Removing Cords

1. Sit comfortably straight in your chair; breathe gently and deeply into your belly.
2. With a playful curiosity bring your awareness into the center of your head.
3. Cut off your old grounding cord, put it in a rose, and explode it.
4. Male- or female-ground.
5. From the center of your head, become aware of the energy of your fifth chakra in the notch of the throat.
6. Imagine golden cosmic energy streaming down from well above your crown, down through the back of your crown and head, down your neck, and into your fifth chakra.
7. Allow it to flow in, around, and through the fifth chakra and out into the entire area surrounding the fifth chakra, to a radius of about 4 inches.
8. Create and destroy roses in and around your fifth chakra.
9. Remove cords in and around your fifth chakra.
10. Vacuum energies in and around your fifth chakra.
11. From the center of your head, bring in lots of golden suns to fill your fifth chakra and your aura, allowing any excess energy to flow down your grounding cord.
12. From the center of the Earth bring up just the right amount of fresh earth energy for your body at this time.
13. To help you integrate the clearing, cut off your old grounding cord, put it in a rose, and explode it.
14. Playfully create a new male or female grounding cord.
15. When ready stand up, stretch, and reverse polarities.
16. You may find it useful to make some notes of your experience.

More on Designing Your Daily Practice

In your own daily practice, we encourage everyone to spend at least five minutes a day grounding and clearing. If you have twenty or thirty minutes by all means do so. If you have ten minutes in the morning and ten minutes at night, you might clear your feet chakras and your first, second, and third chakras in the morning, and your fourth, fifth, sixth, seventh, and hand chakras at night, or even the other way around. Or you might spread your clearing out over a week, working with one chakra at a time. Some folks ground and clear their first chakra while brushing their teeth, or showering, or getting ready for work. Fold your meditation in where you can, and ideally you also have some quality time to sit and meditate. Be creative—even five minutes will make a difference in your vitality and relationships.

John's teacher, Jane Roberts, used to say that spontaneity knows its own discipline. The other side of that polarity is that discipline knows its own spontaneity. Like exercise, you will probably find it more effective to set time aside to meditate every day rather than to meditate when you find the time.

It is true, however, that there is often an initial obstacle when sitting down and meditating: your unexamined pain of the day will often light up. A teacher we greatly respect, John Fulton, refers to "going through the moat" to get to a meditative space. In the same way that it is worthwhile to brush your teeth every day so you don't get a tartar buildup and gum disease, it's worth meditating every day so that you don't get a buildup of pain and resistance. It helps you stay fresh and current, and not only will you enjoy life more, people will find you more enjoyable.

You now have the three large-scale clearing methods with which to work with the chakra system: vacuuming energy, creating and destroying roses, and removing cords. As you clear your chakras with these three clearing tools, you will find yourself enjoying and improving the way that you engage the world. Putting these ideas and skills into practice will help you develop more and more capacity to perceive psychically. You can use your growing skills to know what's going on in your space and in your relationships and to clear your energy. As you become ever more psychic, the pace at which you become more psychic accelerates because the very tools you use to become more psychic become more powerful and effective as you perceive more. Clearing your energy also generates more kindness, generosity, and authenticity because you have released ever more resistance to life as it is.

CHAPTER 9

Opening to Life As It Is:
Resistance and Neutrality

We have presented the core energy tools of psychic psychology, the tools we use to work on the aura. We now explore neutrality, the most important state of mind for working in this system, and its opposite state of mind, resistance. If you can imagine the tools you have learned so far as being similar to the steering wheel, brakes, and accelerator of a car, then neutrality can be thought of as similar to developing a skillful attitude—a calm, alert, and balanced focus on driving that would enable you to be a good driver. Neutrality, found in the sixth chakra, is the state of mind in which you are open to all your experience, including your experience of your own reactions of pleasure and pain, likes and dislikes. Resistance occurs when you fail to be open to a part of your experience.

A person in neutrality, upon learning of the death of a beloved uncle, might experience and be open to the experience of many emotions at once. She might cry even as she remembers and laughs about the wonderful times they had together, even as she worries about her aunt, and so on. Resistance often shows up in ways that aren't obvious, e.g., many people trying to learn to cope with anger repress anger and express only love. A person in neutrality dealing with anger would acknowledge his or her anger, and try to find a skillful way to behave and communicate. (See Chapter 23, "Anger.")

As you develop your psychic perception and clarify your aura, you will notice a simple way to tell the difference between an authentic decision to take skillful action and repression. When you are in resistance (repression), you squeeze or cover up part of the energy in your aura in response to your experience. When you are in neutrality, you allow every part of your aura to flow naturally in responding to an event. You are open to all your energies, whether you "approve" of them or not. Then, from a still point in the center of your head, you can decide how to respond in the moment. Later you can revisit a situation and decide what type of growth you want to make with regard to the energies you earlier found in your space.

As you cultivate neutrality, you have more openness to life because you have more openness to who you are. You have a variety of skillful options for confronting difficult or unpleasant situations. You make changes in yourself more easily. You are increasingly open to uncovering what unexamined contradictions undercut your pursuit of your goals.

As a concept neutrality is very subtle. There is no ordinary word to convey the true meaning that we are seeking in this psychic context. Fortunately, as you grow in skill and understanding, you can grasp the utility of neutrality as you discover different ways of engaging energy. First, neutrality (as we use the word) is not forcibly smoothing an energy out so that it is nice and calm. In fact, as you will come to see, forcing an energy into a particular form is the opposite of neutrality.

Neutrality is giving an energy its natural psychic space (usually we use the word "space" to refer to psychic space). To understand what it means for an energy to have space, natural or not, we will explore the energy nature of experience and space through the next several pages and exercises.

When we say an experience takes "space" we are referring to the space filled by the vibrational energy of that experience. You don't merely create your reality according to your aura. Every experience you have—every physical sensation, emotion, and thought—is, at the time you have the experience, vibrating as an energy in your aura. Even when you are remembering an experience, the energy of your memory is vibrating in your aura.

The tie between your bodily experience and your aura's vibration works both ways. A physical body sensation, emotion, or thought simultaneously generates a unique energy flow in your aura. An energy flow in your aura simultaneously generates the physical body experience, usually unrecognized.

So when you experience emotions such as pleasure, anger, disgust, love, fear, courage, and so on, unique energies vibrate in your aura. An experience of pleasure will always have certain recognizable, vibrational similarities with other experiences of pleasure, and will always be recognizably different from the vibration of disgust (for example). While the energy vibration of each experience of pleasure will be similar to the energy vibration of other experiences of pleasure, each experience will have its own vibrational nuances.

There is one additional helpful point to understand before beginning to explore what it means to give an energy its natural space. You can move an energy from inside your aura to outside your aura without disturbing its vibration. It is often easier to observe and understand an energy outside your aura because inside your aura there's always so much more than one energy vibration going on at a time.

The next exercise then will be to observe the energies, one at a time, of the emotions of anger, happiness, impatience, and love by remembering and exploring, one at a time, specific instances when you experienced those emotions. The energy of every specific instance of a particular emotion will resemble the energy of other instances of that emotion, so when you become familiar with what a representative example feels or looks like, you will learn to recognize what the psychic energy of that emotion feels or looks like.

So, to look at an emotion, remember a specific instance or two where you had that emotion, or think about something that generates the emotion in current time. You'll explore one emotion at a time. Try to notice that the vibrational energy of that emotional event takes space. When you are done looking at the space, create and destroy roses for any pictures that got lit up and replenish your aura.

EXERCISE 39: Observe the Space of Anger, Happiness, Impatience, and Love

1. Breathe gently and deeply, and with openness be in the center of your head.
2. Explode your old grounding cord and male- or female-ground.

3. **Anger:** Remember a specific instance where you were angry, or think about something that generates anger in current time.

4. From the center of your head, pay particular attention to the amount of space that anger takes up in your aura.

5. After you get a sense of the space that anger takes up in your aura, create and destroy roses for any pictures that lit up.

6. **Happiness:** Remember a specific instance where you were happy, or think about something that generates happiness in current time.

7. From the center of your head, pay particular attention to the amount of space that happiness takes up in your aura.

8. After you get a sense of the space that happiness takes up in your aura, create and destroy roses for any pictures that lit up.

9. **Impatience:** Remember a specific instance where you were impatient, or think about something that generates impatience in current time.

10. From the center of your head, pay particular attention to the amount of space that impatience takes up in your aura.

11. After you get a sense of the space that impatience takes up in your aura, create and destroy roses for any pictures that lit up.

12. **Love:** Remember a specific instance of love, or think about something that generates love in current time.

13. From the center of your head, pay particular attention to the amount of space that love takes up in your aura.

14. After you get a sense of the space that love takes up in your aura, create and destroy roses for any pictures that lit up.

15. When through, recycle the energy from your pictures back through your crown.

16. Explode your old grounding cord and male- or female-ground.

17. Replenish your body and aura with golden cosmic energy.

18. Bring up just the right amount of earth energy for your body and aura at this time.

19. Thank your body for being willing to change and grow.

20. Breathe gently and deeply, stand up, stretch, and reverse polarities.
21. You may find it useful to make some notes of your experience.

EXERCISE 40: Comparing How Emotions Occupy Space

Another exercise that might help you notice how the vibrations of different emotional experiences occupy space is to pick something you have a slight emotion about and notice how much space it seems to take naturally, then compare that with something you feel strongly about. The experiences won't necessarily take different amounts of space. The difference could be merely in the intensity of the energy in that space, but usually a stronger emotion will naturally take more space.

1. Breathe gently and deeply, and with openness be in the center of your head.
2. Explode your old grounding cord and male- or female-ground.
3. From the center of your head, recall an issue or incidence that generates a slight emotion for you.
4. Notice the amount of space your emotion occupies in your aura.
5. Next, recall an issue or incidence about which you feel a much stronger emotion.
6. From the center of your head, notice the amount of space your stronger emotion occupies in your aura.
7. Compare and contrast the two, noting how much space each occupies as well as their intensity.
8. When through, create and destroy roses for any pictures that lit up, and recycle the energy from your pictures back through your crown.
9. Explode your old grounding cord and male- or female-ground.
10. Replenish your body and aura with golden cosmic energy.
11. Bring up just the right amount of earth energy for your body and aura at this time.
12. Thank your body for being willing to change and grow.
13. Breathe gently and deeply, stand up, stretch, and reverse polarities.
14. You may find it useful to make some notes of your experience.

EXERCISE 41: Giving Your Mild Anger All the Space It
Naturally "Wants" to Unfold

For the next exercise, you will think about something that makes you
mildly angry, then you will put the energy of the anger out in front of
you and allow that anger to expand and fill however much space it seems
to naturally "want." When the emotion seems to have expanded sufficiently, create and destroy roses. What is new in this exercise is letting
the vibration of your emotion expand to take the space it "wants" to
unfold.

1. Breathe gently and deeply, and with openness be in the center of
   your head.
2. Explode your old grounding cord and male- or female-ground.
3. From the center of your head, recall an issue or incidence about
   which you are mildly angry.
4. Allow your mild anger to go out in front of you and observe as it
   expands and fills however much space it seems to naturally
   "want."
5. When the emotion seems to have expanded and taken up all the
   space it naturally "wants," create and destroy roses.
6. Then recycle the energy from your pictures back through your
   crown.
7. Explode your old grounding cord and male- or female-ground.
8. Replenish your body and aura with golden cosmic energy.
9. Bring up just the right amount of earth energy for your body and
   aura at this time.
10. Thank your body for being willing to change and grow.
11. Breathe gently and deeply, stand up, stretch, and reverse
    polarities.
12. You may find it useful to make some notes of your experience.

For this exercise you chose an instance of anger that was mild. Mild emotions normally take a small to moderate amount of space. The object of
this exercise is to get a sense of the vibrations of an emotion unfolding
to its natural and comfortable size. This is why you used a mild instance

of anger. Over time you can choose more intense emotions to observe and see how they unfold to their natural and comfortable size when you let them. Sometimes when you are very emotional, or more emotional than you realized, the emotion will take up more space than is readily available. A technique to mitigate that lack of space is explained in Chapter 23, "Anger."

EXERCISE 42: Observing If a Difficult Emotion Is Compressed or Taking Its Space

With the preceding exercises you can begin to understand that an energy can be compressed or it can expand to its natural space. The next phase of understanding involves the effect of either compressing an energy or giving that energy its own natural space. In the next exercise you will take an emotion you have a really hard time with. You will put it out in front of you and observe if it is taking its full natural space. Our expectation is that it will not. Observe your emotions. Then ground, breathe, and let the energy take its full natural space. Notice your emotions again. Our expectation is that you will feel more comfortable, balanced, and capable of handling the emotion. The energy itself may change in color, shape, and quality. More important for the skill of neutrality, your emotions about the energy will probably change.

1. Breathe gently and deeply, and with openness be in the center of your head.
2. Explode your old grounding cord and male- or female-ground.
3. Recall your difficult emotion.
4. Allow your difficult emotion to go out in front of you, and observe it and your emotional response to it.
5. Pay particular attention to whether or not it is taking its full and natural space.
6. Then update your grounding, breathe, and let the energy of your difficult emotion expand to its full and natural space, and notice your emotions again.
7. When through, create and destroy roses, then recycle the energy from your pictures back through your crown.

8. Explode your old grounding cord and male- or female-ground.
9. Replenish your body and aura with golden cosmic energy.
10. Bring up just the right amount of earth energy for your body and aura at this time.
11. Thank your body for being willing to change and grow.
12. Breathe gently and deeply, stand up, stretch, and reverse polarities.
13. You may find it useful to make some notes of your experience.

This may be a new experience for you, noticing that there is an emotion and a "you" having that emotion. You are, in some sense, separate from the emotion even as you experience it. Throughout the rest of this chapter you will be developing skills to enhance your awareness of a separate you. Surprisingly, this separate you will be more and more capable of intimacy and engagement throughout all areas of your life.

EXERCISE 43: Noticing That You Are Not Your Emotions

1. Breathe gently and deeply, and with openness be in the center of your head.
2. Explode your old grounding cord and male- or female-ground.
3. Allow the energy of an emotion to go out in front of you, let it unfold, and notice the space it initially takes. Explore how it changes.
4. Notice that there is a "you" that isn't your emotion.
5. Allow your emotion to take its full and natural size.
6. Continue to notice how "you" experience your emotion but aren't your emotion.
7. When through, create and destroy roses, then recycle the energy from your pictures back through your crown.
8. Explode your old grounding cord and male- or female-ground.
9. Replenish your body and aura with golden cosmic energy.
10. Bring up just the right amount of earth energy for your body and aura at this time.
11. Thank your body for being willing to change and grow.

12. Breathe gently and deeply, stand up, stretch, and reverse polarities.
13. You may find it useful to make some notes of your experience.

If you can sense an emotion unfolding to take its natural space, you can start to understand how when you are in neutrality you do not flatten your emotion. In fact, you allow each emotion the space to develop according to its natural flow.

Resistance

We are now going to explore neutrality's opposite, resistance, after which we will explore a number of techniques to be neutral. The goal is to help you be open to the world as it is.

This next exercise will help you learn what resistance feels like. Think of someone or something you really dislike. Most of us have some politician or political ideology we really dislike, but use whatever works for you. It is possible to place your attention on something you really dislike while you cultivate neutrality, and that is the very skill we ultimately wish to cultivate.

To understand what not having neutrality feels like, purposely be ungrounded, and wait to explode your pictures until the end of the exercise. Put the energy of the politician, ideology, or something else that you really dislike on a rose out in front of you and turn your attention to that energy. Dwell on just how terrible you think that situation is. As you dwell, you will probably be able to notice a tightening of your body. More subtly, if you have achieved the ability to notice energy, you may notice that the energy of the politician or whatever it is that you dislike starts streaming towards you and into your aura. Then you can notice yourself pushing against that energy. It is this pushing that is called *resisting an energy*. In the earlier exercises, to allow your emotions to unfold and take their natural space you consciously or unconsciously stopped pushing against the energies, thus becoming neutral and open to the entire experience of that event which triggered the emotion.

EXERCISE 44: Dwelling on Someone or an Ideology You Really Dislike

1. Explode your old grounding cord and remain ungrounded.
2. Create a rose for a politician, ideology, or something that you really dislike.
3. Let yourself dwell on just how terrible you think that person or situation is.
4. Notice your physical and emotional responses: Does your body tighten? Do your emotions intensify? Does your breathing change?
5. It may be subtle, but see if you can notice the energy of the politician, ideology, or whatever it is that you dislike streaming towards you into your aura.
6. See if you can notice yourself pushing against that energy.
7. When through, male- or female-ground and explode your rose and any pictures that lit up.
8. If you worked with a person, intend that his or her energy return to him or her, or his or her guide.
9. Recycle your energy back through your crown.
10. Replenish your body and aura with golden cosmic energy.
11. Bring up just the right amount of earth energy for your body and aura at this time.
12. Thank your body for being willing to change and grow.
13. Breathe gently and deeply, stand up, stretch, and reverse polarities.
14. You may find it useful to make some notes of your experience.

Pushing against something squeezes or covers up an energy you are resisting. What is fascinating and a little chilling is the fact that to push against an energy you must match its colors and qualities. Otherwise the energy would pass right by you. When you match the colors and qualities of an energy you are resisting, even or especially if it's an energy you hate, you vibrate with its very colors and qualities. The vibrations of your aura are who you are. Thus you become what you resist.

Of course when you resist a politician whose politics you despise, you don't suddenly change your politics. What is the same in you and the despised politician are the vibrations in your auras. This is perhaps the hardest spiritual truth to understand. How can you share the same vibrations with your opposite? Moving away from the politician example, how can you share a vibration with someone despicable just because you resist him or her? It's true that your aura may be mostly different in important ways from the despicable person you are resisting, and that makes you, in an important sense, a different, better person. Nevertheless, to the extent that you resist another person, to that extent you match them, and that match has profound consequences in your reality creation. What you resist you become. The most wonderful people, if not aware and not cultivating an authentic openness to life as it is, can resist and thus match the most awful people.[1] In our terminology there is a difference between *resisting* and *opposing*. Other people use different terminologies. When Gandhi engaged in nonviolent resistance, he was, in our terminology, opposing rather than resisting. By virtue of his deep spiritual clarity, Gandhi was able to oppose the English colonization of India without matching their energy of fear or hatred. Underneath the seeming opposites involved in resistance (as we use the term), there will be matching, constrained fear. Even fear can be acknowledged and given space in neutrality. When it is not acknowledged and given space, it generates resistance. We talk more about this in Chapter 18, "Matching Pictures and Unconditional Responsibility."

Seniority

You can't have your whole aura neutral and remain engaged in your personal life. It is possible to flood your aura with white light and be nearly without experience of personal preferences. Underneath the white light, as long as you have a physical body, there will still be personal preferences, but if you flooded your aura with white light you wouldn't experience them. You'd have no personal self that you recognized.

We the authors are committed to the value of having a personal self, and that self will have at least some resistance in its personal aura. What you can learn to do is find a still, quiet place in your aura in which to engage the world with neutrality, which is facilitated by a quality we call *seniority*.

EXERCISE 45: Seniority

In the following exercise please take a little time to explore what energy or emotion reigns in your crown at this moment.

1. Breathe gently and deeply, and with openness be in the center of your head.
2. Explode your old grounding cord and male- or female-ground.
3. Observe your crown to see what emotion or energy is "senior" in your aura.
4. Just observe it, and notice how it lights up pictures in your space.
5. Playfully imagine your crown chakra vibrating at a golden color and explode pictures. (You'll learn an easy way to set your crown to gold in Exercise 49: A Golden Crown in Ten Seconds.)
6. Ground out any energies that are not yours.
7. Explode your old grounding cord and male- or female-ground.
8. Replenish your body and aura with golden cosmic energy.
9. Bring up just the right amount of earth energy for your body and aura at this time.
10. Thank your body for being willing to change and grow.
11. Breathe gently and deeply, stand up, stretch, and reverse polarities.
12. You may find it useful to make some notes of your experience.

Intentionally Lighting Yourself Up

A picture forms in response to some particular quality of energy, pleasant or unpleasant. Basically resistance is a form of fear. The fear becomes an active combatant in your energy experience. Whenever the picture contains fear of a particular energy, you will resist that energy. Whenever the energy you fear runs through your aura, your fear will mobilize its energy to oppose that energy. It literally matches the energy in color and quality, but in the opposite direction.

For example, if you were bullied by your brother when you were two and you are still resisting that experience, then certain new experiences (unique to you) will trigger that picture. Perhaps every time you see your brother you will get triggered, but perhaps not. If you have worked through your issues with your brother, but not your overall issues with bullying, you might be comfortable with him. Still, seeing a playground or seeing a two-year old-child might trigger your bullying picture.[2] There is a psychic coding that determines what triggers a picture and what does not.

Remember, a picture lighting up in your aura operates on the same principle as an incandescent light bulb. Contained in the enclosed space of the bulb is a filament, which is resistant to the flow of energy. As the current passes through the resistant filament, the energy is transformed into light. In the aura, a picture results whenever you are stuck in an energy pattern that obstructs the free and full range of vibration in your energy. Each picture arises out of resistance to a particular quality or frequency of energy. So each picture is resistant only to the particular energy flow that relates to its subject matter.

EXERCISE 46: Intentionally Lighting Yourself Up
1. Breathe gently and deeply, and with openness be in the center of your head.
2. Explode your old grounding cord and male- or female-ground.
3. Create a rose for a scenario you'd like to explore.
4. Imagine the worst possible outcome, let it light you up, and explode those pictures.
5. Imagine getting blindsided, let it light you up, and then explode those pictures.
6. Imagine, for example, realizing that you don't like the job you sought after all, and explode those pictures.
7. Imagine the best possible outcome, let it light you up, and then explode those pictures.
8. Explode your rose, and recycle its energy and the energy from all your pictures back through your crown.
9. Explode your old grounding cord and male- or female-ground.
10. Replenish your body and aura with golden cosmic energy.
11. Bring up just the right amount of earth energy for your body and aura at this time.

12. Thank your body for being willing to change and grow.
13. Breathe gently and deeply, stand up, stretch, and reverse polarities.
14. You may find it useful to make some notes of your experience.

EXERCISE 47: Non-Judgmentalness: Letting Someone Be Who He or She Is

You can still fiercely dislike what the other is doing. And you can still vigorously oppose what is going on. You can even take action against it. What makes an attitude judgmental is coercively seeking to close down the other person's space, whether you are conscious of this or not. What makes your attitude then non-judgmental is allowing other people to have their space even as you oppose them.

Now, allow yourself to stop resisting him or her. Simply observe and let him or her be who they are even as you let your emotions be what they are. This requires that you continue to clear your aura by creating and destroying roses. Try to stay senior to your emotions.

1. Breathe gently and deeply, and with openness be in the center of your head.
2. Explode your old grounding cord and male- or female-ground.
3. Create a rose for someone whose views deeply trouble you.
4. Without judgment, notice how he or she affects your grounding, your mood, your aura.
5. Without judging him or her, simply observe and let him or her be who they are.
6. Also allow your own emotions without judging them.
7. Notice how that non-judgmentalness affects your grounding, mood, and aura.
8. Notice your breath naturally deepening as you give it space to be what it is.
9. When ready, create and destroy roses.
10. Explode your rose, and recycle its energy and the energy from all your pictures back through your crown.
11. Explode your old grounding cord and male- or female-ground.

12. Replenish your body and aura with golden cosmic energy.
13. Bring up just the right amount of earth energy for your body and aura at this time.
14. Thank your body for being willing to change and grow.
15. Breathe gently and deeply, stand up, stretch, and reverse polarities.
16. You may find it useful to make some notes of your experience.

Seeing All Experience as Sacred and Meaning-Filled

Appreciating all experience as sacred and meaning-filled, and embracing experience as an opportunity for you to learn and grow, are seemingly magical attitudes to cultivate your neutrality and compassion.

EXERCISE 48: Seeing Experience as Sacred and an Opportunity to Grow

Imagine a situation that troubles you deeply and contemplate its underlying sacredness and meaning.

1. Breathe gently and deeply, and with openness be in the center of your head.
2. Explode your old grounding cord and male- or female-ground.
3. Create a rose for something that deeply troubles you.
4. Without judging it, consider your event as sacred and meaning-filled.
5. Ask what it is that you are to learn about yourself from this event.
6. When ready, create and destroy roses.
7. Explode your rose, and recycle its energy and the energy from all your pictures back through your crown.
8. Explode your old grounding cord and male- or female-ground.
9. Replenish your body and aura with golden cosmic energy.
10. Bring up just the right amount of earth energy for your body and aura at this time.
11. Thank your body for being willing to change and grow.

12. Breathe gently and deeply, stand up, stretch, and reverse polarities.
13. You may find it useful to make some notes of your experience.

Two Approaches for Cultivating Neutrality: In-the-Body and Out-of-Body

In the following discussions we'll explore two approaches for cultivating neutrality. The first is to consciously and skillfully stay in the body, and the second is to consciously and skillfully go out of the body. There are numerous ways in which to cultivate neutrality, and this section offers several of our favorites.

In-the-Body Neutrality

Whatever color is senior in your crown chakra represents the attitude and tone with which you will engage that moment. For instance, when you are angry certain ranges of reds will be senior in your crown, and when happy brilliant yellows, pinks, and blues can be seen to reign.

When wishing more perspective and neutrality on something, a very quick and effective technique is to vibrate your crown chakra at a neutral golden frequency. You may recall from our discussion on colors in Chapter 5 that gold is one of the highest-frequency colors you can run in your body and stay in your body; it is also one of the most neutral.

Of course, simply vibrating your crown at gold will not magically "make" you neutral and all-wise, but it will help you find the space for a more open and calm perspective. It will help provide quick breathing room so you can engage whatever is challenging you with respect and resourcefulness.

An easy way to bring your crown to gold is to imagine a golden rose and then touch it to your crown, allowing the color to transfer into your crown. You may not always have the time to ground and clear, so we've included two versions to bring your crown to gold—one that will take you about ten seconds, and the other for when you have time to meditate.

With a little practice, you will eventually be able to simply tell your crown to "go to gold" and your crown will find the frequency instantaneously.

EXERCISE 49: A Golden Crown in Ten Seconds

1. Be in the center of your head.
2. Create a playful golden rose.
3. Touch your golden rose to your crown chakra and let your crown become golden.
4. Intend that any pictures that are lit up by your challenge explode.

EXERCISE 50: Bringing Your Crown to Gold with a Clearing

1. Breathe gently and deeply, and with openness be in the center of your head.
2. Explode your old grounding cord and male- or female-ground.
3. Create a beautiful and playful golden rose.
4. Touch your golden rose to your crown chakra and let your crown become golden.
5. Explode any pictures that are lit up throughout your body and aura.
6. Explode your rose, and recycle its energy and the energy from all your pictures back through your crown.
7. Explode your old grounding cord and male- or female-ground.
8. Replenish your body and aura with golden cosmic energy.
9. Bring up just the right amount of earth energy for your body and aura at this time.
10. Thank your body for being willing to change and grow.
11. Breathe gently and deeply, stand up, stretch, and reverse polarities.
12. You may find it useful to make some notes of your experience.

EXERCISE 51: Moving Something Further Away

In the following exercise please notice your grounding, mood, and aura as you practice moving a troubling issue away from you.

1. Breathe gently and deeply, and with openness be in the center of your head.
2. Explode your old grounding cord and male- or female-ground.
3. Create a rose for something that deeply troubles you.
4. Notice how it affects your grounding, your mood, and your aura.
5. Move the rose first 10 feet, then 50 feet, then 100 feet out in front of you.
6. Notice how it affects your grounding, mood, and aura at each distance.
7. Create and destroy roses.
8. Explode your rose, and recycle its energy and the energy from all your pictures back through your crown.
9. Explode your old grounding cord and male- or female-ground.
10. Replenish your body and aura with golden cosmic energy.
11. Bring up just the right amount of earth energy for your body and aura at this time.
12. Thank your body for being willing to change and grow.
13. Breathe gently and deeply, stand up, stretch, and reverse polarities.
14. You may find it useful to make some notes of your experience.

EXERCISE 52: Making Your Challenge Smaller

Sometimes the things that trouble you may seem daunting because they appear too big to handle. In that case you can first imagine the challenge as big as it seems, then allow it to grow smaller and smaller until it is a size that you feel you can look at it with more neutrality. The goal is not to make it disappear; just that it becomes a manageable size.

1. Breathe gently and deeply, and with openness be in the center of your head.
2. Explode your old grounding cord and male- or female-ground.
3. Create a big rose for your challenge.
4. Notice how it affects your grounding, your mood, your aura.
5. Slowly allow the rose to grow smaller and smaller.

6. Notice how it affects your grounding, mood, aura, and resource-fulness.
7. Create and destroy roses.
8. Explode your rose, and recycle its energy and the energy from all your pictures back through your crown.
9. Explode your old grounding cord and male- or female-ground.
10. Replenish your body and aura with golden cosmic energy.
11. Bring up just the right amount of earth energy for your body and aura at this time.
12. Thank your body for being willing to change and grow.
13. Breathe gently and deeply, stand up, stretch, and reverse polarities.
14. You may find it useful to make some notes of your experience.

EXERCISE 53: Changing the Color of a Challenge

One last favorite in-the-body technique for cultivating neutrality is to simply imagine that you can change the color of something so that you are more comfortable addressing the challenge. For instance, if a challenge seems to have lots of sickly greens or grays, imagine that you can clean up the color so that it seems easier to manage.

1. Breathe gently and deeply, and with openness be in the center of your head.
2. Explode your old grounding cord and male- or female-ground.
3. Create a rose for something that deeply troubles you.
4. Notice its color, and how it affects your grounding, your mood, and your aura.
5. Change the color of the rose to a color you prefer. (It might be helpful to create a vacuum cleaner rose or a grounding cord, and to vacuum or drain the sickly colors out of the rose.)
6. Notice how it affects your grounding, mood, and aura.
7. Create and destroy roses.
8. Explode your rose, and recycle its energy and the energy from all your pictures back through your crown.
9. Explode your old grounding cord and male- or female-ground.

10. Replenish your body and aura with golden cosmic energy.
11. Bring up just the right amount of earth energy for your body and aura at this time.
12. Thank your body for being willing to change and grow.
13. Breathe gently and deeply, stand up, stretch, and reverse polarities.
14. You may find it useful to make some notes of your experience.

Going Out-of-Body to Gain Neutrality

When you are in the middle of a difficult emotion, so many stress hormones can course through your body that your attempts to find neutrality are overwhelmed. An out-of-body view can often give much-needed space between you and your body, between you and the challenge. For a short while, being out of the body allows you to consider the challenge's many facets and gives you time to design your strategy for more neutrality. From out of the body, you can clear your lit-up pictures so that fairly soon you can return to your body and find in-body neutrality.

The following four exercises explore varying degrees of distance with which to investigate your neutrality. Following each exercise please remember to update your grounding and replenish your aura before going about your day. Should you feel the least bit spacey you can make your grounding cord a more earthy color and/or increase the diameter of your grounding cord to the size of your body, or even to the size of the boundary of your aura, until you feel comfortably grounded.

EXERCISE 54: Go to Your Crown or Just Above

If being in the center of the head is difficult, go to the crown or just above.

In the midst of really intense experiences it is sometimes difficult to stay in the center of your head. And it would be counter-productive for you to insist that you can and *must* always be in the center of your head. Should you encounter such an intense situation, it is often easier to allow your awareness to go up to your crown or just above your crown, which can also be very effective.

Note: As with any time you go out of body, please remember to come fully back into your body and reground.

1. Breathe gently and deeply, and with openness be in the center of your head.
2. Explode your old grounding cord and male- or female-ground.
3. Create a rose for something that deeply troubles you.
4. Notice how it affects your grounding, your mood, and your aura.
5. Imagine your awareness simply going to or above your crown to look at the rose.
6. Notice how the new perspective affects your grounding, mood, and aura.
7. Create and destroy roses.
8. Explode your rose, and recycle its energy and the energy from your pictures back through your crown.
9. Explode your old grounding cord and male- or female-ground.
10. Replenish your body and aura with golden cosmic energy.
11. Bring up just the right amount of earth energy for your body and aura at this time.
12. Thank your body for being willing to change and grow.
13. Breathe gently and deeply, stand up, stretch, and reverse polarities.
14. You may find it useful to make some notes of your experience.

EXERCISE 55: Go Back Behind Yourself to View Something

Another technique that people find very effective for viewing something that is troubling them is to "get some distance" on it by simply stepping back behind their body, and going slightly above their body. You don't go far out of body—perhaps about 3 feet behind and 3 feet above. You may actually see the back of your head, but if not, imagine that you can and that perspective will help you find the space.

Note: Whenever you go out of body, please remember to come fully back into your body and reground.

1. Breathe gently and deeply, and with openness be in the center of your head.
2. Explode your old grounding cord and male- or female-ground.
3. Create a rose for something that deeply troubles you.

4. Notice how it affects your grounding, your mood, your aura.
5. Imagine stepping back about 3 feet behind yourself and up about 3 feet above your body.
6. Notice how it affects your grounding, mood, and aura.
7. Create and destroy roses.
8. Explode your rose, and recycle its energy and the energy from your pictures back through your crown.
9. Explode your old grounding cord and male- or female-ground.
10. Replenish your body and aura with golden cosmic energy.
11. Bring up just the right amount of earth energy for your body and aura at this time.
12. Thank your body for being willing to change and grow.
13. Breathe gently and deeply, stand up, stretch, and reverse polarities.
14. You may find it useful to make some notes of your experience.

EXERCISE 56: Going Up into the Corner of the Room

A time-honored favorite metaphor for many philosophies is to see the world as a stage, with life making up the scenes from a play. Going up into the corner of the room to look upon yourself or a scene is a powerful way to view the "stage" and gain a healthy perspective and neutrality. From there you can take the time to notice detail and nuance. This technique has infinite potential, so create a version of play that suits your needs.

Note: Whenever you go out of body, please remember to come fully back into your body and reground.

1. Breathe gently and deeply, and with openness be in the center of your head.
2. Explode your old grounding cord and male- or female-ground.
3. Imagine stepping up and out of your body and going up into the corner of the room.
4. Take a few moments to notice how being up in the corner of the room affects your grounding, breathing, mood, and aura.

5. Look back and notice all the details you can about you and your environment. Acknowledge all that you perceive, no matter how fleeting or subtle.
6. Create and destroy roses.
7. When ready come fully back into your body and into the center of your head.
8. Next, recycle the energy from your pictures back through your crown.
9. Explode your old grounding cord and male- or female-ground.
10. Replenish your body and aura with golden cosmic energy.
11. Bring up just the right amount of earth energy for your body and aura at this time.
12. Thank your body for being willing to change and grow.
13. Breathe gently and deeply, stand up, stretch, and reverse polarities.
14. You may find it useful to make some notes of your experience.

EXERCISE 57: Going to the Edge of the Universe

The further you go out, the less something will tend to disturb you and the more resourcefulness and space you can gain. For the last out-of-body exercise you will move progressively further away from your challenge to view it—from your crown to the edge of the universe. Comfortably ground your body before you begin your journey. If at any time you become uncomfortable, simply return your awareness to your body, explode pictures, and reground.

Note: Whenever you go out of body, please remember to come fully back into your body and reground.

1. Breathe gently and deeply, and with openness be in the center of your head.
2. Explode your old grounding cord and male- or female-ground.
3. Create a rose for an issue that troubles you; observe it and your reaction.

When sufficiently lit up:

4. Have your awareness step up to your crown and observe your response.
5. Have your awareness rise to the ceiling and observe your response.
6. Have your awareness move 500 feet above you and observe your response.
7. Have your awareness move to the moon and observe your response.
8. Have your awareness move to the edge of the solar system and observe your response.
9. Have your awareness move to the edge of the universe and observe your response.
10. Step by step, have your awareness come back in and observe your response: From the edge of the universe, the edge of the solar system, the moon, 500 feet above you, the ceiling, above your crown, and into the center of your head.
11. Explode all the pictures that are lit up throughout your body and aura.
12. Next, recycle the energy from your pictures back through your crown.
13. Explode your old grounding cord and male- or female-ground.
14. Replenish your body and aura with golden cosmic energy.
15. Bring up just the right amount of earth energy for your body and aura at this time.
16. Thank your body for being willing to change and grow.
17. Breathe gently and deeply, stand up, stretch, and reverse polarities.
18. You may find it useful to make some notes of your experience.

Perfect Pictures

Perfect pictures are energy fantasies that can never come about. Perfect pictures are not objectively perfect; they are the fantasy of the person who generates the picture. One person's perfect picture might strike another person as being terrible. They vibrate at a white-light level and seem to promise release from all tension. If you are without a job, getting a job might seem to offer relief from all your worries. If you miss someone you love, your picture of your reunion can become a perfect picture. Getting that job or reuniting with your loved one might be wonderful, just not perfect. Because perfect pictures vibrate at a white-light level, they carry a promise of freedom from any tension that won't be borne out in your real-life experience, which must vibrate in the lower frequencies of the personality color range. Real life always has tensions that come from the play of polarities.

The reason perfect pictures can be such a comforting fantasy is that when you focus on the picture or fantasy and match your crown to it, you step out of the personal aura and above the tensions of your personal life. This stepping out will make you spacey or dreamy, so if you are spacey or dreamy around your goal, your goal may be a perfect picture. A quick trip to fantasyland occasionally can be a nice vacation, but even a moderate amount of fantasizing driven by a perfect picture is self-defeating. The biggest problem with perfect pictures is they distance you from real life. You can end up rejecting everything you are ready to create for what you think you must have.

If you are a woman, you'll have a special set of perfect pictures that are intended to be idealized, modeled, and made part of your instinctual functioning. You have a special set of perfect pictures connected with your ovaries. (See the section entitled "Two Drives: Responsibility and Supporting 'Potential'" in Chapter 6.) You choose not to explode them because exploding them would disrupt your hormonal balance. Instead you female-ground so that you can stay senior to the pictures, so that you're not driven by your instinct. Then you can bring all your wisdom and understanding to the task of fashioning a more personal and considered response to the situation. Unless we're talking specifically about female grounding, usually when we talk about perfect pictures, we mean perfect pictures other than the instinctual reproductive perfect pictures.

If you find you're working off a perfect picture other than your own female reproductive perfect pictures, use your techniques to find out whose energy it is. Remove the energy that is not yours from the picture.

Once you remove that energy, the picture will probably move out of the white-light range and into the personality color range. Then it will be something you can work on after you bring it into current time.

Spiritual Freedom

Spiritual freedom is the ability to run a full range of energy frequencies and qualities throughout your body and aura, not perfectly, but flexibly and reasonably unobstructed. While no meditation engages the personal aura as profoundly and deeply as everyday life richly encountered over time, one way to think about and work on your spiritual freedom is to observe how various colors of energy move or don't move through your aura. The exact relationship among colors, frequencies, and qualities of energy cannot be specified. A single named color, say red, can vibrate at different frequencies and have different qualities. Each specific instance of red will feel or look different to the intuition even though all the instances will be described by the word "red." Still, by exploring the flow of a series of colors as we do in the next exercise, you will gather a lot of information and make excellent changes in your aura. It is not at all uncommon to find that some colors don't flow comfortably, while others seem to flow effortlessly. You may also find some colors that flow relatively easily through one part of your aura but not easily through another part. In some cases it may take months or even years to open to a comfortable and flexible flow with certain colors. (If you don't see colors, you may be surprised that you can "feel" or "hear" variations in different-colored energy. For instance, when you try to run a red color and then a green color, each color will feel or sound different even though you can't see the color.)

Your spiritual freedom grows every time you release resistance. As we discuss in the next part of the book, committing to pursuing your desires *without* ego rigidity or thinking that your happiness depends upon attaining those desires is the very best way to generate spiritual freedom. As you pursue spiritual freedom, you will be learning how to generate reliable happiness and how to participate in the joy that is always and already present in all creation.

EXERCISE 58: Running the Colors of the Rainbow through Your Aura

In this exercise you will invite the colors of the rainbow, one at a time, to permeate and flow throughout your body and aura. Then, without judging, observe where each color naturally flows and where it seems obstructed, and explode the pictures that each color lights up. This exercise is best explored over time, so we suggest that you play with it once a week or every two weeks, patiently clearing the obstructions revealed by the colors you choose.

1. Breathe gently and deeply, and with openness be in the center of your head.
2. Explode your old grounding cord and male- or female-ground.
3. From the center of your head invite the scintillating rainbow color *red* down through your crown and allow it to gently and playfully permeate your entire body and aura.
4. Without judging, observe where it flows freely and where it seems obstructed.
5. When you have a sense of the flow, explode the pictures that the color red has lit up.
6. Next, from the center of your head, invite the scintillating rainbow color *orange* down through your crown and allow it to gently and playfully permeate your entire body and aura.
7. Without judging, observe where it flows freely and where it seems obstructed.
8. When you have a sense of the flow explode the pictures that the color orange has lit up.
9. From the center of your head invite the scintillating rainbow color *yellow* down through your crown and allow it to gently and playfully permeate your entire body and aura.
10. Without judging, observe where it flows freely and where it seems obstructed.
11. When you have a sense of the flow, explode the pictures that the color yellow has lit up.

12. From the center of your head invite the scintillating rainbow color *green* down through your crown and allow it to gently and playfully permeate your entire body and aura.
13. Without judging, observe where it flows freely and where it seems obstructed.
14. When you have a sense of the flow, explode the pictures that the color green has lit up.
15. From the center of your head invite the scintillating rainbow color *blue* down through your crown and allow it to gently and playfully permeate your entire body and aura.
16. Without judging, observe where it flows freely and where it seems obstructed.
17. When you have a sense of the flow, explode the pictures that the color blue lit up.
18. From the center of your head invite the scintillating rainbow color *indigo* down through your crown and allow it to gently and playfully permeate your entire body and aura.
19. Without judging, observe where it flows freely and where it seems obstructed.
20. When you have a sense of the flow, explode the pictures that the color indigo lit up.
21. From the center of your head invite the scintillating rainbow color *violet* down through your crown and allow it to gently and playfully permeate your entire body and aura.
22. Without judging, observe where it flows freely and where it seems obstructed.
23. When you have a sense of the flow, explode the pictures that the color violet lit up.
24. When through, recycle your energy back through your crown.
25. Explode your old grounding cord and male- or female-ground.
26. Replenish your body and aura with golden cosmic energy.
27. Bring up just the right amount of earth energy for your body and aura at this time.
28. Thank your body for being willing to change and grow.

29. Breathe gently and deeply, stand up, stretch, and reverse
    polarities.
30. You may find it useful to make some notes of your experience.

In the previous exercise you explored the mechanics of spiritual freedom. For more on how your spiritual freedom works in everyday life,
see Chapter 17, "Creating Your Own Reality According to Your Aura."

Part Two

The Mysticism of Everyday Life

"All life expands in all directions."
—Seth

The mysticism of everyday life is more than just focusing on daily activity. It's embracing everyday life and your individuality as a nexus of an ecstatic meaningful conversation between the Earth, your soul, and innumerable other consciousnesses—all supporting, and in some sense relying on you to be human. It's true you may not consciously notice this larger part of your conversation with life, but it does affect your happiness and the meaning you find. Chapters 10 through 14 explain just how your individuality flows meaningfully through eternity. Chapters 15 through 20 discuss how to follow your desires skillfully in ways that engage you deeply with that conversation, increasing your personal spiritual freedom and leading to a cultivation of happiness.

CHAPTER 10

What Is the You That Creates
Your Reality?

Seth's idea that you create or attract your own reality is not a new one. It may not be obvious, but properly understood it is logically equivalent to the Hindu phrase *Tat tvam asi* (I am that); to the Buddhist principles that nothing exists in isolation from other aspects of All That Is (Interdependent Origination) and that change is ceaseless (Impermanence); and to the Hermetic principle, as above, so below. What is new is how Seth's formulation centers your waking spiritual focus in everyday life, which becomes a purpose in and of itself. Seth talks about a universe in which every bit of consciousness, in whatever form, is sacred and its sacredness expands ecstatically in all directions.

As a result of the centrality of ordinary human experience, desires and the ego sense that there is both an internal world that is me and an external world that is not become valuable rather than something to be transcended. Of course it is also true that this sense of separation is an illusion. Otherwise, why would the external world reflect your internal belief? It is this interplay between the illusion of separateness and the interdependent connection of everything that creates the dance of human life with its order and its ineradicable spontaneity and creativity, often called chaos.

There's a paradox at your core. There's no objective you. There's nothing you can draw a bright line around and say, "This is the real me." This could be depressing but in fact it is why you do not cease to exist at death. It is because you are divinely and eternally a subjective existence expanding throughout eternity that you continue to exist. And that perpetual subjective expansion is why a joy you can become familiar with underlies your every moment.

What makes your subjectivity real is the spontaneous appearance of self-organizing systems called *gestalts* and the eternal expansion of All That Is in every aspect and every bit, including yourself. If the gestalt ever stopped expanding, its existence would collapse. It's hard to imagine how objectivity could expand eternally, but subjectivity moves smoothly through the apparent objective forms in a dance of joy. We're not going to try to define "subjective" and "objective" absolutely clearly because such distinctions cannot ever be fully tied down for the very reasons we are discussing. Our lives are objective in the sense that they are meaningful but not in the sense that they can be tied down.

Because life is ever-expanding, no part of life can ever be tied down and finished. The ever-expanding dance of spontaneous creativity generates an ineradicable tension, because desire naturally seeks permanence. This ineradicable tension as well as the always-present joy is symbolized in Taoism as the play of polarities, which is represented by the famous Yin-Yang symbol.

You can learn to stop fighting that tension, and when you do you become reliably happy and supported by joy. Enlightenment or nondual awareness is one way to accomplish this objective, but to become enlightened, the practitioner must shatter the psychic ground (filters) on which the self-reflective ego is based. Our guides prefer that you keep the self-reflective ego, both for the contribution it makes to your eternally growing personal self and for the contribution the ego structure will make to all of humanity after further evolution over the next few hundred years. The ego will expand to provide ever more magnificent forms of human awareness called group consciousness. Instead of shattering the filters that help generate the self-reflective ego, our guides counsel developing neutrality and openness by engaging everyday life.

Your greatest passions, worst agonies, and finest achievements are dust in that they pass away and disappear quickly in the external world, but the ever-growing web of subjective, expansive joy is eternal. It takes a fairly advanced perception to "see" that expansion, but touching the meaningfulness of all things is something a lot of people can begin cultivating at a comparatively early stage. We give one fairly straightforward method to experience this meaningfulness in Chapter 20, "Pleasure, Happiness, and Joy." This sense of meaning that cannot be lost is the ground of what we call the *Sethian synthesis*. Throughout all the Seth writings, in ways that sometimes got covered up by the excitement of understanding that you create your own reality, is an understanding that every life and every action is a meaningful part of the ever-expanding ecstatic dance of life.

CHAPTER 11

Humanity Has Chosen to Have a Self-Reflective Ego

There is a particularly intense alienation that humans can experience because they have a self-reflective ego. Other consciousnesses do not experience that alienation, and, to a limited extent, that particular human alienation can be eradicated by a strenuous discipline leading to what is called enlightenment or nondual awareness. Yet Seth and the authors' guides discourage pursuing enlightenment for technical energy reasons and for practical experiential reasons. Instead they value the ego. They teach methods set out in this book to heal the alienation and to cultivate happiness and joy; and they are setting out the beginnings of a program that will expand the ego to something unimaginably graceful.[1]

In this chapter we briefly sketch how in the distant past humanity moved to develop the self-reflective ego. Then in the next few chapters we develop a multidimensional perspective that helps explain why both the ego and desire make profound and irreplaceable contributions to the meaning of our lives, even though rigidly pursuing the aims of either is unskillful and counterproductive.

Much of what follows comes from our own guides and from Seth's work in his book, *The "Unknown" Reality*.[2]

There have been many stages of human consciousness. A long time ago human consciousness was centered in what we would currently call the dream state. In the dream state, many directions of human consciousness were and are being followed. One track, the one current humans know, has progressively become more and more centered in physical reality. Over time, human consciousness "burst" from its focus in the dream state and entered into the density we now experience as our psychic energy home—that is, physical reality. Psychically, physical reality is itself an energy, a very dense energy not freely transformable with our minds into a different psychic energy pattern. Unlike the dream state, which is very changeable and immediately responsive to our thoughts, almost all changes to physical structures require action in the physical world itself. There was a transition, over eons, when humankind wedded its consciousness to the physical forms that are our physical bodies.

Long after humanity burst out of the dream-state centering and created its focus in physicality, human awareness retained a flexibility that is foreign to the awareness of humans in our contemporary, global, industrial society. While humans knew themselves as beings related to and centered on the human body, their consciousnesses freely flowed and participated in other forms of consciousness.

For example, a human hunter might have flowed, as energy, into the consciousness of a stream, becoming one with it. As that stream, he could then travel downstream to see where it went and what food might be available. This free-flowing consciousness existed long prior to humans gathering in agriculturally based cities where people used writing for record-keeping.

Prior to gathering in cities thousands of years ago, humans, for their own purposes that they worked out en masse in the dream state, decided to go on a different kind of grand adventure, the grand adventure of generating a self-reflective ego. This was an adventure to engage the sharp contrasts of a life that was no longer fluidly moving from one form of consciousness to another. It was solid and stably fixed to the physical body during the waking state. This consciousness perceived the world beyond the physical body as being outside itself, separate and entirely distinct. Over a period of thousands of years, humankind moved progressively towards the limited, stable individuality that we know now. As part of this transformation, mankind's relationship to time narrowed so that time came to be universally perceived in its one line of development. This progression reached a certain critical point in the period when agricultural cities began, and from that point to this, the form of ego awareness that humans now know became more and more concrete. The pace of concretization accelerated again with the development of industrial societies with their managed time.

Humans came to consider themselves the center of the consciousness in the universe. It was often said that not only was the human incarnation precious, it was the only place from which one could gain enlightenment.[3] This human folding back on itself was part of the process by which we humans developed our current ego identity. But even on this planet there are other chains of consciousness growing, developing, and evolving in their own way, such as angels and cetaceans. In common parlance an angel is a human who has passed on. But psychics identify angels as a whole range of non-physical consciousness associated with the planet, which is a consciousness that travels in an entirely different chain of evolution. Angels evolve in their own sublime direction without need of developing the particular kind of self-reflective ego that humans chose. Angels reach out spontaneously and joyfully, seeking ever more interrelationship with all consciousness. They reach out with a natural un-self-reflective grace. Their reaching out is as natural as the way plants reach out to the sun.

Similarly, cetaceans (whales, dolphins, and porpoises) have their own spiritual evolution that parallels but is not identical to humans. They do not develop the kind of self-reflective alienation that humans do even though they have filters similar to but much larger and more inclusive than those of humans. The physical bodies that we see are a minor part of their consciousness. Most of their awareness is focused in directions humans cannot follow.

Quite intentionally, most of humanity embarked on a journey that hardened its sense of physical separateness until eventually most humans grant no consciousness to the world except to animals and humans, and each consciousness seems to be bound up within one body unable to transition into and participate freely in the consciousness of any other animals, or any other things.

Humanity made this shift because at inner levels of awareness it wanted to develop the self-reflective ego in order to explore a whole universe of physical, emotional, and mental contrasts that arise when we consider ourselves to be separate beings and think of everything outside the boundary of our skin as utterly outside our self. To further the goal of a sense of separateness it was necessary for the guides whose consciousness is larger than humans' to withdraw from interacting with humans so that humans could focus increasingly upon what it means to be human—what it means to understand yourself as limited to a physical body. This artificial, stark separation allows humans to engage in a rich, creative, adventurous conversation between what is our self and what appears to be other than our self. Through a series of lifetimes we can learn to coordinate our energy in such a way that we honor the boundaries of both our personal ego identity and that of others. We do this by learning authenticity, kindness, and generosity, which allows us to reintegrate into the greater gestalts that we are naturally a part of and add something completely original—our own unique self-reflection and meaning-making—to the whole and to those greater gestalts.

Another feature of human specialization and the exploration of ourselves as separate from the rest of reality has been an adherence to one track of time. While the particular experience of clock time that we use throughout our modern world is relatively new, for the last several thousand years increased attention has been focused on time's one-directional movement in the sense of having a past, present, and future; and consequently each human's development appears to progress in one and only one direction, along a single arrow of time moving forward. Just as each human has become ever more constrained into the one identity connected with the one body, so we have ever more rigid categories of past, present, and future. This unidirectionality of experience has been extremely valuable in that it allowed humans to focus on human ego development. This focus comes with limitations that particularly affect how we understand development and reincarnation. In the reincarnation chapter (Chapter 14) we explore what happens to the ego after death, and instead of tracking it in one direction only, we'll track it in at least two directions.

There is a development that is just beginning for the human race. Over the next few hundred years, our guides say, humans' neurological system will be transformed to support a currently unattainable, enhanced ego. This new ego will retain the self-reflective, interpretive qualities of our current egos while adding the ability to interpenetrate and collaborate with numerous other human egos and other consciousnesses with an intimacy and clarity of boundaries not currently achievable.

Out of this interpenetration and collaboration will come a group consciousness that retains each individual as an individual, even while each individual simultaneously experiences directly the new group consciousness. It might help to think of how cells have their consciousness at one level and together create a different kind of consciousness as you, the person. In the future of humanity, individuals will know themselves through their individual consciousness, yet will simultaneously partake in a larger, different kind of consciousness. They will know themselves just as much as the larger consciousness as they know themselves as the individual person. Neither will be more real than the other.

CHAPTER 12

What's New About the New Age?
Enlightenment, Mastery, and the Spacious Ego

"You think of yourself physically as 'top dogs,' so that in effect you limit your own experience of your psyche."

—Seth[1]

"... what it would be like for a mother to become so much a part of the tree underneath which her children played that she could keep track of them from the tree's viewpoint, though she was herself far away."

—Seth[2]

All life expands in all directions. Seth and the authors' guides encourage humanity to embrace the everyday life of the personality, with its self-reflective ego, as the center of our spiritual adventure. Our waking life is nested in larger joyous and compassionate gestalts, without which life would be impossible, and cultivating awareness of their support can help give joy and meaning to life. Still, it is the intimately personal that is the impossible-to-duplicate source of human sacredness and meaning. Two other spiritual systems, as some people interpret them, seem to demand the transcendence of the self-reflective ego. They are the great mystical traditions of the East, which are aimed at developing nondual awareness or enlightenment; and Theosophy, a relatively new system that arose in and was colored by the Victorian period. Theosophy borrowed heavily from the great Eastern mystical traditions, integrating Victorian enthusiasm for progress as well as some Victorian moralism, and most importantly, it foreshadowed the reintegration of humanity out of its protected cocoon (in which humanity seems to be the highest and most important consciousness, as discussed in Chapter 11, "Humanity Has Chosen to Have a Self-Reflective Ego"). A discussion of these two systems will help set a stage to explore a Sethian universe in which all consciousness expands in all directions and in which humans are urged to embrace their humanity, not as a platform from which to approach nondual awareness or mastership, but as a value in and of itself, contributing to all consciousnesses and having its own eternal validity.

Even though we are going to suggest an alternative to nondual or enlightened awareness, we want to acknowledge the continuing sublimity of that path. The great enlightened spiritual teachers are rightly held in enormous respect. One of the authors' favorites is Mata Amritanandamayi Devi (called "Ammachi"). Every year the authors try to attend a weekend intensive with Ammachi. Ammachi is a spiritual figure of thrilling power and compassion. She is known worldwide as the Hugging Saint, a name she's been given because she transmits her spiritual blessings through her hugs of individuals. At her appearances she sits on a dais and radiates enormous spiritual vitality and generosity. Hour after hour she sits and hugs, one at a time, an almost endless line of attendees.

When you observe clairvoyantly Ammachi hugging thousands of individuals, one at a time, you can see that even though she seems to be performing essentially the same sweet hug, in fact she instantly changes and adapts her energy for each person. She gives each person his or her own specialized energy hug, providing exactly the energy blessing that is appropriate at that moment. From time to time, the vast hall in which she is making her appearance will seem to give an inner shudder as she gives a particularly powerful healing to an individual or family for whom such a powerful healing is appropriate, all without interrupting her continuous march of sharing her love personally with each of the thousands of people present.

There is no one definition for the terms "nondual awareness" or "enlightenment," nor is an in-depth investigation of these terms necessary for this book. As far as the authors know, most usages of those words describe the result of a process that includes the destruction of the psychic structures that create the self-reflective ego.[3] It is the destruction of those structures that the authors' guides discourage (the structures look like small filters to the authors).

Our bodies and the psychic underpinnings of the self-reflective ego are like virtual-reality goggles that create the perception and suggest the sense of me and not me, self and other. When a person gains nondual awareness he or she changes his or her etheric body and removes the filters that have created the apparent sense of a self utterly distinct from others. This removal of the filters takes enormous power and focus. Some claim that in all the universe only humans can become enlightened. Our teachers turn that assertion on its head, saying that only a consciousness similar to humans' (and there are innumerable such consciousnesses) with a self-reflective ego has "need" for enlightenment. All consciousnesses—bigger, smaller, or parallel in complexity to human consciousness—are forever expanding in all directions, exactly as humans do. A human consciousness is to be treasured, not because it's the only platform from which one can become enlightened, but because it's a magnificent experience in the dance of consciousness. Later in this chapter we discuss how that self-reflective ego will become the building block for group consciousness over the next several hundred years.

The Value of Personality

The Eastern systems' focus on nondual or enlightened consciousness involves a timeless state. While attaining nondual awareness requires enormous skill and effort, and its achievement is almost always part of an intention to aid all creation, within the terms of the spiritual practice to attain nondual awareness, nothing new is created.[4]

Theosophy's aims are radically different. Theosophy explores a universe of evolution without end. Of course the ground of being, that simple sense of being[5] comprising nondual awareness, is the ground of being for all consciousness and for all evolution. Nondual reality is the unchanging ground to which nothing can be added or taken away. But Theosophy explores another direction, the direction of perpetual evolution. Using an appealing straightforward structural model, the Victorian Theosophists redirected the mystical quest into a businesslike engagement of the world. Unfortunately, from the authors' perspective, they denigrated the merely personal and sought, like some mystics of the East, to transcend the personality and to achieve an impeccable, impersonal objectivity.

In Theosophy, the soul is the center of human life. The soul, in Theosophical terms, is that eternal gestalt that seeds an incarnation into physical reality, learns from it, moves to its next incarnation, and learns from it. Through a linear series of incarnations, the soul (and deeper aspects still) achieves mastership rather than enlightenment. No mention is made of nondual awareness. Instead the excitement is focused on ever-greater kindness and generosity, and on an ever-greater objective impeccability (more like the evolutionary chain of angels rather than humans).

The Theosophists imagined the soul as aloof, rarely expending its energy with a personality unless the personality was abstractly spiritual, rising above sensations and emotions. As awesome as Theosophical seers were, especially C.W. Leadbeater, they were only tracking a narrow line of progress. Much of interest occurs in what Seth called "the spacious awareness." Looking in directions other than linear time and a single direction of progress, one can see the soul ensconced in everything. While the Theosophists assumed a linear time frame, whispers of a rambunctious, multidirectional approach peek through the Theosophical literature, perhaps unrecognized.

The authors' guides respect the Theosophical tradition, with its sense of purpose and progress in human development. Still, according to our guides, it fails to value each person's life and personality in and of itself. It values only the progress that the personality makes for the soul. They missed the essential value of each life in its own terms because they were looking down the one track of linear time and did not notice the personality continuing to exist and actively grow, even while collaborating with the soul. The active growth of the personality as a personality is what the next chapters discuss.

The Limitations of Enlightenment

We are now going to address what we and our guides see as fundamental limitations of having enlightenment or nondual consciousness as a goal. We address these limitations even while having enormous respect for the many enlightened saints, and we recognize that there are solid grounds for seeking enlightenment. It is true that there's a ground of being that is nondual awareness, and that nondual awareness can generate happiness.

Still, seeking enlightenment requires a practitioner to divert enormous effort away from everyday reality, which is where the greatest values of human waking life are addressed; and it requires a practitioner to engage in the potentially dangerous process of gathering and diverting enough of his or her energy to shatter the ego's etheric filters. As a consequence of the technical difficulty of shattering those filters, almost all practitioners must turn over a large part of their authority to a guru, thereby short-circuiting important personality developments that would otherwise contribute to the eternal personality, to the soul, and to the richness of the group consciousness towards which humanity is moving.

Furthermore, the gurus can err, or even misbehave. For example, at least a few of the Eastern masters have stated that homosexuality is wrong. One, Mother Meera, suffered a great blow to her reputation and is consequently underutilized as a global treasure. The problem isn't with her enlightenment. She brought a new energy to the Earth in the '80s, a higher energy than anyone prior had utilized in any meaningful way. The problem is in thinking that the enlightened have no social programming that clouds their awareness. Even more seriously, there is a history of gurus, even great ones, misusing their power over their disciples for sex.

When you look at consciousness expanding in all directions you see at least two directions that undercut the desirability of enlightenment. First, as we discuss in the next several chapters leading to the claim of eternal validity for the personality, every person eventually achieves nondual awareness. It ordinarily takes a few hundred to several hundred years after death. It could take millions of years for people who commit atrocities. Achieving nondual awareness can happen within a week or two for a person like the late Jane Roberts. Whatever the timing, it does happen in multidirectional time in such a way that each and every individual finds both fulfillment and nondual awareness. Second, an attraction of enlightenment is the idea that it represents the height of human consciousness. Many even claim that enlightenment or nondual consciousness is the height of all consciousness, human or not, but now that humans are reintegrating into the realm of all consciousness, few would argue that any human is, in any meaningful sense, larger than Mother Earth or other even larger consciousnesses like the sun or a galaxy. Thousands of years ago, to allow the self-reflective ego to grow in its sense of separateness, some guides stepped back—they were so big that awareness of them (even for mystics) would have undercut the separation process. Now, channels like Jane Roberts can reliably channel nondual beings whose perspectives are larger than any human being's, enlightened or not. Even vis-à-vis humans, clairvoyant observation establishes that a life in which a person gains enlightenment or nondual consciousness often isn't the last life of the soul's reincarnational cycle. A personality may shatter the ego's etheric filters and gain nondual awareness in a life, or become a saintly compassionate being, even though the soul is comparatively young and still requires much more experience before its investigation of being human is done. The converse is also increasingly true for the human race. More and more in contemporary times, the last life of the soul does not involve nondual awareness while the personality lives. Instead the personality often lives an outwardly unremarkable existence in which it integrates understandings of boundaries, desires, kindness, and generosity in the dance of everyday life.

One might argue that even if everyone eventually achieves nondual awareness after death, nondual awareness remains the only true relief from suffering and hence the most appropriate goal during life. However, nondual awareness and enlightenment are a relief from suffering only in a technical sense. It is true that once the pause for self-reflection has been obliterated, there is no separate self to suffer or to experience alienation. This is a real accomplishment. Some practitioners of the path of enlightenment also add huge energies of bliss into their aura on top of their enlightenment. But that same bliss can be achieved without nondual awareness—this was one of the fundamental insights of the Buddha. Most contemporary practitioners, especially those influenced by Buddhism, never cultivate that kind of overwhelming bliss. Zen has long talked of enlightenment as involving the ordinary events of life; and so a Zen Master who is beaten with a stick screams in pain just as an ordinary person would.[6] Both Ken Wilber and Traktung Khepa, experts on nondual awareness, state that pain is, at times, part of nondual awareness. What changes for those with nondual awareness is their relationship to pain. Again this is a very real accomplishment. Still, our guides say the cultivation of seniority and neutrality is a better way to change one's relationship to pain because it more easily integrates with all the values of humanity that prompted one's incarnation as a human in the first place, even if those values are often hard to recognize in linear time. Instead of radically obliterating the ego at the level of the etheric body, our guides advise that one cultivate the kind of neutrality and seniority taught in this book while deeply engaging in everyday life.

The techniques taught in this book are not the only techniques by which humans can retain their ego and move towards a more spacious version of that ego. (Even those people who destroy their ego can, in a roundabout way, reengage the personal self with its personal emotions and ideas suitably to rejoin humanity's move towards the spacious ego.) Humans are not currently capable of achieving a fully spacious ego, in part because it would require a critical mass of individuals able to use their spaciousness, a critical mass that currently isn't available. Still, big steps can be taken in the direction of a spacious ego, according to our guides, who tell us that four figures moved substantially in that direction by 1990, by gaining a clarity of consciousness and as deep a mystical engagement as a human can *without* shattering their etheric filters. The first two people are unknown to the authors. Our guides identify the third as Shirdi Sai Baba. It's interesting to note that in the multidirectional, multidimensional universe, he is a prior incarnation of Sathya Sai Baba, who only recently passed away in 2011 and who did go the enlightenment or nondual direction of eradicating the ego etheric filters.

The last figure was J. Krishnamurti. According to our guides, Krishnamurti chose not to eradicate his etheric filters and achieved a new crystal-clear consciousness with ego awareness. Krishnamurti himself claimed repeatedly and specifically that what he was teaching was different from what other Eastern Masters were teaching. The authors are not very familiar with his work, but they can see what their guides are referring to.

The information about the etheric filters comes from the authors' guides. The authors are beginning to see those filters themselves. They can see the obliteration of those filters in various people who have obtained nondual awareness. When they look at the energy of Krishnamurti, they see that not only did he not obliterate the filters, he sharpened and strengthened them. Further, according to our guides, Krishnamurti enriched what was unique in his humanity to a degree unapproachable by those who shatter the etheric filters. They're not saying he was a better or more saintly person. They are saying that at a personality level, he developed something needed for the coming group consciousness that was special. Perhaps as an indication of the value of etheric filters for those species that choose to develop them, the etheric filters of cetaceans are much bigger than humans' and have capacities that the authors cannot now follow.

Several thousand years ago, large consciousnesses and guides stepped back from humans, creating the illusion that humanity is the only center of the universe, that humans are the highest consciousness. They withdrew to allow humanity to turn in on itself and develop the self-reflective ego that humanity has in fact developed. Humans are reemerging into the larger universe, a universe where everything is conscious and expanding in all directions, a universe in which humans are neither the single center nor the highest or best-evolved form of consciousness. Recognizing this actually allows us to value what is unique—our self-reflective ego—in a way that mysticism has not done up until now.

Because humans were isolated for the last three thousand years or so, non-mystical people quite rightly focused on ego satisfaction as mystical people quite rightly focused on the eradication of the ego. There were two paths that seemed starkly separate. As humanity again encounters consciousnesses that are far larger than us and consciousnesses that are organized radically differently from our own, we will develop capacities to collaborate and integrate with those other consciousnesses that are currently unimaginable. This collaboration will bring our nearly complete development of ego consciousness into a much larger arena. Instead of eradicating ego consciousness, we will expand its uniqueness into new territory—in a sense synthesizing the apparent duality of ego consciousness and mysticism.

Through each person's ego engagement with human life, part of the Earth, like an Earth womb energy, is brought up into the personality and the soul in a way that can only develop through the relationship of the human's self-reflective individuated ego and the Earth. Without the threads of the ego's evaluations and interpretations of its own Earth experience, the weaving together of Mother Earth, the personality, and the soul in its own plane could never have emerged. Though we have always been part of the tapestry of interdependent consciousnesses, we are now capable of bringing a stronger, more vibrant, more robust, more supportive strand to the infrastructure of the coming group consciousness.

In the future each of us will have more capacity to commit to the ego structure of our lives without ego rigidity. Rather than a few great saints of compassion whose transcendental love comes from beyond and outside the personality, an ever larger percentage of people will find deep and abiding love and compassion in the small and intimate moments and conversations of the self-reflective ego. Rather than humans pursuing transcendence by destroying the ego, they will develop an ego structure that is so strong, flexible, and secure that each person will be able to shift into other and even multiple identity gestalts. A mother or father could become the tree under which their children played, or with fully conscious awareness, part of the dream gestalt in which family, business, or global conflicts could be addressed; or transcendent gestalts of love and joy; and eventually all of these at once. For example, Chapter 14 introduces John's friend

Will, who died in 1976 and currently participates simultaneously in many focuses of consciousness with intimacy, clarity, and a deep serene joy. What he has accomplished after death, humans will come to accomplish during life, opening new interconnections of joy for the Earth, humans, and their souls.

CHAPTER 13

Rambunctious Multidirectional Time

Humanity's linear time focus has narrowed our attention, even the attention of mystics and of the Theosophists. We track just one line of development; one person or thing can't move into two futures at once. This one-line focus has rendered invisible the eternal validity of the personality, the redemption of all experience ranging from horrible mistakes to kindness and generosity, and the eventual attaining of non-dual awareness by every personality (even if it takes a few twenty million years and experiences on another planet). These realities are not factored in because all those developments happen "off to the side" from where humans' current primary linear time focus directs them. After death the personality develops in at least two different directions: the direction where it is absorbed completely by the soul, and a somewhat independent direction taken by the personality.

Surprisingly, Theosophy's straightforward, unambiguous, linear model of the universe provides an excellent platform from which to develop a more multidimensional, multidirectional understanding. Theosophy divides spiritual/psychic energies relevant to the human consciousness into seven frequency ranges in a manner similar to the seven chakras. (See Figure 5, "The Seven Planes of Consciousness," page 195.) But whereas the chakras are complex and multidimensional, the Theosophical scheme is as straightforward as the keys on a piano. Both the chakra system and the Theosophical system have advantages and disadvantages relative to one another. (By focusing on the personal aura, this book leaves out some of the multidimensional complexity of the chakras. That complexity is for other books.)

One could compare the Theosophical energy system to a piano with its keys, each key set at a well-defined frequency. Just as a piano's keys move straightforwardly from low-frequency notes at the bottom of the keyboard to high-frequency notes at the top, so in the Theosophical scheme there are discrete energy notes relevant to humans. (Notes extend far beyond the human range for large consciousnesses like the Earth and the Sun.[1])

The Theosophical system contains forty-nine notes arranged in groups of seven each, much like octaves on a piano; by convention, these groups are called *planes.* John has released a four-CD set (*Navigating the Seven Planes of Consciousness*[2]) discussing the Theosophical system, with guided meditations to find each of the forty-nine notes (called "sub-planes" in the Theosophical system). The CD set teaches how to use the forty-nine-note sub-plane system to explore useful psychic skills like finding the exact frequencies of different aspects of your soul. For the present book there are two important aspects of reality that the Theosophical system helps clarify: 1) the etheric nature of ego awareness and nondual awareness, and 2) the significance, for the eternal validity of the personality, of multidirectional time.

The last chapter discussed the fact that nondual awareness is generated by the radical removal of etheric filters on human awareness. Understanding the relationships among the three lowest-frequency Theosophical planes (octaves) will make clearer the purpose of the self-reflective ego and just how specific nondual awareness is. Remember that the forty-nine frequencies of the Theosophical system are divided into seven groups called planes, each with seven frequencies. Each frequency moves one step higher than the frequency before it. Through each step of a plane and as you move from plane to plane, each step moves exactly the same degree, one step higher for forty-nine steps.

Everything in the universe is vibration at a particular frequency. By "universe," we don't mean merely the physical universe. We include also the psychic universe with its increasingly higher vibrations or frequencies. The densest or lowest-frequency plane in the Theosophical system includes all the vibrational steps comprising the physical universe—there are three such steps—together with four vibrational steps that comprise

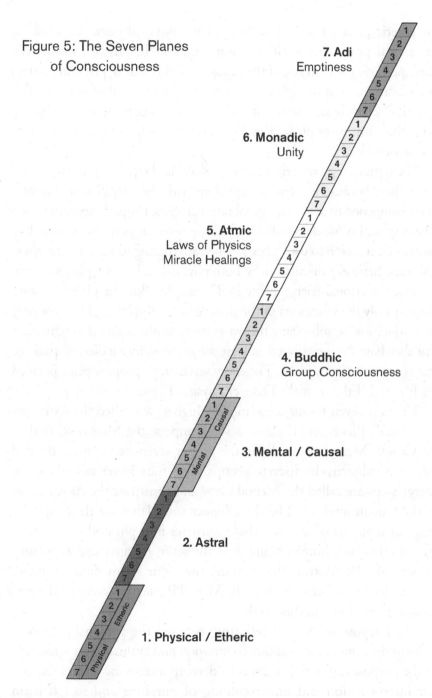

Figure 5: The Seven Planes
of Consciousness

7. Adi
Emptiness

6. Monadic
Unity

5. Atmic
Laws of Physics
Miracle Healings

4. Buddhic
Group Consciousness

3. Mental / Causal

2. Astral

1. Physical / Etheric

Chart by Brian Greminger

the etheric plane. The "vibrations" of the physical plane are what we perceive as physicality itself, as the material of the physical world. We don't perceive the material of the physical world (that is, physical matter) as a vibration, even though we do perceive the material of our aura as a vibration. Our physical senses are calibrated to register the kind of "vibration" that comprises physical reality as reality itself, as physical material, not as vibration.

The terminology referring to the physical and etheric "planes" is confusing here because it seems inconsistent with the overall structure of a plane composed of seven energy vibrational steps. Properly speaking, each Theosophical plane does consist of exactly seven steps or sub-planes. It is another convention to use "planes" when attempting to separate the physical and etheric in a discussion. So both physical and etheric planes exist in the first vibrational-energy plane in Theosophy. But our physical senses perceive only the vibrations of the three lowest sub-planes. This grouping of the three lowest sub-planes that we perceive as physicality is so significant that they have been separated, at least subjectively, into a discrete package that is its own type of plane. The entire seven-step "proper" plane is called the Physical/Etheric or the Etheric/Physical Plane.

The next seven frequencies (moving higher) are called the Astral (or Emotional) Plane, and the next seven comprise the Mental/Causal or the Causal/Mental Plane. Again the proper seven-step plane is divided into two subjectively discrete groups. The four lower sub-planes or energy steps are called the Mental Plane and constitute the energy range of the human intellect. The three higher sub-planes are the frequency range of that part of the soul that incarnates into physical life, lifetime after lifetime as a human being. It is the seven frequencies/steps/sub-planes of the Astral Plane plus the four immediately higher frequencies/steps/sub-planes of the Mental Plane that comprise the personal aura explored in this book.

The purpose of the self-reflecting ego and the personal aura is to develop the human race's ability to interpret and evaluate. In a sense, one of the purposes of each human is to develop interesting stories that are our interpretation and understanding of our lives and to tell them throughout the universe.

To keep the levels of contrast and freedom manageable for the developing ego, several thousand years ago time hardened into a linear track as one-directional as a piano keyboard or, to change images, as one-directional as the Theosophical ladder of frequencies/steps/sub-planes by which a meditator can climb to ever higher frequencies. Within this linear framework, abnormalities in time don't show up. However, early in John's work with Jane Roberts, Seth encouraged Jane and his readers to explore psychic energies not just in the direction of higher and lower frequencies, but also sideways. It's from these sideways directions that time becomes playful, all action is redeemed, each personality is eternal, and all lives—not just those of sages or the enlightened—have their unique, divine validity. Each life, whether it is recognized or not, is saturated with eternal meaning, in its own terms, as well as in terms meaningful for its soul, for humanity, for the earth, for All That Is.

CHAPTER 14

The Reincarnational Process and the Eternal Validity of the Personality

We want to discuss an idea of reincarnation that we expect will be new to our readers. We find that this understanding places desire in a reassuring light and helps explain the very nature of our desires, allowing us to relax and be open to life as it is.

Most readers of this book can easily imagine that the soul exists eternally.[1] Most readers then find it comforting that whatever they're suffering, all their experience has meaning for the soul. Some people, however, say, "No. What good does it do me, the personality? I suffer and die. My experience is used by my soul, but I am not there as Jack or Donna or whoever. How does it help me if the soul makes meaning out of my personal suffering?" While it does help you as a personality when the soul makes meaning of your suffering, answering that question would take us off track for this book. Instead, we address the underlying assumption that the personality ends at or shortly after death with the breakdown of the physical and psychic vehicles that composed the personality.

This assumption is, perhaps, universal amongst psychics and mystics, and it is consistent with much of what one sees clairvoyantly in watching the dissolution process after death *when you look at the process along one direction of time.* When you look in multiple directions you see something dramatically different.

Your soul doesn't gobble up the personality or strip it like a wreck for parts. Not only is the personality's experience gathered and embraced by the soul, the personality itself continues to grow after death, as itself, in the embrace of the soul and in the embrace of even larger consciousnesses than the soul. The personality continues to exercise its own will and uniqueness with recognizably human characteristics (though no physical body) even as it also grows in ways marvelously different from the embodied human consciousness or ego consciousness that we all presently know.[2] The soul completely absorbs the experience of the personality and reorganizes that experience to be unrecognizable by the old personality. The concept that the personality could be ongoing in another direction to freely continue exploring, as itself, violates our normal notions that something can only be one thing at a time. Multidirectional time allows the personality's experience to go in multiple directions at once, and to exist in many forms at once—one form integrated unrecognizably in the soul, other forms as part of larger consciousnesses, and at least one recognizable as the personality as it knows itself.

Seth pointed to this continuation of the personality in a class Jane Roberts gave on May 15, 1971, in which he spoke about his own physical incarnations, detailing one incarnation in particular—his incarnation as a minor pope of the Catholic Church around 300 CE. Seth indicated that he could not remember the details of his life as pope. He could, however, get a more accurate rendering of the details by checking with his past incarnation, the pope. Seth indicated that while getting the details was possible, it was not worth the effort at the time, since that pope, a past life of his/Seth's, was off doing other things. "But as I now recall them, without directly checking on our friend the pope, who has, you must understand, gone his own way...."[3]

John remembers noticing this statement, as well as several others, in *Seth Speaks*, but the significance of Seth's clear indication that the personality continues didn't register for John until John observed the afterdeath continuation and extraordinary growth of someone he had known in life.

John's first observation of this continuation was in the early '90s and concerned a dear friend. In February 1976, John's friend and fellow Seth class member, Will Ives, committed suicide. In a meditation in the early '90s, John saw a beautiful violet ribbon of light. As he observed and interacted with the beautiful ribbon of light John noticed that it contained the consciousness of Will. It *was* Will, the old Will, just much happier. John had earlier observed that Will had already reincarnated twice, but this Will was not a later incarnation who had gobbled up John's friend Will—this was Will with John's friend's memories and flavorings. This was the Will that John had known: wiser, with a deep serenity and joyousness, participating in something John couldn't then follow.

Over time John's communication with and perception of Will has expanded. Today John easily communicates with Will as Will. He also can perceive Will ecstatically participating in several gestalt consciousnesses: a few huge, a few small explorations, and at least one person-to-person, i.e., the one where Will communicates with John. In some way, while honoring boundaries, Will sees through and is affected by John's experience, and vice versa. Will became what we call a *co-personality* to John, which we will explain over the next few pages.

After Death

Here's what the authors see as the normal after-death process. Please understand that the creativity and multidimensionality of this process render all accounts simplifications. Physical death occurs and the personality moves into higher planes of energy. If this is the soul's final incarnation, the soul itself moves into a higher energy range than it had occupied, reconfigures itself with the last personality being vitally important, and engages in continued evolution. For example, the late Jane Roberts, who was the final life of her soul, has become an integral part of a large entity that acts as a guide (primarily in the dream state) for numerous people simultaneously.

If the deceased personality is not the soul's final incarnation, the personality gives a copy of all its experience to the soul. The personality has several additional avenues to pursue its own further growth. Even though the personality eventually loses all the earthly vehicles that had held it together and supported its individuality in life, the personality continues to be held together by at least three sources: its soul, by even larger beings, and by an individualized spark that it received from All That Is when it initially incarnated.

After death the personality continues to train with guides and explore its new environment. After engaging in various trainings and explorations, most personalities have a set of questions and challenges that they personally take back into the reincarnational process (again, without losing themselves in the incarnation, see below). For example, if the personality in physical life was narrowly intellectual and arrogant about its intellect, it might choose to explore a lifetime with less intellect to experience the validity of such a life and to learn how to live skillfully with having a lower status.

The personality will never again have another physical lifetime that is exactly like the physicality it once experienced. Instead there is an amazing way in which it becomes a co-personality in other incarnations, actively participating as itself, just a slight energy distance away from the energy field of the new physical incarnation. The personality collaborates with its soul, All That Is, and other larger beings, as well as some other personalities from its soul's other incarnations, to form a new "baby being." The baby being is comprised of its own spark of uniqueness from All That Is, of challenges and questions arising from the multiple past incarnations, and of projects bestowed by the soul itself and other larger beings that gave birth to it. From now on this being has its own spark and initiatives even while it is a part of others greater than itself. It, too, will live as a human and then continue eternally, both as itself and as a part of other greater energy gestalts, especially as a part of its soul. The baby being's psychic DNA is formed out of the desires that gave it birth. It will be motivated by those desires. In a way hard to understand given our existence in linear time, the baby being, through its own divine spark, gets to choose, in an important sense, the desires that give it birth. The nature of the baby being's creation and birth sheds light on the nature of desire and the challenges that all humans face.

The Co-Personality

Remember the narrowly intellectual and arrogant personality whose after-death adventure we proposed above. Let's call him Daniel. Daniel wanted to explore a life with less intellect and lower status in order to develop compassion and to learn a simple happiness. After death, Daniel consults with other personalities of the soul, with the soul itself, with guides, with other souls that may want to interact with him in his next incarnation, and with All That Is. Together they plan a new incarnation, a new baby being whom we'll call Beth. Daniel, who took part in planning the Beth incarnation, does not get lost in the Beth baby being but participates in the new incarnation from a nearby energy platform that's part of Beth's subconscious mind. He will be what we call a *co-personality.* Other personalities from his soul will also participate as co-personalities from an energy distance.[4] Their environment will not be structured in simple linear time as is Beth's physical reality in her new incarnation. Instead, each past personality will experience a vibrant, engrossing, somewhat dreamlike environment. Each personality, like Daniel, will seem to be the center of his or her own experience. Daniel affects and is affected by Beth. And each has free will. One could say that the new incarnation of Beth's becomes an aspect of Daniel's reality, part of Daniel's subconscious mind, just as Daniel is an aspect of Beth's incarnation, an aspect of her subconscious mind. The new incarnation, Beth, will be fully free to accept, in part or in whole, or to reject altogether the sensory, emotional, and intellectual responses of her co-personalities, including Daniel.

Daniel will engage only the times in Beth's life relevant to his own unfinished, unassimilated experience. Eventually Daniel obtains enough experience to move to his next question, and the process is initiated again as a co-personality to a new incarnation. Again a new baby being is formed. Let's call him Christopher. And again Daniel becomes a portion of Christopher's subconscious; Daniel affects and is affected by Christopher, and each exercises free will in their respective energy vehicles. Eventually Daniel answers his questions sufficiently so that he moves forward to the stage that John's friend Will now experiences: nondual awareness.

Every personality is eventually redeemed through this process, even if its actions and physical life were cruel and repellent. In the case of extreme cruelty it could take a million years on another planet before the personality is redeemed, but eventually every personality is able to function fully in the realm of nondual divine play.

Returning again to Beth, the baby being created out of the questions of Daniel, it is the very nature of Beth to want to know how to be happy while being less intellectual and having a lower status than her soul's incarnations had in recent (earlier) lives. In multidimensional time, we, the personality, choose the life situation into which we will be born for the adventure it offers. This is hard to understand from our normal experience of time—how can we choose before we exit? In multidimensional time we do choose before we exit, and we feel free to choose challenges, knowing that ultimately all our actions will be redeemed as we·expand eternally as a personality. Understanding this helps us understand why we engage life as we do with the strength and weaknesses that we have, and reassures us that we can and eventually will experience a wholeness that every bit of prior experience contributes to in its own unique way.

A few personalities move, with minimal further training, fairly directly to the Unity level (where John's deceased friend Will is centered), which most personalities don't reach until much further along in their experience. The personality goes to the Unity level only if it has no major unfinished business.

For example, personalities who come at the end of a lengthy series of their soul's lifetimes (in which the soul investigated an issue in depth) might be relatively complete at death, even if the soul has other issues to investigate. An example might be a soul that explored issues of war and anger, having multiple lives as a combatant at various levels of rank, for various ideologies, and in various styles of combat; and also as a noncombatant affected by the wars, in some lives adversely, and in some lives by being liberated, as many slaves were in the Civil War, or other advantageous ways; lives as war hawks and others as doves; and many lives learning how to deal with anger in daily life, again sometimes as the aggressor and sometimes as the recipient. Perhaps the last life in this series could be one where the incarnated personality is especially good at addressing anger—say, a hospital administrator confronting the turmoil of patients and their families and conflicts over insurance. Such a person might be relatively complete at the end of their life and ready to move rapidly to the nondual awareness of Unity.

Yet another type of person in our experience who goes relatively directly to nondual reality is someone who attains fearlessness in meeting the world as it is. John had a client who died of ALS (commonly known as Lou Gehrig's disease). He spent his last year or so in the world-famous healing community of John of God.[5] A few months prior to his death he told his wife that he had never been happier. It took only about five years in John's time for this gentleman to make his way to the Unity level. His soul may still have many more lifetimes to complete, but this particular personality was ready to move almost directly to the Unity level.

CHAPTER 15

The Limitations of the Ego
and the Assets Available to It

The ego was always meant to be a specialist in evaluating and interpreting physical life, but it was never meant to be the sole or even dominant voice in your life.

The human ego gives us a unique capacity for self-reflection, evaluation, and interpretation. While these ego capacities are wonderful and are capacities that humankind will develop even further in the coming Aquarian Age, the ego has its drawbacks, at times serious. Understanding how the ego operates in the aura will help you understand the process of creating your reality and the place of desires.

Whenever you think, feel, or act, energy flows through parts of your aura. That energy and any resistances it encounters as it flows through your aura cause those parts of the aura to glow. While usually most of a person's aura has at least a light glow all the time, thinking, feeling, and acting increase the glow in part of the aura. The thinking, feeling, or acting triggers an increased energy flow, in particular when you are thinking, feeling, or acting in terms of yourself. For example, with "I want an apple" or "I wouldn't accept that treatment," portions of the aura involved in your sense of "I" light up. Your sense of "I" arises out of your sense that your "I" is discrete from the rest of the world. This sense of discreteness or separation generates self-reflection and in turn, self-reflection generates a sense of discreteness and separation.

Humankind developed self-reflection through neurological changes over thousands of years, as discussed in Chapter 11, "Humanity Has Chosen to Have a Self-Reflective Ego." This self-reflection has become the ground of human experience. Your sense of "I" arises out of self-reflection, and this sense of "I" is what we mean when we refer to the "ego" in this book. Humans have a unique capacity for self-reflection, evaluation, and interpretation. Other consciousnesses, even other complex consciousnesses in other chains of evolution, engage experience very differently.

This capacity for self-reflection is humanity's distinctive contribution to the universe; it is humans' niche in the ecology of consciousness.

In infancy your neurological system and aura develop so that your sense of "I" is the foundation of your experience. This sense of "I" allows you to focus and direct your attention; it allows you to engage the world. In this book, that part of your aura which generates your sense of "I" is called the ego. Ego, as used in this book, is not the same concept as the Freudian ego. Nor does it necessarily relate to ego rigidity or arrogance that people often refer to as simply "ego." For the discussions in this book, the ego is the part of the aura that directs the focus of your awareness and engages in self-reflection, evaluation, and interpretation. The ego is a self-sustaining though ideally ever-changing gestalt or subsystem of energy in your aura. In turn, the ego's self-reflection, evaluation, and interpretations constantly sustain, reinforce, and change both the self-organizing gestalt of the ego and the self-organizing gestalt of the whole personal self.

Clairvoyantly, when you observe a person's aura, you can see those parts that they include in their ego, those parts that they recognize as themselves, those parts of their personal self that engage in self-reflection, evaluation, and interpretation. A different kind of energy flows through those parts of their aura. Every physical body activity is paralleled by a unique aura activity, each of which generates the other. Every time a person's brain reflects, evaluates, or interprets their lives, energy flows through certain habitual portions of their aura. Identically, whenever energy of self-reflection, evaluation, or interpretation flows through those habitual parts of the aura, the person's brain and neurological system generate reflection, evaluation, and interpretation at a physical level.

In humans, ego self-reflection, evaluation, and interpretation are generated by the fifth chakra, the chakra that governs talking. So the stories we tell ourselves via the fifth chakra control our self-concept, control what we will look at in ourselves and what we won't. The stories we tell ourselves fashion our egos, turning our attention in some directions and possibly refusing to turn our attention in directions that might be productive.

The energy of self-reflection, evaluation, and interpretation, for most people, runs in habitual patterns through the aura. Aspects about themselves they could recognize if only their egos weren't rigid become hidden—not because their conscious mind doesn't have access to the information, but because their habitual patterns of thought have walled off parts of their personal thoughts, emotions, and beliefs. Consequently there is a down side to having an ego. It can be seriously mistaken as to its own self-interest.

Since the rigid ego is aware of only some of the contents of the conscious mind and usually unaware of the personal self's place in the larger scheme of things, its evaluation of the personal self's self-interest is often inadequate. The ego may experience pleasure or pain when the whole personal self's experience is opposite. A child taunting another child may, at the ego level, experience pleasure while at the larger level of the whole conscious mind (remember, the ego is just one storyline or a snapshot of the conscious mind) the overall experience is pain. Clairvoyantly the difference between the ego's experience and the person's whole conscious mind shows up brilliantly. In a person with a rigid ego, the clairvoyant can see the relatively small, inflexible, and highly conditioned part of that person's aura that, by habit, they respond to. Far more of the aura that the conscious mind has a natural capacity to respond to remains unaddressed. But the whole aura creates a person's life, not just that part referenced by the ego. The example of the taunting child will help illustrate the process.

The ego of the taunting child thinks that taunting another child is a good idea. It, that part of the aura, can be filled with pleasure in seeing the distress in the other child. But a clairvoyant can see that the taunting ego is a small part of the overall aura. The clairvoyant can see a larger part of the aura that vibrates in just as much pain as the child who is taunted.

The total aura then creates the bully's experience, and so his or her pain comes back into his or her life as an outside experience unfair and painful in some way, often not obvious. Perhaps, for example, a bad economy may hurt his or her family's finances if the aura of other family members is consistent, causing the bully distress that matches the target of his or her earlier repeated bullying. Over time, this feedback from the outside world will teach the bully compassion. Chapter 22, "Self-Talk and Stories: Conversation vs. Commands," addresses some of the practical issues of helping your ego stay flexible and more in touch with your real self-interest.

One might ask, why the disconnect between the outside world and the personal self? Why punish a child for an admitted bad choice? Isn't that harsh? The world of the ego is often harsh. The inexplicable pain that the child experiences as a result of the bad economy mirrors the inexplicable pain the child as a bully imposed on the child he or she bullied. This pain isn't imposed to punish the bully but to educate him or her, an education in contrast that the soul, in its own dimension, cannot get. The soul experiences no sense of separation.

By entering the world of separation through its collaboration with your personality, and especially your ego, the soul experiences the ego's sense of sharp contrast and meanings separated out into individual packages. Thus what the soul experiences holistically in its nonphysical sphere can be divided into numerous specialized packages of experience that allow implications and meanings to show up that the soul alone could not notice.

That is to say, a soul may experience alienation in its own realm that it can't find the cause of, but incarnated as you, it may explore learning how to live with difficult emotions and difficult conversations. When they are separated out and intensified, issues of boundaries and balance that lack clarity in the soul's own realm can become clear lessons. For example, in its own realm, the soul has no access to the rich ambivalence and complexity of loving and rearing a child.

Like everything else in the manifested world, there is an extent to which the ego is intrinsically limited in any moment of its existence, though it constantly expands in all directions. By itself, the ego has inadequate access to the big picture and to a full understanding of what's in its own best interest. Fortunately there are partners a flexible ego can turn to that help support it and bring it reliable happiness and joy. The ego was always meant to be a specialist in evaluating and interpreting physical life, but it was never meant to be the sole or even dominant voice in your life. There are deeper levels of your being that we are calling, after the fashion of Seth, "the inner ego." The inner ego is a gestalt composed mainly of collaborating contributions of energy/consciousness from the soul, from All That Is, and from the eternal spark that gives rise to your individual personality.

These collaborators bring several capacities to a flexible ego. They are aware of a bigger picture than the ego is focused on. They provide a joyous support of unity that the ego can draw on to lessen its sense of isolation, even though its job is to embrace its sense that it exists separately from other aspects of the universe. Those unity aspects of the inner ego can help the outer ego find neutrality. Then the ego can look at and evaluate all of the personality's experience rather than getting stuck on its assumptions.

Sadly, it's quite possible for very good, psychically aware people to get stuck in seemingly endless and terrible challenges. They may be flexible in large parts of their life, but in some important part of their ego, they have a hard time opening to a new direction. The promises of creating their reality or the laws of attraction can make their despair even worse, because as far as they can tell, they're doing all the right things they've been told to do.

In these cases, the best resource for people who are stuck isn't usually to find one more technique that promises relief from their difficulty. By all means it's a good idea for them to continue pursuing their goals with increasing skill, but with flexibility. (See Chapter 9 for more on flexibility.) Additionally, maybe even more fundamentally, when a person understands the nature of pleasure, happiness, and joy, and the nature of spiritual freedom, then their primary goal changes. Instead of being rigidly focused on their desires, they use their desires to commit to life and to explore the development of happiness, joy, spiritual freedom, and meaning. Chapter 20 describes what is distinctive about each of these and how focusing on them as your primary goals can bring happiness and often free up progress towards the secondary goals of fulfilling your desires. Part Three gives some practical approaches to committing to life through your desires while staying flexible and opening the limitations of the ego.

CHAPTER 16

Desire and Trust

Your desires are an unerring prompt to explore and discover. At each point they and your experience, in dialog, will provide course corrections, often small, but occasionally onto a radically different path.

Desire is the paradoxical force that draws us into life. Desires, rather than instincts, are the principal force prompting human behavior. It is desires that draw us into unexpectedly complex relationships, and it's that unexpected complexity that brings richness to our lives.

Take the example of a young man, Alan, who loves Evelyn. She wants to settle down and have children, but he's reluctant to take on the responsibilities of being a husband and father. He wants to keep things just as they are; he likes his freedom. However, he does love her and doesn't want her to leave. If he creates his own reality, can't he just create a reality in which she's content to continue with him as they have been doing unless he decides he'd like to marry?

Of course there's something wrong with that idea—it turns Evelyn into an automaton. The idea is that Alan is to be able to choose spontaneously whatever he wants, but Evelyn's choices must move in lockstep with his. Imagining that through the magic of synchronicity or probable realities that others will exercise their spontaneous free choices in ways that never conflict with your desires is merely getting lost in a semantic logic maze. In reality, the fact that you explore your dance of desires in a world with other people who have their own desires is what gives your whole experience depth, richness, and contrast—all of which make incarnating as a human unique and meaningful. Desires require choices with accompanying limitations, and require expansion into experience you cannot fully anticipate.

If Alan marries Evelyn there will be limitations on his freedom. There will be far more limitations on his freedom when they have children. Yet many men who have feared the responsibility of fatherhood love it when it comes; some do not. On the other hand, if Alan separates from Evelyn without marrying her, he is free but uninvolved. If he convinces Evelyn to change her mind and stay with him without getting married, then he won't have children. There's no one right answer for every man facing Alan's choice. Every person making a decision faces real uncertainty.

If You Could Make Your Desires Come True

Desire has a peculiar relationship with happiness. Most people expect the fulfillment of their desires to bring happiness. Presumably there is a strong biological programming to expect happiness to follow upon getting your desires; otherwise you wouldn't be motivated to pursue them. But you don't have to be too old before you have seen both yourself and other people desire passionately what later experience shows to be harmful, and to resist passionately the very experiences that could have led to happiness.

Just because you are now twenty, thirty, forty, eighty, or ninety and passionately desire something does not mean that getting it would bring you happiness or bring you relief or bring you whatever it is you imagine. That is because each moment of life experience always changes you, always gives you back more understanding (conscious or unconscious) than you brought to that moment. It's desire that commits you to engaging your humanity.

EXERCISE 59: Imagine You Could Make Someone Love You According to Your Design

In the following exercise, please imagine you could make someone love you without there being any significant differences between what they desire and what you want. You can use as your imagined lover someone who actually is an unrequited past love, or someone you now know, or you can make up a scenario with a fantasy figure. Notice how satisfying or unsatisfying the enforced love seems, and notice how long it remains satisfying. That an enforced love would be unsatisfying is obvious, but many of us still retain fragments of the fantasy that have surprisingly powerful invisible undertones and effects in our psyche. Let your experience be whatever it is, and explode any pictures that light up.

1. Breathe gently and deeply, and with openness be in the center of your head.
2. Explode your old grounding cord and male- or female-ground.
3. From the center of your head bring to mind someone you would like to or would have liked to make fall in love with you, and imagine him or her being in love with you.
4. Further, imagine that his or her desires always fall in line with yours.
5. Acknowledge how satisfying that is.
6. Explode your unrealistic pictures.
7. Looking out through time, notice how long it remains functional and satisfying.
8. Notice the amount of space your emotion occupies in your aura.
9. When through, create and destroy roses for any pictures that lit up, and recycle the energy back through your crown.
10. Explode your old grounding cord and male- or female-ground.
11. Replenish your body and aura with golden cosmic energy.
12. Bring up just the right amount of earth energy for your body and aura at this time.
13. Thank your body for being willing to change and grow.
14. Breathe gently and deeply, stand up, stretch, and reverse polarities.
15. You may find it useful to make some notes of your experience.

As a thought experiment, think of something you want but currently do not have, and create a rose for your current energy in respect to your desire. Give the rose a grounding cord and put it off to your left a couple of feet. Next create a rose for what your energy would be like if you had your desire. Check that energy and see if you like it, if your subjective sense of it is favorable. If so, then ask your inner wisdom to set up a pathway that involves, amongst other changes, the development of real-life skills and the clearing of what might be called weaknesses so that your energy moves towards the fulfillment of your desire.

EXERCISE 60: Consulting Inner Wisdom

1. Breathe gently and deeply, and with openness be in the center of your head.
2. Explode your old grounding cord and male- or female-ground.
3. From the center of your head, create a rose for your current energy in respect to your desire and let it fill in.
4. Give the rose a grounding cord and put it off to your left a couple of feet.
5. Next create a rose for what your energy would be like if you attained your desire.
6. Check that energy and see if you like it, if your subjective sense of achieving that desire is favorable.
7. While exploding pictures, compare and contrast your two roses.
8. If your subjective sense is favorable, then ask your inner wisdom to set up a pathway that involves, amongst other changes, the development of real-life skills and the clearing of what might be called weaknesses so that your energy moves towards the fulfillment of your desire.
9. When through, create and destroy roses for any pictures that lit up, and recycle the energy back through your crown.
10. Explode your old grounding cord and male- or female-ground.
11. Replenish your body and aura with golden cosmic energy.
12. Bring up just the right amount of earth energy for your body and aura at this time.
13. Thank your body for being willing to change and grow.
14. Breathe gently and deeply, stand up, stretch, and reverse polarities.
15. You may find it useful to make some notes of your experience.

What to Trust

There are at least two important aspects of trust that many people struggle with. The first concerns whether to trust themselves or others. If themselves, what portions of themselves? The second aspect concerns trusting that they will like the outcome. Both aspects of trust are potentially confusing.

One student said she had made a terrible choice in her marriage because she hadn't trusted herself. Upon analysis, it wasn't clear what "trusting herself" meant. At the time she married, she trusted herself that she was making the best decision that she could. She had trusted some emotions while discounting others. Since we're never completely congruent, we always face that decision of deciding what to trust. Only upon looking back did she feel that she hadn't trusted the right aspects of herself. She hadn't trusted her intuition. So, at the time of the class, "trusting herself" meant trusting her intuitions, rather than trusting what other people might say or trusting her own emotions and reasoning.

The authors don't think trusting your intuition works as a hard and fast rule, either. Making your own decisions is a good idea, but that's not a guarantee. You can rigidly follow your intuitions and rigidly make your own decisions and still have unfortunate outcomes. Before this student married, someone probably had reservations about the man. Listening to others is important also.

Two Examples of the Imperfection of Intuition

Decades ago, John had noticed that certain of his dreams that had a vividness and spontaneity in describing future events always came true. As a result of this accumulated experience, when John had a dream one night that a particular editor would warmly support one of John's book ideas, John confidently contacted the editor. To John's shock, the editor utterly rejected his idea with an impersonality completely inconsistent with John's dream conversation.

In 1987, John attended another channel's class. A woman asked the channeled entity what to do about the criticism she was getting from her in-laws about raising her children. The entity told her that she must trust herself. "I knew it!" she exclaimed. Now adding her husband to the mix, she continued, "My husband and in-laws are telling me I shouldn't be breast-feeding my four-and-a-half-year-old son, but I know my son's needs better than anyone else." The entity quickly backtracked in his advice to say that sometimes it's a good idea to listen to others.

A mature trust in yourself, we suggest, will allow you to engage your perceptions, your emotions, thoughts, and intuitions, and will allow you to listen to others (both those you respect and those you don't) who may or may not have your best interest at heart. Then you develop your own best understanding and act on it.

The second aspect of trust that people refer to is trusting that they/you will like the outcome. Often people are counseled that in creating or attracting what they want, it is important to believe or trust they will get what they want. This advice is explored in depth in Chapter 26 when discussing affirmations and visualizations. As a quick summary now: we believe that, depending upon what you mean by "believe" or "trust," the advice can be useful. However, many people work hard to eliminate all doubt, alienating themselves from the very content of their own mind. Mere overriding or repressing parts of your mind is a bad strategy for cultivating the awareness that brings spiritual freedom and happiness.

One of John's clients is a very talented developing psychic. As she and John were talking one day, John noticed a cap she was placing on her psychic development. Together they explored the cap, and it became clear that she was afraid that she and her daughters would be socially ostracized by her community if it were known that she was a psychic. The way she was addressing her concern was to say to herself, "My guides would never lead me down the wrong path." As she and John talked more they decided that while that may be true, and even if she were correctly understanding where her guides were leading her, there remained issues requiring her attention.

It very well might be that people would socially ostracize her. She could prepare to meet their objections in an authentic, kind, and generous way, giving them the space to have their own opinion. She would do that by exploding her matching pictures. Had she just reassured herself, she would have lost the opportunity to get lit up by what she feared and to clear her resistance to it. As she and John explored further still, they looked at ways in which she could talk to her daughters, because the children of psychics can find themselves in difficult social situations, and it's important for them to be prepared to address such encounters. John's client and John brainstormed about what she could say to her daughters and how they would handle the kinds of interactions that normally arise. Preparation offered an opportunity to turn what could be an unpleasant life experience into a genuine chance to learn and grow for her daughters. So, trusting that things will work out for the best doesn't mean not addressing your concerns. Addressing those concerns is part of engaging life. By coping with her own shame and embarrassment pictures, she developed her spiritual freedom, opened her psychic abilities even more, and was prepared for any potential social ostracism. Consequently, since she was no longer in so much resistance to the possibility, it was less likely to happen.

There is a rock-bottom absolute trust that you can skillfully cultivate. That rock-bottom trust includes the conviction that all things good, bad, or indifferent have spiritual meaning and fit in an overall meaningful and joyful existence. Each experience makes you more than you were, appearances to the contrary notwithstanding. You can go backwards in what you have, but never in what you are. For example, you can be rich and then go bankrupt. You'll have less money, and in that meaningful sense you've gone backwards. You may experience great pain. However, simultaneously you have learned more about money, value, relationships, and compassion. So you can have less money, but you, the eternal being, cannot know less about money. Fundamentally, after the experience you have more spiritual freedom, spiritual meaning, and spiritual capacity for life. You can learn to experience the ever-increasing joy that is augmented moment to moment by your growing spiritual core. Trust that all your experience has spiritual meaning and spiritual joy. That meaning grows and contributes to your potential for current personal happiness and joy. This kind of trust will lead you to enjoy life more and to be more resourceful and resilient.

Getting Your Desires Is Not a Good Predictor of Happiness

Your own experience and scientific studies will show you that getting your desires is not a good predictor of happiness. However, pursuing your desires with a balance of self-acceptance, curiosity, and a sense of adventure will bring meaning and happiness.

Example: Let's say your desire is to have money to provide your children the intellectual and social advantages you want to give them. By all means pursue making more money, but remember there are numerous deeper values that can be seen as the real goals. Pursue money with the intent of developing your own skills to recognize what other people will value, and to build your ability to provide value and to communicate value to other people. Also remember that the purpose of providing money to your children's support is always in service of helping them become more balanced, capable, self-sufficient, and socially skilled children now and adults in the future. Until you have money you can still help them develop all those goals around your lack of money or through your lack of money. So while you might provide tutoring if you have the money, you can model resourcefulness and self-sufficiency in making do with the assets you have. While providing tutoring might give them advantages, learning to live gracefully with lacks will also provide advantages. What's in the way is also the way.

CHAPTER 17

Creating Your Own Reality
According to Your Aura

Rather than life being a mere competition with a world waiting for you to impose your will, life is a conversation expanding uncontrollably, ecstatically in all directions.

It is widely known among readers of books like this one that *you create your own reality*, as John's teacher Seth proclaimed in the '60s. Looking at this process of creation in terms of the personal aura clarifies several hard-to-understand aspects of what creating your reality means in practice.

There is a paradox that underlies the very essence of creating your own reality. You can create your own reality only because you are part of and unified with All That Is. On the other hand, you experience your desires in your human way only because you stand separate from the external world and All That Is. This paradox creates tension. The word "tension" is used here a little differently than normal. Tension, here, is a simple direct consequence of life, not (as that word is normally used) an extensive physical, emotional, and psychological embellishment stemming from the rigid ego. More tension is generated by the fact that your desires are no more or less sacred than anyone else's. Everything is interdependent, dynamic, and impermanent. All this apparent contradiction and interplay sets up an ecstatic dance of order and chaos, tension and completion, pleasure and pain. Humans constantly strive to reach a point of no tension, but the tension between a human's unity and his or her separateness is at the very center of the whole dance of ecstasy. Again, you only have the particular intensity and dynamism of your desires because of this interplay. Your commitment to your desires is a commitment to the play of polarities and to a certain inevitable tension. Much of the rest of this book involves strategies to become more resourceful, skillful, and happy so that when you experience the inevitable tensions in your life with people and polarities, you don't resist them, making the challenges more problematic than necessary.

Pursuing your desires leads you (just as it is meant to lead you) into this play of polarities. When you are resourceful and skillful, pursuing your desires leads you to discover barriers in your aura and to make connections with various parts of yourself that have been alienated from one another. Pursuing your desires leads you to meet the world. Meeting the world is how a human meets him or herself. In meeting yourself, you make more of yourself, increasing your achieved connection with the external world as well as your overall capacity for connection. While connection with your soul and other deep aspects of yourself is important for a full life, it is no substitute for everyday life experience. It is the engagements of daily life that form the core of your personality during and after your life. As a result of the centrality of daily experience to your eternal self, shortcuts in creating your reality are rarely available. Just as you cannot pay someone to exercise for you, you cannot usually get your soul or one of the many miracle workers (who do exist) to remove entirely your burdens. You can, however, learn to find pleasure, happiness, joy, and meaning in everyday life, hard times as well as easy times, and in doing so everyday life becomes easier. To understand why everyday experience is so important, we will look at several aspects of creating your reality.

While you create your reality according to the vibrations of your aura, that reality attains its concreteness and stability in a magnificent collaboration of consciousnesses from the tiniest sub-atomic particle to the sun and even other stars. Just as you have an individual personal aura, so you participate in a global reality aura that vibrates through many ranges of energy. Through your integration with the global reality aura, events that originate solely in your personal aura manifest as objective events in the world at large, which anyone can observe. Your physicality itself and the changes you wish to make in your body depend on the laws of nature, which are established by innumerable consciousnesses, including most prominently Mother Earth and the angelic chain of being. Emotional and mental events take place in a psychic atmosphere collaboratively held together by innumerable consciousnesses including Mother Earth and, most importantly, other human beings. Interestingly, men collectively generate a psychic atmosphere supporting activity for both men and women, while women collectively generate a psychic activity supporting relationship or space for both men and women.[1]

All events you wish to have manifest in the external world require some structural integration into the forms of this physical world. That structural integration almost always comes from, at least in part, your own activity in the concrete external world, and activity in a form recognized by the relevant consciousnesses as meaningful. For some events, the structural integration can come from the concrete world efforts of other people or from your own karma.

Examples of the effect of karma would be winning a lottery or the family conditions into which you were born. Note, we are not saying here that you are controlled by karma. You can change karma at any time by learning the underlying lessons. We are saying that the group energy necessary to allow an event to manifest in the external world can flow through time as karma into your present body and thereby into the global reality aura (into which your body is integrated).

Aspects of physical reality like linear time and gravity are created for you in the part of the global reality aura that coordinates the observed laws of science. Your entry into that part of the global reality aura comes automatically when you are awake in your physical body. When you dream and leave your body, you are in a different part of the global aura in which neither linear time nor gravity applies. That part of life experience is real but is not a part of the physical reality in which your waking desires manifest.

The foregoing might suggest why your soul cannot simply give you what your ego wants. Your soul's access to the global reality aura is through your personality aura. Your soul cannot vibrate by itself in that physical manifesting range. When your personality aura's internal contradictions are significant enough, they block your soul's access to the global reality aura. You yourself, by your contradictions, close the doorway—i.e., you close down your personality aura, the passageway to transmit and translate the soul's vibration.

It isn't just the soul's vibrations that don't transmit to the global reality aura when you are conflicted. Even your own ego's goals don't get transmitted. Instead the conflicted vibration of your whole personality aura gets transmitted and manifested as conflict.

While your aura will never be perfectly clear, manifestation will require that your aura be reasonably clear in the energy ranges relevant to your desires. Pursuing your desires in everyday life, in the give and take of human relationships, whether good, bad, or indifferent, is the fastest way to clear conflicts in your aura. While meditation practices such as that taught in Part One and affirmations and visualizations can help, there's no substitute for real-life experience. This is because your internal conflict between your ego awareness and your whole personality can be hard to find.

Take the example of Roger, a very capable, idealistic man with high aspirations for genuine spiritual growth. He's also a very angry person, deeply resentful of his father for the way he treated Roger in childhood, resentful of the government for taking taxes and giving some of that money to others, and resentful of a whole series of bosses and coworkers who didn't appreciate him.

He learned about the laws of attraction and, misreading them, decided that he could insulate himself from all these things he found so distasteful by tapping into the abundance of the universe. He worked hard on his intent, went into day trading, and lost all his money.

There are several issues that Roger's failed strategy illustrates. First, it can be hard to know what you really want. Roger's ego wanted to be free from interacting with a world he thought was unfair. But his whole personality wanted to be well-integrated with society. Had Roger made the millions he expected, he would have closed in even more self-protectively and angrily.

There were hints in Roger's own awareness that Roger could have used to change his course had he been more flexible. Roger could see how he was closing other people down. Roger knew that he wanted spiritual clarity most of all. Had he been able to attend to his own feelings carefully, he would have noticed that when he thought of his coming millions, his body tightened and his feelings became even more cramped.

John noticed that Roger's aura blackened when Roger focused on how his energy work on abundance was going to free him from the world he found to be so unfair. John tried to tell Roger, but just as John had ignored all advice when he was new to the notion of creating one's reality, so did Roger.

Fascinatingly, when Roger told John a year and a half later that he'd lost all his money, Roger's aura looked dramatically healthier. It's ironic that had Roger been a much younger soul, he might have found a way to make a lot of money even as he ran away from society (though probably not by day trading, see below). Younger souls often concentrate on one facet of humanity at a time. They aren't called upon to integrate multiple aspects of themselves like older souls. A younger soul might get away with being disgusted with the world even as he or she made lots of money. He or she would be concentrating solely on learning how to perform a service that people would value. The older you are as a soul, the more aspects of yourself you are called upon to integrate and use in harmony with society at large.[2]

Compare Sarah's experience to Roger's. Sarah, after working hard for decades, wanted to retire and write poetry. Instead, when a promotion into an administration post opened up, she decided to take on the challenge. It was hard, but with resources like the book *Difficult Conversations* and her developing psychic tools, she did so well that she got another promotion after only a year. More importantly to her, she was rapidly developing more and more spiritual freedom. She cleared so much of her aura energy that work challenges lit up; and her physical, emotional, and mental health improved. After a while in her second new job, she found herself starting to work with arts organizations. Clairvoyantly, one can see that her poetic aspirations had manifested as an inner poetry, whose rhythms reverberate around the world. The older you are as a soul, the less likely you are to become famous as a poet; the more likely you are to develop spiritual freedom that grows into a reliable happiness and inner contribution to the world.

The next mistake Roger's strategy illustrates is trying to obtain his goal while stripping away any meaningful engagement with the world. By choosing day trading, Roger would never have to please anyone—no bosses, coworkers, or customers. But it's just those kinds of interactions that lead to growth. You can always leave an awful situation and continue to learn from it (see Chapter 18, "Matching Pictures and Unconditional Responsibility").

However, if you continue to find yourself in awful situations, there's something you're missing. Many of the remaining chapters in this book may be particularly useful if you have such a challenge. One of the reasons real-life experience is so vital is its rich specificity. Nothing else works as well to help you develop your strengths and address your weaknesses. Looking at the aura helps illustrate this fact. In Part One you explored a technique to help you understand the mechanics of spiritual freedom— the ability to run a full range of energy frequencies and qualities through- out your body and aura. (See Chapter 9, Exercise 58, "Running the Colors of the Rainbow through your Aura.") Here's how spiritual free- dom plays out in everyday life.

All life experience generates flows of energy through your aura. The specifics of the experience determine the colors and qualities of the energy. Unless an energy you run through your aura is keyed very specifi- cally to the colors and qualities of your conflict, the energy won't high- light or activate them. Life experience generates very specific flows through your aura—the specific energy flows of real skills and meaning- ful experience like how to create real abundance (create value) and how to have a great relationship (learn how to communicate). When those conflicts are highlighted and activated, they start to dissipate and allow greater freedom in your aura for that kind of energy to flow and express itself in ever more comprehensive, inclusive, and integrated ways. When this flowing, expressive freedom develops, both your internal and external realities become freer flowing, richer, more subtle, and integrated. They expand in advantageous ways. Similarly, everyday life experience activates and exercises your strengths, and you spontaneously see ways to expand and integrate them into other areas. You generate even more relationships and meaning.

We call your ability to run many qualities and colors through large parts of your aura your "spiritual freedom." All experiences generate more and more spiritual freedom, and this spiritual freedom adds to your competency and generates joy.[3]

The next deficit that Roger's strategy illustrates is trying to take abundance from life without generating a skillful presence in life. Roger intended to be a philanthropist when he made his money, but he was going to make the money essentially out of air. Essentially, he was telling the universe, "With my brains and your money. . . ." Roger's strategy wasn't designed to integrate and support commerce; his strategy proceeded from a deep denial that society at large had worth (a belief inconsistent with a true appreciation of universal abundance).

John's early adult experience illustrates that kind of failure to create a presence in the world. The idea that you can create your own reality seems to undervalue the cultivation of skills for making money, developing relationships, building your health, and other such desires.

John's early life experience with long-term unemployment in 1975 shows how subtle creating your reality can be. John had graduated from Harvard Law School and wanted a job as a lawyer. Because of his prestigious education, and because he had studied with both Jane Roberts and Lewis Bostwick, he had a very high opinion of himself and expected to find a job—not just any job, but a high-paying job in a lovely locale where he would be able to use all the valuable understandings he felt uniquely prepared to impart. Actually, he was abysmally ignorant and deficient in almost all skills he needed to be a valuable employee. Harvard Law School best prepares students for entry-level jobs in large law firms in big cities, and John wanted to live in a small town. Even for those big-city jobs, John was useless. Somehow he'd gotten through school without learning to write clearly, a necessary skill for lawyers. Mostly John suffered from having poor people skills and poor judgment. For example, he was asking prospective employers for big-city wages, not understanding the economics of small-town practice.

John suffered many months of unemployment. Finally, a friend introduced John to a sole practitioner named John Lo Pinto, who had trained the friend in small-town practice. This older man, Lo Pinto, was well known as a tough, even belligerent litigator. Somehow he helped John begin learning what it would mean to be a lawyer. He pointed out that John couldn't produce anything of economic value to him without learning a lot more. Though John was a lawyer, Lo Pinto's secretary knew far more of the daily practice of law than John did, even without knowing how to do the academic work John had learned in law school. Lo Pinto put John to work without pay. Or rather, the payoff was that Lo Pinto was able to help John learn how to write so that the logic of an argument was clear. Though it was many years before John developed people skills and judgment, at least now John had something: an emerging ability to write. John soon got a paid job, and though there were several more hard years, he at least had a start.

No amount of purely psychic work would suffice to manifest John's desire for a good job. It required years of learning, full of starts and stops. Ideally, if John had been more open to what life had to teach him, it would have been much easier. John's first father-in-law used to say, "You can tell a Harvard man, you just can't tell him much." John heard the joke but didn't understand that he was the Harvard man who was going to have to learn the hard way, because he just didn't get the lessons he needed without resisting them.

When he was suffering so, a channeled entity told John that he would come to look back on this time as a short period of intense transformation. Now, more than thirty-five years later, John does see it as a short period; and he sees how impoverished his life would have been had he found a job that gave him what he wanted without requiring him to learn the lessons in humanity that John was forced to face.

Rarely, maybe never, is any significant desire fulfilled just by getting what we think we want on the surface. Desire naturally carries us into life complexities and richness we can't even imagine before we get to them. Often people rebel against this fact. Whenever we suffer and fail to receive what we desire, it seems as if the soul receives the value of the richness and complexity, while we (the personality) just suffer. After all, we may be suffering for a long-term goal of the soul that we won't be around to enjoy. We discuss elsewhere how the personality both fully chooses to participate in those longer-term goals, and how it directly benefits (see Chapter 14).

Yet another weakness that Roger's strategy illustrates follows from his determination to use intensity or passion to overcome resistance. Many people try to overwhelm obstructions rather than addressing them—rather than learning from them and integrating that part of themselves. Overwhelming rather than addressing obstructions makes people afraid of their own mind. Doubt becomes the enemy. It is important to be able to commit to your activity without constantly second-guessing yourself. And it's important to be able to integrate new or contradictory feelings, thoughts, or information. Computer programmers work like mad to build a program, and at regular intervals bring equally intense concentration to trying to "break" the program. That is, they test the program rigorously to see where it might have gaps. One of the greatest benefits of neutrality is that it increases your capacity both to commit to a path and to be open to integrating contrary information.

Some people employ a strategy of overwhelming the objecting portions of their mind by powerful programming. This powerful programming can temporarily bring them what they think they want, but it further clogs the aura; and while not fundamentally lessening the amount of spiritual freedom they have, it lessens the amount of *accessible* spiritual freedom. In other words, their aura, unfortunately, is not as open to creating a full experience.

Another aspect that's deceptive about creating your own reality is that sometimes you can seem to go backwards. Here's the kind of process that can occur. After you've successfully lost weight and stabilized at a comfortable level, you might notice in your meditation one day that a picture containing someone else's energy has been coordinating and generating your weight loss. (Remember, pictures are psychic structures that coordinate psychic vibrations, and are troublesome only when they get stuck in repetitive patterns or, as here, when they are composed of someone else's energy.) Upon your noticing that the energy driving your weight loss hasn't been your own, the energy might return to the owner. Unless you had already developed your own resources, you might once again struggle with your weight.

You might wonder: wouldn't you have been better off not meditating? But for meditating, you might think, you would have retained your slim body using someone else's energy. Being unaware might have worked for a while, but using someone else's energy would leave your aura and your spiritual freedom with a gap. Recognized or unrecognized, that gap would itself generate an inner alienation that eventually manifested itself outwardly as a more serious problem, maybe a health problem or something that made you unattractive not withstanding your slim body. Clearing the other person's energy opens more space in your aura for your overall happiness and overall energy coordination, making more and more of your authentic goals manifest.

Matching Pictures and Unconditional Responsibility

Our guides encourage people to respond to difficulty and even defeat on multiple levels. The first level is to have all the emotions you have without censoring what is an acceptable emotion. Of course, you try to behave skillfully in response to your emotions. Whatever your emotion, you have the potential for a full range of behavioral responses to it. All emotions, both so-called positive emotions and so-called negative emotions, contain information and energy vital to your learning, growing, and becoming authentically kind and generous. Being fully open to emotions such as despair or rage doesn't imply that one need behave foolishly or meanly. Fully having so-called negative emotions while acting as skillfully as possible is the focus of Chapter 23, "Anger," and giving your emotions their natural space is the focus of Chapter 9, "Opening to Life As It Is: Resistance and Neutrality."

The next level is to grieve your losses. One doesn't want to get lost in them; instead, one uses psychic tools like giving the emotion its natural space while staying senior and exploding matching pictures. Still, it's important not to prematurely pronounce yourself "over it." Friends and relatives can be a real support in times of loss. Then there comes the time to assimilate the lessons of the defeat, disaster, loss, or even just a stressful or annoying event. Now your natural tendencies for self-justification (which probably have their own evolutionary benefits) or even your friends' support can short-circuit the learning process. Friends, being on your side, will often rush to reassure you how wonderful you are and how awful the person who hurt you was, and they may be right; but if you stop there you will be wasting the opportunity that your pain and suffering is presenting. Regardless of who is at fault, since you create your own reality, if you have an unpleasant experience there are aspects of your aura that you can fruitfully change. Here are some examples of evaluations that may be accurate, but by digging deeper you may open to make fruitful changes in yourself: "I worked harder than my coworkers and they got angry." Were you radiating resentment or superiority? "Men don't like strong women." How's your female grounding? Do you think being right entitles you to get what you want? "She wouldn't listen." Did you really seek to elicit and understand why she found your reasons unconvincing or did you insist all the harder? "I was ahead of my time." Did you address your audience's concerns? It also often helps to ask how an enemy would characterize your actions. While their characterization might be wrong, it might still help you break through your own self-justification. Some people will object to this approach, saying that such a focus on what they could change would just make them feel bad about themselves. It might, and if this kind of self-reflection makes you feel bad, you could explore why addressing your own fallibility makes you feel bad about yourself. (See the section entitled "Mistakes" in Chapter 24, "Self-Evaluation.") When you cultivate neutrality, you will have an easier time drawing value from the things that go wrong.

Native peoples, after a successful hunt, will use all of the animal that they've killed, not just the meat, but the hide, hooves, bones, etc. Inside the bones is the marrow, a source of important nutrients. Only if you penetrate the bones of your losses, break them apart and see what's in the marrow, do you fully engage your life. Only if you get past the self-congratulatory explanations do you move directly towards better times. When you do, the payoff is wisdom and spiritual freedom. Whether you notice it or not, your body, emotions, and thoughts will be freer, more comfortable, and happier.

Most of us stop learning when we decide another person is at fault. Taking unconditional responsibility for what happens in your aura is a path to spiritual freedom and more pleasant outcomes. Taking unconditional responsibility means letting go of whether someone else is guilty of terrible behavior or has treated you unfairly, and similar concepts that can short-circuit your analysis of what you want to change about yourself. Let's examine an extreme hypothetical case. Both the names and the situation are made up to illustrate how even in a black-and-white situation, the victim can benefit if he or she takes unconditional responsibility.

Addie was married to an alcoholic batterer. She left and got a divorce. How does she now go about creating a different kind of relationship for herself with a different man? Often the advice she hears is to have self-respect and to demand to be treated well. Like much advice, this advice can work if she understands and acts on it flexibly enough that she makes a deep and wide range of changes in herself.

The answer is more than "don't marry an alcoholic abuser." It's vital to not get stuck on the same unconscious behavior for decades, or marriage after marriage. Try to go below the surface of appearances. In Part Three we put forth a number of approaches to life that will help you get to the underlying issues. Particularly relevant will be self-talk and "shoulds, have tos, and oughts," discussed in Chapter 22, "Self-Talk and Stories: Conversations vs. Commands."

You create your reality according to your aura. The implications of energies and beliefs are often not apparent or easily decipherable by your ego, especially difficult problems. It isn't the label that generates an outcome. Fixing a serious problem requires penetrating beneath the label to the underlying energies or beliefs—and often more difficult, understanding the implications of a belief or an aura energy system. You can't just fix the problem by telling yourself and others that you want to be treated well—who doesn't? An energy that brings someone into a marriage with an abusive batterer arises from several kinds of resistances. You can discover what those resistances are by exploring your aura clairvoyantly or by asking yourself what emotions and ideas lead someone to be an alcoholic batterer. Then the person marrying him will have matching pictures. A picture in one person's aura "matches" a picture in another person's aura if it lights up when they interact. On the surface, the matching pictures may be complete opposites, different but complementary, or much the same; but beneath the surface there will be an underlying shared resistance. The person who is so afraid of anger that he or she never expresses anger but always tries to speak of love may eventually lose touch with anger altogether. She may marry an alcoholic batterer. (See Chapter 23, "Anger," for a discussion of the aura mechanics of anger.)

A person who responds to his or her anger by taking no responsibility for his or her emotion, but instead hurls abuse at other people, is similarly unwilling or unable to do the work to learn how to behave and respond skillfully when angry. He or she may become an alcoholic batterer.

Someone becomes an alcoholic batterer from a set of interlocking issues that will usually include anger, guilt, pain, aggression, boundaries, and other issues. Someone is attracted to and marries an alcoholic batterer because their aura has set up a kind of magnetism based on matching pictures. The person who marries the batterer will also have issues with anger, guilt, pain, aggression, boundaries, and other issues.

Noticing whether pictures match has nothing to do with who is culpable and who is blameless. There are victimizers who commit acts of horror on the blameless. There are always matching pictures between the victimizers and the victim. For the victim, no matter what the horror, there is always an active path to clear the matching pictures and to gain his or her own spiritual freedom. He or she can do this regardless of what the guilty party does or whether the guilty party is punished or not.

Matching pictures, the process by which we draw unpleasant experiences into our lives, can be really hard to understand. Creation through matching pictures works through a different kind of mechanism than what we assume in our culture.

For the following exercise please brainstorm by yourself or with another about what kinds of beliefs might bring two seemingly different groups together. You might consider native peoples and colonizers, Republicans and Democrats, men and women, or a pairing of your own choosing. Explode your matching pictures throughout the exercise.

EXERCISE 61: Brainstorm About Beliefs That Might Bring Seemingly Different Groups Together

1. Breathe gently and deeply, and with openness be in the center of your head.
2. Explode your old grounding cord and male- or female-ground.

3. By yourself, or with another person, brainstorm about what kinds of beliefs might bring two seemingly different groups together.
4. Explode your matching pictures throughout the exercise.
5. When through, recycle the energy back through your crown.
6. Explode your old grounding cord and male- or female-ground.
7. Replenish your body and aura with golden cosmic energy.
8. Bring up just the right amount of earth energy for your body and aura at this time.
9. Thank your body for being willing to change and grow.
10. Breathe gently and deeply, stand up, stretch, and reverse polarities.
11. You may find it useful to make some notes of your experience.

EXERCISE 62: Finding Matching Pictures by Revisiting an Unfair and Unpleasant Interaction

For the following exercise go back to a time in your life, or into the life of someone you know, when you, or he or she, experienced unpleasant interactions that seemed unfair. Notice whether the incident still lights you up. If so, then you have matching pictures that you still resist. It is helpful to remember that these pictures can sometimes take years to clear.

1. Breathe gently and deeply, and with openness be in the center of your head.
2. Explode your old grounding cord and male- or female-ground.
3. From the center of your head create a rose out in front of you for a time in your life when you experienced unpleasant interactions that seemed unfair. (Or you might choose to look at the life of someone you know.)
4. Does the incident still light you up? If so, you have a matching picture that you are still resisting. Explode whatever pictures light up.
5. When through, recycle your energy back through your crown.
6. Explode your old grounding cord and male- or female-ground.
7. Replenish your body and aura with golden cosmic energy.

8. Bring up just the right amount of earth energy for your body and aura at this time.
9. Thank your body for being willing to change and grow.
10. Breathe gently and deeply, stand up, stretch, and reverse polarities.
11. You may find it useful to make some notes of your experience.

Matching Picture Issues Don't Require Proportionality

Your weakness may be minor compared to the weakness of the person you're matching. The point is always the matching, and your power is always to change yourself.

Letting go of the idea of proportionality can allow you to learn lessons much more easily. You create your own reality, and therefore what you see outside of you is a reading of your own internal state. So if you are frequently seeing people do things that you really disapprove of, check and see where you could possibly have matching fears, constrictions in your space. For example, let's say that it makes you very angry that people ignorantly dismiss ESP without really understanding the nature of ESP based upon what they think is scientific authority. If you look you may find that you frequently expect people to accept what you say if the emotional grounding of it is compelling. In both cases there's a lack of understanding that there are different systems operative in the universe, and in the one case there are laws of science for fields like physics and chemistry, but those "laws" are not going to be operative in the same sort of way in a field where the connections are often connections of meaning rather than of power. And for you it's important to learn that while you might consider emotional grounding a good and sufficient reason to do something, other people may have different styles of understanding events and finding their motivations.

Accepting People as They Are

It may not seem like part of unconditional responsibility at first glance, but accepting that people are who they are is a major part of unconditional responsibility. For example, many people complain that their parents or in-laws don't treat them with respect. Of course, it's completely appropriate to communicate with them skillfully to help them understand how you would like to be treated; but at the end of the day even if you are skillful your parents or in-laws may never treat you with the respect that you would like. At some point, unconditional responsibility parallels the Serenity Prayer:

God, grant me the serenity to accept the things I cannot change,
Courage to change the things I can,
And wisdom to know the difference.

—Reinhold Niebuhr

Just because the universe is infinitely abundant doesn't mean that you're entitled to a big or even a small piece of it without changing and growing.

- If what is unpleasant for you is a relationship with a lover, friend, enemy, or boss—don't merely try to change the people; change how you communicate with, judge, and evaluate people.
- If it's money—learn to create value in a form that others recognize.
- If it's health—learn to collaborate with the body to run energy smoothly and appropriately through the body.
- If the past bothers you, learn from it.
- If the future frightens you, address your fears, change what you can, accept what you can't, and develop the wisdom to tell the difference (The Serenity Prayer).

CHAPTER 19

Pain and Punishment

L ife often hurts. The Buddha was right when he observed that life inevitably brings loss. We love someone and they suffer a sudden setback. We age and even if our health is wonderful, we're not like twenty-year-olds. Desires are inexhaustible and no matter how many desires are fulfilled, others are not. Until you can accept the fact that there is pain, you're not going to have a reliable happiness.

Because humans use pain to punish other humans, we come to associate pain with punishment. Many of us start to think that whenever we suffer pain, we are being punished by the universe.

Intrinsic to the notion of punishment is taking something away from the wrongdoer. The idea of punishment only fits in the relative world in which we subjectively experience pleasure and pain. In this relative world, one of us can punish another by restricting pleasure or inflicting pain.

In the deeper world where all things expand in all directions and in which the extent of our personal existence is equivalent to the extent of the meaning we create, every experience brings us more, makes us more, and generates more of us.

In this deeper world pain is an elegant truth—we experience pain because and only because we are alienated from that part of us that is in pain. If we are in pain because we are lonely, some portion of our aura is cramped and twisted. Some portion of our aura is unable to vibrate throughout its entire natural range. Pain focuses our awareness on that area of consciousness that is hurting, and this very energy of awareness will inevitably bring about an expansion of awareness that unties the constrictions and relieves the pain. Growth and spiritual freedom are inevitable, the speed and ease of that growth depending primarily on the degree with which we engage life openly as it is. Resistance to our lives cannot stop growth; it just slows growth down.

Guilt and Pain

When our actions hurt others in violation of our own inner knowing, we feel guilt. The guilt that arises spontaneously from our own inner knowing is a form of healing and moving forward that Seth called "natural guilt." Natural guilt feels bad and redirects us to break free of our own limitations and lack of understanding to become more authentically kind and generous. As part of that kindness and generosity we may make moves to reconcile with and/or compensate those whom we hurt. The thrust of our response to natural guilt is to move forward.

Responding to natural guilt by growth is very different from becoming enmeshed in punishing guilt. Punishing guilt focuses on inflicting pain upon the guilty party. It is backwards-looking, and while it may be accompanied by an intent to teach, the punishing guilt in itself is not authentic. Your own energy can never seek to punish you, because your own energy is always seeking paths of expansion. Your own energy may utilize pain to help you expand and move forward, but your own energy will never utilize pain merely to pay you back for something you did in the past. Punishment seeks to lessen and control. Natural guilt seeks to expand consciousness and create new meaning and joy.

Pain Doesn't Actually Originate in the External World

In one sense pain has nothing to do with what happens in the external world. The pain you are experiencing arises from your inability to run a full range of energy through your aura. Wherever your aura is constricted, the energy you're trying to run crashes into those contractions. If you can clear the constriction you'll experience delight. If instead when your energy crashes into those constrictions you make them harder and more rigid, thinking you are going after your desires, you will experience pain. Pain is not punishment. Pain is the universe telling you that you are constricting your own aura and cutting yourself off from joy.

So, in some sense there would be no need for an external world if you could directly engage your polarities and contradictions. The reason you incarnate at all is to engage a graceful dance or conversation that, among other things, shows you where your contradictions are.

Neutrality allows you to stop running away from your pain. With neutrality you look at your aura and life and clear the obstructions that cause your pain. Neutrality also allows you to be more open to pleasure by clearing the incongruities that even your pleasures often contain.

CHAPTER 20

Pleasure, Happiness, and Joy

The inner ego provides a joyous support of Unity that the outer ego can draw on to lessen its sense of isolation, even though its job is to embrace its sense that it exists separately from other aspects of the universe. Those Unity aspects of the inner ego can help the outer ego find neutrality. Then the ego can look at and evaluate all of the personality's experience rather than getting stuck on its assumptions.

Distinguishing among pleasure, happiness, and joy can highlight three different though interacting energies, each of which is important for life but serves a very different function. Pleasure is what you often feel when the ego's desires match its experience. Pleasure may or may not serve your true interests. Joy, as we are using the word, is always part of your moment-to-moment existence, flowing eternally from deeper parts of yourself that do not experience ego separation. Your experience of joy is often, maybe usually, blocked by your own ego rigidity; but you can learn to be open to joy's permanently bubbling-up presence. Happiness then, as we are using the word, results from a long-term style of interacting with the world that flows directly from having a flexible, resilient ego and is augmented by openness to the percolating joy that supports us in every moment. Happiness and joy do not depend upon pleasure or pain.

Pleasure is an experience of the ego. You won't experience pleasure every time you get your ego's desires. Even that can sometimes be disappointing. But pleasure, as we are using the word, is solely a function of ego satisfaction. Since the ego is inherently limited in its understanding, pleasure is inherently limited in its long-term effects. Pleasure is linked to its opposite polarity—pain—and the two are constantly appearing and disappearing in our lives. Because we naturally seek pleasure and the avoidance of pain, we find ourselves seeking to control life and force life to provide us only with pleasant experiences, but as the Buddha pointed out, perpetual avoidance of pain is impossible. Furthermore, as discussed in Chapter 11 on the nature of the ego, what we take pleasure in is not always wise. School children may take pleasure in taunting another child. What we find painful may be the best experience for our long-term happiness.

Still, pleasure is a lovely part of life and it is good to pursue pleasure as long as we do not get excessively caught up in obtaining our desired outcome. Getting caught up in our desires will not only inevitably generate disappointment, it will lead to ego rigidity, which blocks happiness and joy. Pursuing pleasure is good because that pursuit brings us into contact with the give and take of life, thus generating spiritual freedom, happiness, and joy.

Happiness and Joy as Functions of Meaning

Happiness becomes reliable when the ego is skillful at finding meaning in every event; joy comes from the meaning that doesn't need to be found but is always and already present. The purpose of the ego is to give us a sense of "me" and "not me," an inside that is me and an outside that is not. This ego then develops richness through its unique interpretations of reality. When the ego is excessively attached to its version of pleasure and excessively resistant to its version of pain, it becomes rigid and unable to find meaning in life.

There are two forms of meaning relevant to our discussion, which we will call *strategic meaning* and *absolute meaning*. You, the ego you, find experience strategically meaningful when you can use it to further your ego's goals. Since some pain rather than pure pleasure is inevitable, if your principal goal is pleasure or relief from pain, you are likely to interpret large parts of your experience as meaningless whenever they don't seem to lead towards or produce pleasure, or whenever they seem to thwart pleasure.

You can, however, change your strategy so that all experience is meaningful. When your principal goal is one like cultivating authenticity, wisdom, kindness, and generosity, then all experience strategically supports achieving these qualities. You can secondarily seek pleasure and seek to avoid pain, but you will always be successfully and meaningfully pursuing your principal goal, and this brings reliable happiness.

Joy

Joy, as we are using the word, supports your ego, but it is not a function of the ego. Instead, joy is an intrinsic part of all experience. Joy isn't the result of anything and doesn't flow from any particular outcome. Joy occurs in a pure knowingness without the ego's categories and without any sense of an inside that is me and an outside that is not. In fact, the joy that you experience and are supported by is not the personal emotion of any particular person. Joy as we are using the term is a much larger energy that a particular person can open up to but not contain within him- or herself. Joy occurs outside time and is independent of outcomes; yet paradoxically joy, in a way that logical thoughts and human concepts cannot explain, always increases in profoundly important ways as a result of your unique engagement with life.

As long as you engage in waking experience in your personal body with a fully functioning ego, the joy that dances through all consciousnesses cannot be experienced as your primary awareness. Still, that joy can be perceived as a perpetually supporting presence that percolates up through every atom and quark, through every psychic energy that composes your being. Also, in your meditation you can rise to energy states beyond the ego and drink in joy more directly. According to our guides, staying at that level as your primary awareness is inconsistent with deeply encountering your personal life. Therefore they suggest choosing to stay involved in everyday life as an individual supported by joy but centered in happiness. This approach mysteriously adds to the universe of joy.

You would have no being as a human unless every bit of you arose, as it does, from deeper fields of joy and meaning, to which in turn your every action, good, bad, or even despicable, contributes mightily. The joy we seek arises from no single source, not even from source itself. Our ever-greater encounter with joy arises from gracefully engaging the intrinsic play of polarities. In Hindu mysticism, this is called the play of consciousness.

There Is Always a "You" That Is More Intrinsic

As you become more psychic you can start to notice that your moods and desires are energies that in some sense are a part of you, but there is always a "you" that is more intrinsic than the whole bundle of moods and desires. There is a you that *has* those moods and desires and can *notice* that those energies are often not energies that you really identify with. The moods and desires are things that are passing through your aura.

With development, sometimes even early on, you begin to perceive a part of you that's engaged in all the phenomena—that is to say, sensations, emotions, and thoughts of your life—and yet you retain a core that isn't at the mercy of your sensations, emotions, and thoughts. This core is augmented or increased by every phenomenon, but at no time is it fundamentally limited or constrained by your experience of life. You could reasonably call this your soul, though in some ways it goes much deeper than even your soul. This is the part that we refer to as "you" when we suggest, for example, that you learn to have your sensations, emotions, and thoughts without becoming them. Only when you lose this awareness of a deeper self do you become reactive rather than skillful, sensing yourself as alienated or fundamentally oppressed.

In the following exercise you will try to find this part of you. Until you've cleared your aura considerably, this part will often be somewhere other than the center of your head, and even broken into pieces. So the first task is to find this part of you. You usually do this by asking yourself, "Where am I?" Surprisingly, almost everyone gets a sense of where they are. The second step: Measure the distance between this you, wherever it is, and the center of your head. It has a tendency then to come back into the center of your head.

If you can get enough of you to come back into the center of your head long enough, you can observe whatever is going on in your aura and begin to glimpse the fact that your experience is something you have, not something you are.

One might imagine that this "sense of yourself not lost in your experience" might be an alienated sense of yourself. In fact, knowing that you have your experience but are not your experience takes you more and more out of alienation and more and more into genuine heartfelt relationship with All That Is and all other beings.

This is something you may get glimpses of right away, or perhaps not for some time. But for everyone we know this is a practice that grows deeper year by year.

EXERCISE 63: Finding Your Intrinsic You

1. Breathe gently and deeply, and with openness be in the center of your head.
2. Explode your old grounding cord and male- or female-ground.
3. Ask yourself, "Where am I?" and wait a few moments to get a deeper sense of where "you" and other parts of you are.
4. Measure the distance between this you, wherever it is, and the center of your head and allow yourself to coalesce back into the center of your head.
5. Notice that you can have your sensations, emotions, and thoughts without becoming them; that you are augmented but not limited by your experience.
6. Rest in your intrinsic you-ness.
7. When through, create and destroy roses for any pictures that lit up, and recycle the energy from your pictures back through your crown.
8. Explode your old grounding cord and male- or female-ground.
9. Replenish your body and aura with golden cosmic energy.
10. Bring up just the right amount of earth energy for your body and aura at this time.
11. Thank your body for being willing to change and grow.
12. Breathe gently and deeply, stand up, stretch, and reverse polarities.

13. You may find it useful to make some notes of your experience.

EXERCISE 64: Finding Meaning—Observe the Same Event from Two
Perspectives

A sense of meaning allows you to tap into deep healing and joyful energies. Please take a moment to remember an experience that was deeply
meaningful to you. Notice how effortlessly and instantaneously it takes
you to a calmer, more secure space tinged with a joy that rises from
beneath the level of your personal self, while also supporting it. A sense
that all experience has meaning brings you into direct contact with the
infinite support of the universe.

In the following exercise use your imagination to look at the same
external event from two different perspectives: first meaningless, then
meaning-filled. For example, say you've argued with a loved one, made
no progress, and are angry, frustrated, and scared. First, view the experience as meaningless and see how you feel. Then reevaluate it from the
perspective that you can use the experience to learn how to become a
better listener or more grounded, and more resourceful in such moments.
Imagine, for example, that you can more skillfully model to your child
how to respond to such frustrating interactions.

1. Breathe gently and deeply, and with openness be in the center of
   your head.
2. Explode your old grounding cord and male- or female-ground.
3. Imagine or remember an argument with your son, daughter, or
   other loved one, where you made no progress and were angry,
   frustrated, and scared.
4. View that whole experience as meaningless and see how you feel.
5. Then reevaluate your experience, telling yourself that you can use
   it for self-reflection and growth, and that you can model to your
   son, daughter, or loved one how to respond to the earlier frustrating interactions.
6. When through, create and destroy roses for any pictures that lit
   up, and recycle the energy from your pictures back through your
   crown.

7. Explode your old grounding cord and male- or female-ground.
8. Replenish your body and aura with golden cosmic energy.
9. Bring up just the right amount of earth energy for your body and aura at this time.
10. Thank your body for being willing to change and grow.
11. Breathe gently and deeply, stand up, stretch, and reverse polarities.
12. You may find it useful to make some notes of your experience.

EXERCISE 65: Brainstorming with Someone You Trust to Find Meaning in an Event

When you cannot find meaning in a situation, call on a trusted friend or loved one to give you another perspective, and together brainstorm about the event that stymies you.

1. Breathe gently and deeply, and with openness be in the center of your head.
2. Explode your old grounding cord and male- or female-ground.
3. Brainstorm with a partner about how to find meaning in an event that stymies you.
4. As you listen deeply and consider their point of view, explode the pictures that will light up and pay attention to your boundaries.
5. Thank him or her for helping you explore the possible meaning of the issue with you.
6. When through, create and destroy roses for the pictures that lit up, and recycle the energy back through your crown.
7. Explode your old grounding cord and male- or female-ground.
8. Replenish your body and aura with golden cosmic energy.
9. Bring up just the right amount of earth energy for your body and aura at this time.
10. Thank your body for being willing to change and grow.
11. Breathe gently and deeply, stand up, stretch, and reverse polarities.
12. You may find it useful to make some notes of your experience.

Finding the Larger Context of Experience

Even if you are not in touch with it, the meaning of your experience arises in the Buddhic Plane (the Theosophical plane found just above your individual soul), bubbling up eternally as a resource for you. Your experience of meaning will probably be quite subtle at first, more like having beautiful music on in the background while dining. You don't have to listen intently to be soothed and nourished by its melody. As you find meaning more clearly the experience becomes more like tuning into an underlying message of calm, "everything is okay and meaningful," rather than a "knock your socks off" kind of phenomenon. Sooner or later, you will begin to see everything that happens to you from this point of view. You may not like it all, but you will subtly know that everything is okay and that there is purpose and even liberation in whatever you are experiencing.

This higher order of meaning, where things can't help but be meaningful, where meaning is just another way of looking at joy and is always and already present, can most easily be engaged in a transition state between your personal self and larger aspects of yourself. This space can be found roughly three inches above your head, above the crown; and it's where you can make a shift between your personal self and larger aspects of yourself. As you learn to perceive that space you can begin to have fun playing with it.

EXERCISE 66: Finding Your Meaning Space About Three Inches
Above Your Crown

In the following exercise you'll find and explore your meaning space; then, to help you hone in on those energies even more, you'll compare and contrast those energies with the energy you find by moving an inch above and an inch below.

It is a subtle energy, so if you feel you do not find it right away just come back to this exercise in a month or six months, or even a year from now.

1. Breathe gently and deeply, and with openness be in the center of your head.
2. Explode your old grounding cord and male- or female-ground.
3. Allow your awareness to rise up into your crown, and then move about 3 inches above your crown to your meaning space.
4. In that space, find an energy that is yours, an energy that, like a lullaby, assures you that all is well.
5. Continuing to observe carefully, see if you can find its infinite resiliency, an unceasing expansion in all directions.
6. When ready, allow your awareness to rise to a space about an inch higher (about 4 inches above the head) and compare and contrast the energy there with your meaning space.
7. Then move back to your meaning space, about 3 inches above your crown, and reacquaint yourself with your energy.
8. Allow your awareness to move downward an inch (to about 2 inches above your head), and compare and contrast the energy there with your meaning space.
9. Finally, move back into your meaning space and again find the energy that is you—an energy of infinite resiliency, expanding in all directions, which like a lullaby assures you that all is well.
10. When through, create and destroy roses for any pictures that lit up, and recycle the energy back through your crown.
11. Explode your old grounding cord and male- or female-ground.
12. Come fully back into your body and the center of your head.
13. Replenish your body and aura with golden cosmic energy.
14. Bring up just the right amount of earth energy for your body and aura at this time.
15. Thank your body for being willing to change and grow.
16. Breathe gently and deeply, stand up, stretch, and reverse polarities.
17. You may find it useful to make some notes of your experience.

EXERCISE 67: Finding an Event's Essential Meaningfulness

For the following exercise, choose an experience that you haven't come to terms with yet, in any range of emotional intensity, from something mildly unpleasant to something really awful. Then centering your awareness in the meaning space (see exercise above) about three inches above your crown, observe the experience and try to place it in a larger context. Look for its essential meaningfulness.

1. Breathe gently and deeply, and with openness be in the center of your head.
2. Explode your old grounding cord and male- or female-ground.
3. Create a rose for your experience.
4. Allow your awareness to rise up into your meaning space about 3 inches above your crown and find an energy that is yours, an energy like a lullaby assuring you that all is well.
5. From that space look at your experience. See it in its larger context. It may be good, it may be horrible, but search out the essential meaningfulness.
6. Looking further, see if you can find your energy's infinite resiliency, an unceasing expansion in all directions.
7. When through, bring your awareness back into the center of your head.
8. Create and destroy roses for any pictures that lit up, and recycle the energy back through your crown.
9. Explode your old grounding cord and male- or female-ground.
10. Come fully back into your body and the center of your head.
11. Replenish your body and aura with golden cosmic energy.
12. Bring up just the right amount of earth energy for your body and aura at this time.
13. Thank your body for being willing to change and grow.
14. Breathe gently and deeply, stand up, stretch, and reverse polarities.
15. You may find it useful to make some notes of your experience.

EXERCISE 68: Finding Happiness Through Meaning

When you get in touch with meaning it takes you to the level of happiness. In other words, when you find meaning you'll find reliable happiness.

1. Breathe gently and deeply, and with openness be in the center of your head.
2. Explode your old grounding cord and male- or female-ground.
3. Allow your awareness to rise up into your meaning space, about 3 inches above your crown.
4. Find the larger-context space; an infinite resiliency, an unceasing expansion in all directions. Rest there for a while. Like a lullaby, this expansive space assures you that all is well.
5. Next, from the meaning space, allow yourself to sink down into a space of happiness. Rest in the happiness space.
6. When through, create and destroy roses for any pictures that lit up, and recycle the energy back through your crown.
7. Explode your old grounding cord and male- or female-ground.
8. Come fully back into your body and the center of your head.
9. Replenish your body and aura with golden cosmic energy.
10. Bring up just the right amount of earth energy for your body and aura at this time.
11. Thank your body for being willing to change and grow.
12. Breathe gently and deeply, stand up, stretch, and reverse polarities.
13. You may find it useful to make some notes of your experience.

Everything Is Full of Meaning

Because everything is full of meaning, we never throw away any part of our experience, even so-called negative emotions. While we often add emotions, we never substitute one emotion for another. In fact, skillfully navigating so-called negative emotions generates enormous spiritual freedom.

Meaning is not contained within any single consciousness but in the interaction between consciousnesses. All That Is has no meaning in it and breaks itself into pieces in order to create meaning.

All your life has meaning because none of it really stays on the "inside" of you. Life will invariably involve heartache. The people who learn and grow, who make it through the best, are the ones who can perceive the dried bones of their hopes and dreams and break those bones apart to seeing what lies within. What beliefs of their own, what limitations, what pains in their own space triggered that trauma? Just break the bones of that disappointment apart and find the marrow, the sustenance that arises out of that. Tear apart the structure of the disappointment to find the core issues, the hidden core issues.

As human beings we are gathering life experience. Experience becomes psychic information that ultimately is energized meaning. Experience becomes meaning when you assimilate it, when you stop resisting it. To some extent a purpose of your life is to generate enough experience, information, and meaning that you are prepared to move on to what's next. Of course, that's one side of a polarity. It's just as much your purpose to generate meaning in current time. Your life has meaning both in the present and for the future, just as your relationship with a child involves both present goals and future goals. You want the child to be happy now. You want their life to be interesting and meaningful now. It's also important to be training them for adulthood. There is a dynamic interplay. Sometimes you focus more on one and sometimes on the other.

Lewis Bostwick used to say, "If you aren't enjoying what you are doing, enjoy *not* enjoying it." The story that follows is a courageous example. Jackson, who was in his sixties, was shocked when his wife of many years informed him that she wanted to separate and might want a divorce. Understanding the futility of blame, he spent very little time trying to figure out who was at fault. Crushed, he decided to learn everything he could about communication and the value of boundaries. Within a few months his growth was obvious, and within eight months he was calm, grounded, with an easy kindness and generosity. He and his wife weren't back together, but they were interacting and communicating better than ever, and spending more time together. As he mused on how quickly he was growing, and how he developed boundaries that he hadn't known he needed, he said that as agonizing as it was, he'd never been happier.

Part Three

Practical Wisdom

A ll the chapters in Part Three address various kinds of conversations—conversations with yourself, with others and with the world,
or conversation stoppers, one of the latter being rigidity. Rigidity comes
from grasping onto or freezing what you think you know. There's a difference between committing to action based upon your current evaluation, and grasping at a course of action with so much unacknowledged
fear that you lose the ability to take in new information. Another conversation stopper is opting out of a conversation altogether and seeking
to impose your will on the world. There's a difference between vigorously
pursuing your desires with clear boundaries and unconditional respect
for others in the world, and subtly though unilaterally trying to impose
what you think is right. By engaging life as a conversation rather than
pursuing the fantasy of unilaterally commanding life, you develop the
capacity for happiness, joy, and meaning.

By "practical wisdom," we refer to the ability to engage skillfully with
everyday life. Most of the skills addressed in this part involve interactions
for which there is no one right answer. We are learning how to handle
for ourselves ambiguity, ambivalence, contradiction, and the process of
always transforming from one thing to another. We're learning to engage
in conversations with others without objectifying them. In fact, most of
the skills in this part are facilitated by intentionally shifting from trying
to figure out who or what's right to trying to understand all the points
of view. Then decide what you want and proceed with kindness, generosity, authenticity, and skill.

Part Three

Practical Wisdom

CHAPTER 21

Internal Awareness: A Bridge to Change

Becoming Aware in Current Time

In your everyday awareness you keep track of what is going on. You might be mostly focused on what is going on outside you, or maybe inside you, or you might have a balance of the two. In this chapter you will turn your everyday awareness inwards in order to expand and deepen what we will call your *internal awareness*. Your internal awareness is the focus you use to track your sensations, emotions, and thoughts. Also, your internal awareness is how you begin noticing the effects on your aura of momentary experiences like being in a hurry or relaxing and eating a pleasant meal.

Remember that specific sensations, feelings, and thoughts are directly connected to specific energies in your aura, and every energy in your aura is directly connected to what you sense, feel, and think. The next couple of chapters discuss how to become aware of what your sensations, emotions, and thoughts are. Then, by working with them, you can change your aura. You will also use your internal awareness to begin noticing how your aura changes. Your aura is somewhat like your face—it retains its basic character even while showing moment-to-moment changes. Your aura's changes depend upon your sensations, emotions, and thoughts.

In the rest of the chapters you will often be using your skill of internal awareness to change yourself. Then you can respond to events like becoming angry with more openness and authenticity.

EXERCISE 69: Noticing Your Breathing, Sensations, Emotions, and Thoughts in Current Time

The next two exercises may hardly seem like exercises at all, but they will help you build the foundation for deepening your internal awareness. Please acknowledge and accept the information you perceive, no matter how subtle.

1. From the center of your head, male- or female-ground.
2. For the moment turn your awareness inward and notice your breathing: its ease, depth, speed, and fluidity. Feel your body's sensations.
3. Please take a few moments to notice your emotions. Can you notice several emotions at once? Do your emotions change rapidly or slowly? Where in your body do you feel your emotions? See if you can feel your emotions out in your aura.
4. Now gently move to your thoughts. Are they moving rapidly or slowly, in harmony or not? Do you agree with the thoughts that are flowing through your mind? As an advanced question, can you identify whose thoughts they are, whose energy composes your thoughts?
5. When through, explode pictures and recycle the energy from your pictures back into your crown.
6. Explode your old grounding cord and male- or female-ground.
7. Replenish your body and aura with golden cosmic energy.
8. Bring up just the right amount of earth energy for your body and aura at this time.
9. Thank your body for being willing to change and grow.
10. Breathe gently and deeply, stand up, stretch, and reverse polarities.
11. You may find it useful to make some notes of your experience.

EXERCISE 70: Becoming Aware of Your Energy Field in Current Time

1. From the center of your head, male- or female-ground.
2. For the moment, stop and become aware of your energy field, your aura.

3. Some questions you can ask yourself: How is my grounding? Where are the edges of my aura? Is the energy pleasant or unpleasant? Where is the energy free to flow and where is it obstructed? Are any pictures, cords, or energies that are not mine lit up? What color is my crown? What are my chakras doing— are some open more or less than is comfortable?
4. Please acknowledge and accept the information you perceive.
5. When through, explode pictures and recycle the energy from your pictures back into your crown.
6. Explode your old grounding cord and male- or female-ground.
7. Replenish your body and aura with golden cosmic energy.
8. Bring up just the right amount of earth energy for your body and aura at this time.
9. Thank your body for being willing to change and grow.
10. Breathe gently and deeply, stand up, stretch, and reverse polarities.
11. You may find it useful to makes some notes of your experience.

Becoming Aware in Past Time

For each of the next three exercises, please do the exercise first for your sensations, emotions, and thoughts; and then (or in another practice session) repeat the exercise for your aura. If internal awareness comes easily to you, then try combining the two exercises, simultaneously cultivating awareness of sensations, emotions, and thoughts with your aura awareness. You may find it helpful to write down your experience.

EXERCISE 71: Reconnecting with Your Past Thoughts, Feelings, and Sensations from Today
1. From the center of your head, male- or female-ground.
2. Imagine going back to a moment, interaction, or event earlier in your day and reconnect with your attendant thoughts, feelings, and sensations. [Second time through: aura and chakras]
3. When through, explode pictures and recycle the energy from your pictures back into your crown.

4. Explode your old grounding cord and male- or female-ground.
5. Replenish your body and aura with golden cosmic energy.
6. Bring up just the right amount of earth energy for your body and aura at this time.
7. Thank your body for being willing to change and grow.
8. Breathe gently and deeply, stand up, stretch, and reverse polarities.
9. You may find it useful to makes some notes of your experience.

EXERCISE 72: Reconnecting with Your Thoughts, Feelings, and Sensations from Your Distant Past

1. From the center of your head, male- or female-ground.
2. With a sense of adventure, imagine going back to a moment, interaction, or event earlier in your life and reconnect with your attendant thoughts, feelings, and sensations. [Second time: aura and chakras]
3. When through, explode pictures and recycle the energy from your pictures back into your crown.
4. Explode your old grounding cord and male- or female-ground.
5. Replenish your body and aura with golden cosmic energy.
6. Bring up just the right amount of earth energy for your body and aura at this time.
7. Thank your body for being willing to change and grow.
8. Breathe gently and deeply, stand up, stretch, and reverse polarities.
9. You may find it useful to makes some notes of your experience.

EXERCISE 73: Reconnecting with Your Thoughts, Feelings, and Sensations from Various Times in Your Life

For the following exercise, there's nothing magical about the time periods chosen. The object is to learn to use different kinds of time periods.

1. From the center of your head, male- or female-ground.
2. With a sense of adventure, imagine going back approximately 10 minutes ago. Recall an event or moment, and reconnect with your

related thoughts, feelings, and sensations. [Second time: aura and chakra]

3. Imagine going back approximately 10 hours ago to recall an event or moment, and reconnect with your thoughts, feelings, and sensations.

4. Imagine going back 10 days ago to recall an event or moment, and reconnect with your thoughts, feelings, and sensations.

5. Imagine going back 10 weeks ago to recall an event or moment, and reconnect with your thoughts, feelings, and sensations.

6. Imagine going back 10 years ago to recall an event or moment, and reconnect with your thoughts, feelings, and sensations.

7. When through, explode pictures and recycle the energy from your pictures back into your crown.

8. Explode your old grounding cord and male- or female-ground.

9. Replenish your body and aura with golden cosmic energy.

10. Bring up just the right amount of earth energy for your body and aura at this time.

11. Thank your body for being willing to change and grow.

12. Breathe gently and deeply, stand up, stretch, and reverse polarities.

13. You may find it useful to makes some notes of your experience.

Monitoring Your Whole Aura: A Core Skill

In earlier exercises when you opened a chakra, your goal was to feel the energy of the chakra; all your attention was focused narrowly on that chakra. In the following exercise you'll open your third chakra and not only focus your awareness there, but also practice expanding your perception to track the changes that occur simultaneously throughout your whole aura. Of course, in some respects you've been doing this all along, but now you'll begin to refine and utilize your growing awareness.

Developing this ability to pay attention to the particular while also attending to the whole will promote your ability to use these tools to make real-life changes and, ultimately, to use these tools as you go through your day.

EXERCISE 74: Observing Your Aura's Response to Making One Change

In this exercise you'll open your third chakra and see if you can notice two or more changes that automatically and simultaneously take place in your aura. Does it affect the boundary of your aura? If so, how? Does it affect your mood? How does your body respond? Does it lessen your stress level? Does it affect your grounding? Do you feel more empowered? Acknowledge all that you notice.

1. From the center of your head, male- or female-ground.
2. Bring your crown to gold and without judging simply become aware of your body and aura.
3. Next, open your third chakra as far as it will open comfortably and simply observe how your body and aura respond. Did any of the other chakras change when you opened your third chakra? How did your body feel? What happened to the size and shape of the aura?
4. After that, please do the opposite: Close your third chakra down as far as you can and again without judging simply notice any changes. How did your third chakra feel when it was closed down? Did any of the other chakras change when you closed your third chakra? How did your body feel? What happened to the size and shape of the aura?
5. When satisfied with your observations, open your third chakra back to 50% if you are male and 75% if you are female.
6. When through, explode pictures and recycle the energy from your pictures back into your crown.
7. Explode your old grounding cord and male- or female-ground.
8. Replenish your body and aura with golden cosmic energy.
9. Bring up just the right amount of earth energy for your body and aura at this time.
10. Thank your body for being willing to change and grow.
11. Breathe gently and deeply, stand up, stretch, and reverse polarities.
12. You may find it useful to makes some notes of your experience.

Perhaps the next time you practice this exercise you could work with your first chakra. Ideally over time you will explore changing all the chakras in different combinations, perhaps using different amounts of earth and cosmic energy. Your increasing awareness of what your aura is doing and how different portions of your aura affect one another will help you begin to notice and attend to these kinds of changes as they spontaneously occur during the day.

EXERCISE 75: Observing the Effect of Anxiety on Your Aura

If the opportunity presents itself, the next time you are feeling anxious, explore it. Instead of trying to get over being anxious right away, take the time to explore how the emotion affects your chakras and aura, as well as your breathing and other emotions. When you are not feeling anxious it is a good opportunity to put yourself back into a time of feeling anxious and observing those shifts. You can, of course, explore any emotion in this manner, such as anger or grief. In the following exercise you will practice first being ungrounded while anxious. Then re-explore your aura's response to anxiety when you are grounded. Initially, you may not notice much overall change in response to the specific changes you make to your grounding, etc., but with time this practice will help you develop ongoing aura awareness.

1. Drop your grounding cord and remain ungrounded for the first portion of this exercise.
2. Without judging, become aware of an anxiety and let it be what it is.
3. Please note the impact your anxiety has on your breathing, emotions, sensations, and thoughts.
4. Then note the impact your anxiety has on your chakras and aura.
5. Practice grounding and breaking your grounding several times and explore the effects.
6. Then remain grounded, and with a sense of adventure, bring different colors of cosmic energy into your aura and see how that shifts your response to your anxiety.
7. See what happens when you change the size of different chakras.

8. When through, explode pictures and recycle the energy from your pictures back into your crown.
9. Explode your old grounding cord and male- or female-ground.
10. Replenish your body and aura with golden cosmic energy.
11. Bring up just the right amount of earth energy for your body and aura at this time.
12. Thank your body for being willing to change and grow.
13. Breathe gently and deeply, stand up, stretch, and reverse polarities.
14. You may find it useful to makes some notes of your experience.

Becoming Aware of How Your Aura Changes in Specific Situations

The following exercises focus on becoming aware of how your aura changes in specific situations. You can use the ability to return mentally to an event in order to explore any specific issue or event in any time period.

EXERCISE 76: Pure Imagination—Be Angry About the Weather

1. From the center of your head, male- or female-ground.
2. Using solely your imagination, choose a time (in current time, or in the past or future) and imagine what it would feel like to be angry about the weather. As you feel the anger that you have created in your imagination, what are your thoughts, feelings, and sensations? What is your aura doing? Ask yourself questions such as: Have I lost my grounding? Do cords light up in my first chakra, third chakra, liver, etc.? Be curious and explore your aura.
3. When through, explode pictures and recycle the energy from your pictures back into your crown.
4. Explode your old grounding cord and male- or female-ground.
5. Replenish your body and aura with golden cosmic energy.
6. Bring up just the right amount of earth energy for your body and aura at this time.
7. Thank your body for being willing to change and grow.

8. Breathe gently and deeply, stand up, stretch, and reverse polarities.
9. You may find it useful to makes some notes of your experience.

At some point in your psychic development when you're engaged in your internal awareness and looking at an energy, an image of the person who taught, trained, or modeled the behavior for you around this issue, belief, or energy that you're looking at will come to your mind, sometimes clearly and sometimes very subtly. It will most often be a parent or early authority figure, who tend to train you in one world view and then as you move towards adulthood you become increasingly active in transforming that world view to better fit your needs and experience.

If you turn your attention to that image and explode your matching pictures and clear your energy enmeshments with that person, you will achieve excellent clearing. You don't need to clear everything between you and that person. The image that comes up will be from one particular time or style, and since it's the image that you became aware of for this particular clearing, addressing the particular issues that this image lights up is exactly the correct focus of the clearing.

EXERCISE 77: Imagining How Someone Would Respond and Your Own Internal Response

Part of your internal awareness is your ability to imagine how another person would behave in any given situation. Society would be impossible if we had no ability to imagine how another person will or would behave in a theoretical situation. Specifically, it is important to be able to imagine how another person would behave in response to different actions you could take. In recent decades scientists have found the part of the brain where this creative imagination takes place. Those cells in the front of the brain are called *mirror neurons.*

In the following exercise you will use your ability to try out different hypothetical actions and imagine how someone you know would respond. What you'll add (which you might not ordinarily do) is using your internal awareness to notice also what the effect would be on your own energy—noticing your breathing, grounding, sensations, emotions, and thoughts, and your aura in general, as you perform the imaginary action. Thus you will imagine two responses: the other person's response to your action, and then your energy's response to what you believe would be the other person's reaction to you. First you'll explore smiling at a loved one, then three levels of anger: ungrounded anger, blaming anger, and anger with a commitment to having a mature conversation. As always, feel free to experiment.

1. From the center of your head, male- or female-ground.
2. From either a female-grounded or male-grounded space, imagine yourself smiling at a loved one, and imagine his or her response to your smile.
3. Then, with your internal awareness, notice your personal response to him or her: What happens to your own breathing, grounding, sensations, emotions, thoughts, and your aura in general as you smile while grounded?
4. Next, purposely break your grounding and once again imagine yourself smiling at a loved one, this time from an ungrounded space, and imagine his or her response to your smile.
5. Then, with your internal awareness, notice your personal response to him or her: Notice what happens to your own breathing, grounding, sensations, emotions, thoughts, and your aura in general as you smile at him or her while being ungrounded.
6. Breathe gently and deeply into your belly, explode pictures, and male- or female-ground.

Next you'll explore several kinds of anger in a similar process, the first one with your ungrounded anger.

7. Break your grounding and imagine yourself being angry at a loved one, and imagine his or her response to your ungrounded anger.
8. Then, with your internal awareness, notice your personal response to him or her: What happens to your own breathing, grounding, sensations, emotions, thoughts, and your aura in general when you are angry at him or her while ungrounded?

9. Breathe gently and deeply into your belly, explode pictures, and male- or female-ground.

Next you'll explore a blaming anger in a similar process.

10. Break your grounding and imagine yourself having a blaming anger towards someone. Imagine his or her response to your blaming anger.
11. Then, with your internal awareness, notice your personal response to him or her: What happens to your own breathing, grounding, sensations, emotions, thoughts, and your aura in general when you have blaming anger at him or her?
12. Breathe gently and deeply into your belly, explode pictures, and male- or female-ground.

Next explore being angry but committed to having a mature, difficult conversation.

13. Male- or female-ground, and imagine being angry with someone but committed to having a mature conversation. Imagine his or her response to your anger and your commitment to handling it maturely.
14. Then, with your internal awareness, notice your personal response to him or her: What happens to your own breathing, grounding, sensations, emotions, thoughts, and your aura in general when you are angry but committed to a mature conversation?
15. When through, explode pictures and recycle the energy from your pictures back into your crown.
16. Explode your old grounding cord and male- or female-ground.
17. Replenish your body and aura with golden cosmic energy.
18. Bring up just the right amount of earth energy for your body and aura at this time.
19. Thank your body for being willing to change and grow.
20. Breathe gently and deeply, stand up, stretch, and reverse polarities.
21. You may find it useful to makes some notes of your experience.

CHAPTER 22

Self-Talk and Stories:
Conversation vs. Commands

Part Three is devoted to moving into conversation with your world. An excellent place to start is with your *self-talk*. Often when people refer to self-talk they are referring to the kinds of punishing judgments that people repeat to themselves, often without noticing what they are saying. People engaging in that kind of self-talk usually are told to replace the negative self-talk with positive self-talk called *affirmations*. We do affirmations, though differently than others. We discuss our approach in Chapter 26, "Affirmation and Visualization." In this book we do not directly address the punishing, judgmental self-talk. We think most readers will already be actively letting go of that kind of self-talk.

We address the kind of self-talk highlighted by Albert Ellis involving musts, shoulds, have tos, and oughts. We encourage you to read one or more of Dr. Ellis's books, as he addresses these ideas more extensively than we can do here.[1] This kind of self-talk moves your aura focus out of a conversation mode and into a command mode. When you tell another person what they must, should, have to, or ought to do, you take on the mantle of objective truth. Usually the largest part of your awareness pops out of your aura and assumes an objective third-person stance, as if your statement weren't your personal preference but a law of nature. The same effect applies when you use that self-talk on yourself. You pop out of your aura and start ordering yourself around. The authors think that popping out and ordering yourself around will always utilize someone else's energy to turn what may be a good idea into an order. What, you may say, if I am objectively right?

As pointed out in the book *Difficult Conversations,* even when you are objectively right, it's still important to be able to understand what the other person is thinking or feeling. In psychic terms it's important to not just understand what the person is thinking or feeling, but to understand what their resistances are and to engage them in conversations so that you can explode your matching pictures. This also applies when the other person is you. When you order yourself around and try to coerce yourself into doing even what is objectively right, you override and overlook the sources of your resistance rather than addressing them, clearing the energy, and learning what there is to learn from your resistance.

Part of what the authors particularly like about Dr. Ellis's approach is that it allows you to experience all your emotions. When you learn to stop insisting that an external or internal event should be a certain way, for example, you still get to keep your disappointment that it isn't the way you want it to be. Moving away from the stance of objectivity to the one acknowledging that this is your personal preference (and you are willing to experience the world as it is) greatly facilitates your meeting the situation resourcefully.

EXERCISE 78: What Is Your Self-Talk Telling You?
1. From the center of your head, male- or female-ground.
2. Remember a situation when you were feeling angry, anxious, ashamed, or some such emotion.
3. Turn your inner awareness towards the area of your head around your ears and jaws (usually just behind your ears but often moving towards the temples).[2] Take your time and explore what you are saying to yourself about the situation. See if you can notice multiple levels of your self-talk. Though you may not actually use the words "should, have to, or ought," if you explore you'll usually find that a claim of objectivity is somewhere present in the stories you tell yourself.
4. When through, explode pictures and recycle the energy from your pictures back through your crown.
5. Explode your old grounding cord and male- or female-ground.
6. Replenish your body and aura with golden cosmic energy.

7. Bring up just the right amount of earth energy for your body and aura at this time.
8. Thank your body for being willing to change and grow.
9. Breathe gently and deeply, stand up, stretch, and reverse polarities.
10. You may find it useful to makes some notes of your experience.

EXERCISE 79: Exploring Your Self-Talk Regarding Parents or In-Laws

1. From the center of your head, male- or female-ground.
2. Remember a situation with your parents or in-laws where you felt disrespected and/or were feeling angry, anxious, ashamed, or some such emotion.
3. Turn your inner awareness towards the area of your head around your ears and jaws (usually just behind your ears but often moving towards the temples). Discern what you are saying to yourself about the situation. See if you can notice multiple levels of your self-talk. Though you may not actually use the words "should, have to, or ought," if you explore you'll usually find that a claim of objectivity is somewhere present in the stories you tell yourself.
4. When through, explode pictures and recycle the energy from your pictures back through your crown.
5. Explode your old grounding cord and male- or female-ground.
6. Replenish your body and aura with golden cosmic energy.
7. Bring up just the right amount of earth energy for your body and aura at this time.
8. Thank your body for being willing to change and grow.
9. Breathe gently and deeply, stand up, stretch, and reverse polarities.
10. You may find it useful to makes some notes of your experience.

Stories Are How We Tie Our Self-Talk Together

Stories are how we make sense of the world. Through stories it's possible to integrate pieces of self-talk into larger-scale systems of engaging the world, usually without noticing just what is happening. With shoulds, have tos, and oughts you can build self-defeating, though plausible, stories.

ESCALATION: CAROL AND BILL

Carol was angry. Her husband, Bill, was making important decisions affecting both of them without consulting her. Carol had made huge sacrifices in her own life and work to help him raise capital for a new business he had his heart set on, and was working part-time for Bill's new business to help it get off the ground.

She found it incomprehensible that Bill made several important business decisions without consulting her, and she complained passionately. He complained back that she wasn't available when the decisions had to be made and that he didn't understand why she didn't trust him to make that kind of decision anyway. Each felt entitled to get his or her own way, and each felt offended by the other's behavior.

Carol got angry and shared her distress with John, but she and John had no time to problem-solve. They talked a couple of times over the next week but continued to lack the time to problem-solve.

Each time they talked, Carol got angrier and angrier as her complaint slowly changed. What had started as a direct complaint about not being consulted steadily changed to a growing conviction that when Bill refused to consult her, he was showing that he didn't care about her feelings.

The next step in her story about Bill was that his not consulting her was just the kind of interaction style that put the whole world at risk. "People have to consult or talk with each other, or how are we ever going to have world peace?" Carol exclaimed to herself over and over.

With each repetition of her enhanced story, she became more angry and more frightened that the relationship would not last. Each time she told herself or others that Bill's behavior was just the kind of action that made world peace unattainable, the core portion of Carol's identity—which our system encourages people to place in the center of their head—floated further up and outside her aura. With her core floating outside her aura, Carol had less and less of a sense that her dispute with Bill was her own personal issue. More and more Carol was coming to believe that her dispute was really a matter of principle; and that even at the risk of her marriage, she had to stand up and demand that Bill consult with her. She felt compelled to stop behavior like Bill's, so injurious to women everywhere and to world peace. She had to stop it now.

It's surprising how often we all tell ourselves stories, leaving ourselves increasingly unable to listen to and engage another, and making ourselves more and more angry, sad, ashamed, or whatever other emotions render us less happy and effective. When Carol noticed how her story had been changing and how her psychic position had shifted from a personal experience to a sense that her story was an impersonal objective truth, she decided to stop and change. She stopped repeating that story to herself and started to consider her options. She figured out better ways to talk to her husband, to understand his motivations and help him understand what was important to her and why. A situation that had threatened to spin into a marital crisis became a trust-building exercise where each person had important interests and feelings. They had been operating without an understanding of the other person or even an inclination to learn how to understand the other person. Being careful with her self-talk was the key step for Carol's move to becoming more skillful.

Stories Organize the Energy Field of the Personal Aura

We wouldn't be capable of action as human beings without the stories we tell ourselves. Stories prepare the aura to operate as a gestalt, to function in an organized manner. The stories are a mental-plane energy that sets up an inner structure for the energies of the personal aura to coordinate taking action and interpreting and experiencing the consequences of action.

The stories you tell yourself are equivalent to the structure of your ego. A flexible ego utilizes its own stories and updates them smoothly and easily as it gains new experience. An inflexible ego holds onto its stories, unchanged by new experience.

Your stories are what Seth refers to when he says that you create your own reality according to your conscious beliefs. Stories organize the energy field of the personal aura, then become the template for your aura's vibration on all matters that story is relevant to.

What Happens to the Personal Aura When Someone, Gritting Their Teeth, Says, " I Am Loving, I Am Loving, I Am Loving ..."?

It might be a little confusing to use the word "stories" because the real phenomenon is not bound or governed by your ego's censored version of what's going on. The real story is a force that organizes the personal aura in a regime of color, intensity, quality, and interconnection. You can access these uncensored stories though careful openness to and examination of the organization of your aura. You can use any sense to explore your aura's self-organization. Your self-talk (or the stories you tell yourself) is perhaps the most accessible, but you can also feel or see the energies that your ego's story has censored, or even taste or smell them with your inner senses.

So, just because you call something "love" doesn't make it equivalent to what someone else calls love or even what you would call love if you saw it play out in real life. What matters is not the word but the energy of the word.

The very reason that life is a conversation is that many of your concepts will be misunderstood by you until you see them play out in your life. You may consider yourself very loving. The story you tell yourself may contain the word "love." But if the energy that flows when you think "love" contains a conviction that difficult interactions are terrible or horrible and that the only answer to difficult relationships is to find people who aren't difficult, then you will be alienated from a large percentage of the world. You will also be alienated from portions of your physical vitality because your vitality depends upon your access to all your emotions. You can't have access to all your emotions unless you can engage conflict when it arises. So, if constraining your relationships to people you find easy is the true energy associated in your aura with the word "love," then you will find yourself isolated from your own vitality at the energy level of the personal aura.

Two Kinds of Stories: Feeling Tone and Self-Talk

The duration of the effect on your aura of a story will differ, ranging from long-lasting, stable stories that form part of your master narrative to your moment-by-moment self-talk, but the "storytelling" itself is all part of the same process. Just because you can't "hear" yourself telling yourself these stories doesn't mean that you are not organizing your experience moment by moment according to these stories. These stories themselves form a structure throughout the fifth layer of the aura that both organizes your personal aura and feeds into larger networks of energy through which your personal experiences manifest. The narratives themselves are contained in the fifth layer of the aura, but you can access them from anywhere in your aura where you discover a piece of your energy that is being colored by the narrative. So, if you feel a tightening in your third chakra and closing down of your first chakra when you hear a politician make an argument you dislike, the narrative or story you are telling yourself might be that you must fight him or her or some disaster will happen. You could, however, learn to listen to these same ideas that you dislike with a comfortable first chakra and open third chakra, meaning that you had learned to engage in conversation and use this catalyst as a resource on matters you consider to be of great importance. You could still oppose the political position, but you would do so with a profound understanding of the collaboration of all life. Even someone in your life who denies the possibility of collaboration is presenting you with an opportunity to learn the deeper truth that all life is in collaboration with all other life, whether it seems to be the case or not, and to learn the practical skills to understand and work in the world taking unconditional responsibility for your actions.

Indulging Self-Righteousness for a Moment

John: "One day I found myself getting angrier and angrier at my wife. I kept telling myself that there was no excuse for what she had done (and now I can't even remember what it was). But I remember repeatedly thinking to myself that I was being really unskillful; and thinking I am so lost in this emotion I'm just going to indulge in the self-righteousness generated by my story that there was no excuse for what she had done. But even though I indulged in self-righteousness, my behavior never got as extreme as it would have had I not realized how foolish my self-talk was. And I apologized to her more quickly and more sincerely than I would have had I not known that the story I was telling myself was completely counterproductive.

"If that happened to me now I would use the strategy I knew about but didn't think

to use. I'd go as a point of light out of body, way far away so that I could look down on
the event, and more importantly look down on my body with its raging stress hormones.
That would allow me to not be run by those hormones and to use what I knew about
skillful stories. Then as I gained some neutrality outside my body I could explode pictures
and help my body calm down so that I could come back into it and stop being a jerk."

Stories Are the Gatekeeper

Stories are the sieve through which manifestation must flow. You might think of your whole personal reality as floating on an inner sea of infinite possibilities. Then you can think of your stories as the sieve or gatekeeper through which aspects of the world of infinite possibilities that are consistent with your stories bubble up into physical manifestation.

A clairvoyant can see this effect in someone's aura. When someone tells a story, that is, interprets events to themselves, they set their crown at the color of the overall theme of the story or interpretation; and that color and quality of energy ties together all the pictures, cords, and energies that are not yours, in your aura. Even your own energy that is tied with it takes on that color tint and quality so that a large mass of your aura vibrates collectively in an overall feeling tone. These feeling tones last as long as you accept the story or interpretation you're telling yourself (i.e., as long as you frame the experience with that color and quality or feeling tone). Since large portions of your aura are tied together with these feeling tones, they come to impart an overall quality to all your experience.

You can change a feeling tone either by clearing the energies that are held together or by changing the story that ties all the energies together. In fact, doing either of those will end up changing the overall energy, because changing your story will tend to explode your resistance; and clearing the resistance in your aura will free you from the story you've been telling yourself.

One of the exercises is to "reach around in your aura," whereby you turn your attention to your aura and see if you can experience portions of your aura that just naturally seem to vibrate and hang together. They will have a consistent feeling tone.

EXERCISE 80: Finding Feeling Tones

1. Breathe gently and deeply, and with openness be in the center of your head.
2. Explode your old grounding cord and male- or female-ground.
3. From the center of your head, look around in your aura and see if you can experience portions of your aura that naturally seem to vibrate and hang together.
4. When through, recycle the energy from your pictures back through your crown.
5. Explode your old grounding cord and male- or female-ground.
6. Replenish your body and aura with golden cosmic energy.
7. Bring up just the right amount of earth energy for your body and aura at this time.
8. Thank your body for being willing to change and grow.
9. Breathe gently and deeply, stand up, stretch, and reverse polarities.
10. You may find it useful to make some notes of your experience.

EXERCISE 81: Explore the Standard Interpretations You Believe About Life

The next exercise is to explore a kind of standard interpretation that you tend to accept and believe about life. For example, perhaps you believe that people are basically well intended, or that people are out to get what they want and you'd better watch out, or that there's so much pollution in the world right now that your health is really at risk, or if you are a mother you might think that your children's future depends on how happy they are as children. As you think of that story or interpretation, observe what portions of your aura light up. You might enjoy and/or benefit from exploring several of your interpretations or stories that you tend to believe.

1. Breathe gently and deeply, and with openness be in the center of your head.
2. Explode your old grounding cord and male- or female-ground.

3. From the center of your head, contemplate one of your standard interpretations that you tend to believe about life.
4. As you contemplate your story or interpretation, observe what portions of your aura light up.
5. When through, explode the pictures that lit up and recycle the energy back through your crown.
6. Explode your old grounding cord and male- or female-ground.
7. Replenish your body and aura with golden cosmic energy.
8. Bring up just the right amount of earth energy for your body and aura at this time.
9. Thank your body for being willing to change and grow.
10. Breathe gently and deeply, stand up, stretch, and reverse polarities.
11. You may find it useful to make some notes of your experience.

EXERCISE 82: Exploring and Changing Your Inner Landscape

The third exercise in this series is to imagine that you have an inner landscape. (This one comes from Seth.) Let an image of your inner landscape show up in your mind's eye and then notice if there are portions of it that you might like to adjust. Notice where there are any dark areas, ugly areas, and pretty areas; notice how your inner landscape feels or sounds throughout the whole of it, and throughout specific parts. Just notice your inner landscape and then decide if there are some pieces of it that you might like to change. For example, if there's an ugly mountain in your landscape you might want to replace it with a different kind of mountain, or you can try putting in a lake. Another method is to imagine your inner landscape and simply explode pictures until your inner landscape is more to your liking.

1. Breathe gently and deeply, and with openness be in the center of your head.
2. Explode your old grounding cord and male- or female-ground.
3. From the center of your head allow an image of your inner landscape to arise in your mind's eye, then notice if there are portions

of it that seem too dark, or too light, too jagged, or unpleasant in any way, and take a few moments to just observe.

4. Decide if there's some portions of your inner landscape that you would like to change.

5. Choose how you would like to make the changes. You could simply make the change in the landscape like a painter, brushing in your preferred colors or shapes, or explode pictures as you observe the landscape change until the result is more to your liking. Or you might choose to use both techniques.

6. When through, recycle the energy from your pictures back through your crown.

7. Explode your old grounding cord and male- or female-ground.

8. Replenish your body and aura with golden cosmic energy.

9. Bring up just the right amount of earth energy for your body and aura at this time.

10. Thank your body for being willing to change and grow.

11. Breathe gently and deeply, stand up, stretch, and reverse polarities.

12. You may find it useful to make some notes of your experience.

CHAPTER 23

Anger

Gloria: "In 1993 John was channeling his guide to me. The guide, with an energy that was very kind, told me that there was an emotional closet I was about to open. He didn't want me to be too surprised, but the closet was going to be full of many, many pockets of anger....

"At the time that was hard to imagine, since I didn't think I had much anger. I wasn't an angry person. I didn't hold grudges. For the most part, people seemed to like me.... Well, I did find those pockets, and despite his kind warning, I was both shocked and forever grateful. Over the years I have worked through lifetimes of hidden anger, and clearing still-hidden pockets of anger continues to be unimaginably freeing."

Becoming Skillful with Anger

Working skillfully with anger is one of the best ways to develop practical wisdom. Because anger is such a fierce emotion, learning to respond to your own and others' anger teaches you to engage conflicting emotions, energies, and situations with skill, authenticity, kindness, and generosity. Skillfully addressing anger generates deep self-awareness, with an improved flow of energy throughout the aura. In this way anger energizes you to take effective action, to understand yourself and the other. Skill with anger leads to improved, more intimate relationships.

Unfortunately, it can be difficult to address anger skillfully. In fact, many spiritual systems seek to transcend anger altogether, and we can reduce the logic to three reasons: First, people seek to transcend anger because they can see how destructively most people respond to anger. Most people engage in battle as opposed to skillful opposition with the ones they blame for their anger; or they respond to their anger by manipulating or blocking relationships; or they turn it inwards and attack themselves; or a combination of these responses and more. There is a difference between your having an emotion and the behavioral response you have to that emotion.[1] You can be angry and yell, scream and blame; or you can be angry and use the energy of that anger to move you skillfully through difficult conversations and actions. With study, anger can be engaged constructively, improving understanding and relationships.

Second, many traditions urge people to transcend their humanity by becoming perfectly and solely identified with unity, to have no personal self. The sole identification with unity can be accomplished subjectively by flooding your personal aura with white light, blotting out all experience of personal preferences. The price of this sole identification is loss of any personal identity. Our teachers hold all levels of consciousness sacred. They deem it the purpose of humans to embrace their humanity through their personal aura, and consequently they recommend against transcending the personal.

Third, and perhaps most compelling, people seek to transcend anger because they assert that all anger arises from ignorance. The authors agree that all anger arises from ignorance. However, transcending anger can only make sense if you believe that anger and the ignorance that triggers it can be totally eliminated from the personality.

Looking at the aura mechanics of anger shows that it cannot entirely be eliminated as long as you are in touch with your personal preferences. Anger is your natural, biological/psychological response to your aura's sudden collapse. You are meant, as part of your life experience, to explore your energy, beliefs, and desires through your aura. This exploration requires that your aura have sufficient space to hold your experience. A collapsed aura is not an effective aura.

Your aura collapses whenever your current sense of personal identity is threatened. A natural system is in place to prod you to explore just what is occurring whenever your aura collapses. Energy floods through your "action and understanding" chakra, your third chakra. The energy both re-inflates your aura and prods you to develop new understandings about yourself and others. The energy further prods you to take action based on those new understandings. When you are unskillful with anger, your action will involve skipping the development of new understanding and relying solely on polarities such as repressing your anger, attacking others, or transcending your anger. These polarities are unskillful uses of the energy the third chakra provides.

More on the Mechanics of Anger

As mentioned above, anger occurs whenever the boundaries of your personal aura collapse. Normally several energies, including some of your pictures, operate in sync with your third chakra to maintain the boundaries of your aura. What we metaphorically refer to as a person's "boundaries" are reflected in the actual boundaries of the aura, in the actual location in space of the edge of a person's aura. There are two triggers for the collapse of boundaries: a genuine threat to your biological safety, and any threat to your self-concepts around boundaries. The first trigger, a primordial threat to your safety, will generate a kind of anger that is not problematic in itself and consequently not something we will discuss further except to say that this kind of anger can become enmeshed with our self-concepts, with the second kind of anger. You can address that enmeshment by addressing the relevant self-concepts and the issue(s) those self-concepts raise.

It's the second trigger, a threat to your self-concepts, that this chapter addresses. Those portions of your self-concepts that can be threatened will be held in your aura as pictures. If those pictures are made to wobble, you will feel irritated. If the self-concept pictures are so disrupted that they stop (at least for the moment) interacting with your third chakra to maintain your aura boundaries, your aura will collapse and energy will flood your third chakra to re-inflate your aura and prod you into gaining understanding and taking action. It's up to you whether the action you take is skillful or not. That third-chakra energy prodding you into understanding and action will direct your body to produce stress hormones and adrenaline. A cloud of psychic energy that we identify as anger will fill portions of your aura and even jump out into other people's space. This angry psychic energy is made of the pictures and energies that compose your response to the original aura collapse. The cloud of angry energy can become long-lasting and can even build into a relatively permanent pattern of anger in your aura. You can be unaware, at an ego level, of your anger clouds or similar "negative" emotions. You might even cover them up with energies of love or rationality or some other defense. Relatively permanent energy patterns of anger or other insufficiently addressed emotions will affect your attitude, health, and reality creation until you change your self-concepts either intentionally or through spontaneous growth.

You might wonder if it is possible to explode all limited self-concept pictures so that you have no vulnerability to a collapsing aura. We know an advanced meditator who felt that she had risen entirely above anger. She went into business and got so angry with her partner that she threw her shoe at the wall, breaking through the drywall. She only rose above anger when she filled her aura with the white light of impersonality, and when she wanted to get in touch with her personal emotions and desires she found that anger had been there all the time, hiding under the white light. Stories like this are common. Our guides say that it is not possible to remove anger entirely from your personal aura. Since all consciousness expands in all directions, your self-concepts will always be growing, encompassing new territory moment by moment. All self-concepts eventually become limiting. No matter how flexible and encompassing your ego, it always functions in human dimensions by sorting through desires and generating unique perspectives on your life as a human. The very purpose of the ego and the intrinsic impermanence of human experience guarantee that there will always be unexploded pictures in every area of your life—experiences at the edges of your identity that you are in the process of engaging, understanding, and assimilating. Consequently, to ignore or cover up anger under tremendous energies of love or some other transcendental energy is to miss opportunities for the cultivation of your unique self and the subtle, divine, eternal energies that derive from authentically engaging your humanity.

So if you can't completely rid yourself of anger, how can you authentically handle your anger when it arises? We use a three-step process. First, we acknowledge to ourselves that we are angry, and try to give the emotion its full natural space while retaining our seniority. Second, we act as maturely and resourcefully as we are able in the moment. Finally, we look back on our anger later, and use psychic tools and explore our self-talk to clear any particular pictures and limited understandings that generated the anger in the first place. That first step is the subject of Chapter 9 on space. The second step is addressed in Chapter 9's section on seniority; in Chapter 18, "Matching Pictures and Unconditional Responsibility"; and in Chapter 25, "Difficult Conversations." The third step is addressed here.

EXERCISE 83: Breaking Your Grounding to Explore
Ungrounded Anger

In the following exercise you will imagine being angry or you will look at a time when you actually were angry, and deliberately be ungrounded. Then ground.

1. Breathe gently and deeply, and with openness be in the center of your head.
2. Explode your old grounding cord and *remain ungrounded.*
3. Remember or imagine an event when you were very angry, and let the energy build.
4. Notice your various sensory and emotional responses to the event.
5. From the center of your head, male- or female-ground and observe the event from this more resourceful space.
6. Repeat the process if you'd like.
7. When through, create and destroy roses, then recycle the energy from your pictures back through your crown.
8. Explode your old grounding cord and male- or female-ground.
9. Replenish your body and aura with golden cosmic energy.
10. Bring up just the right amount of earth energy for your body and aura at this time.
11. Thank your body for being willing to change and grow.
12. Breathe gently and deeply, stand up, stretch, and reverse polarities.
13. You may find it useful to make some notes of your experience.

EXERCISE 84: Exploring Second-Chakra Enmeshment and Anger

For the following exercise you will recall someone with whom you are now or have been angry with in the past. Pay particular attention to any second-chakra enmeshment. Then pull your energy out of the other person's space and look again.

1. Breathe gently and deeply, and with openness be in the center of your head.
2. Explode your old grounding cord and male- or female-ground.
3. Recall someone with whom you are very angry now or have been in the past, and let his or her energy go out onto a rose.
4. Notice your various sensory and emotional responses to him or her, especially your second-chakra enmeshment. See if you can perceive a concentration of pictures and/or cords, and/or energies that are not yours.
5. Breathe your energy back out of his or her space.
6. Send his or her energy back to him or her, or his or her guide.
7. Observe how you look and feel once you've separated your energy from them.
8. Repeat the process two or three more times.
9. When through, create and destroy roses, then recycle the energy from your pictures back through your crown.
10. Explode your old grounding cord and male- or female-ground.
11. Replenish your body and aura with golden cosmic energy.
12. Bring up just the right amount of earth energy for your body and aura at this time.
13. Thank your body for being willing to change and grow.
14. Breathe gently and deeply, stand up, stretch, and reverse polarities.
15. You may find it useful to make some notes of your experience.

EXERCISE 85: Finding Hidden Anger and Resentment—Throwing Purple Light at Something to Light It Up

A wonderful skill for finding and lighting up obstructive energies in your space is to simply throw purple light at them, at which time it they will light up. This provides you the opportunity to clear them. You might take a few moments to practice the technique before moving on to the next exercise.

1. Breathe gently and deeply, and with openness be in the center of your head.
2. Explode your old grounding cord and male- or female-ground.
3. Think of a space in your body or aura where you would like to light something up so that you can observe it.
4. Imagine throwing purple light at it and lighting it up.
5. Using your various tools, give yourself a healing around the issue.
6. When through, create and destroy roses, and recycle the energy back through your crown.
7. Explode your old grounding cord and male- or female-ground.
8. Replenish your body and aura with golden cosmic energy.
9. Bring up just the right amount of earth energy for your body and aura at this time.
10. Thank your body for being willing to change and grow.
11. Breathe gently and deeply, stand up, stretch, and reverse polarities.
12. You may find it useful to make some notes of your experience.

EXERCISE 86: Clearing Anger and Resentment from Your Spleen and Liver

The spleen functions as part of the circulatory and immune systems and is tucked under the left lower corner of your diaphragm. The liver is responsible for digestion, protein synthesis, and the detoxification of the body; it is the body's largest gland, with the bulk of its mass on the right and extending to the left just past the midline. Both the spleen and liver hold anger and resentment. Please familiarize yourself with the location of both before practicing the following exercise.

1. Breathe gently and deeply, and with openness be in the center of your head.
2. Explode your old grounding cord and male- or female-ground.

3. Bring your crown to gold, and imagine throwing purple light at your spleen to light up any anger or resentment hidden there.
4. Give your spleen a gentle but thorough clearing of any anger and resentment energies you are ready to let go of: explode pictures, remove cords, vacuum energy.
5. When through, replenish your spleen with lots of golden cosmic energy.
6. With a sense of adventure, from the center of your head update your grounding.
7. Bring your crown to gold, and next imagine throwing purple light at your liver to light up any anger or resentment hidden there.
8. Give your liver a gentle but thorough clearing of any anger and resentment energies you are ready to let go of: explode pictures, remove cords, vacuum energy.
9. When through, replenish your liver with lots of golden cosmic energy.
10. Create and destroy roses, and recycle the energy back through your crown.
11. Explode your old grounding cord and male- or female-ground.
12. Replenish your body and aura with golden cosmic energy.
13. Bring up just the right amount of earth energy for your body and aura at this time.
14. Thank your body for being willing to change and grow.
15. Breathe gently and deeply, stand up, stretch, and reverse polarities.
16. You may find it useful to make some notes of your experience.

Compressed Emotions: "I'm So Over It!"

Sometimes when people haven't fully owned and processed an emotion, the emotion literally compresses and hardens somewhere in their body and aura. Like turning air into stone, an emotion can get so compressed, so hardened, that what had begun as a nice flowing energy becomes calcified, dark, and hidden, tucked into a tiny space where, if left unconscious, it can eventually become a health problem or an unpleasant external event. For example, anger is one of those emotions that if left to fester can eventually lead to heart issues.

The compression often occurs when people are convinced that they've moved on, that they are so "over" someone or something, or that they've completely forgiven someone or themselves.

In the next exercise you'll explore an old anger or hurt to see if you have given it its full space and acknowledgment. Whatever you find will be a rich opportunity to explode pictures and come more deeply into current time.

EXERCISE 87: Freeing Hidden and Compressed Emotions

1. With a sense of adventure, from the center of your head male- or female-ground.
2. Recall an event you'd like to explore or something you feel like you've moved on from or forgiven.
3. Take a few moments to simply notice and acknowledge your immediate emotional and physical response to the memory.
4. Ask yourself to estimate how much space you've given the event to be what it is (between 0 to 100%).
5. Create a rose for your compressed emotion and let it expand and morph and become whatever shape and size it wants to take.
6. Observe your physical and emotional reaction.
7. As you let the emotion have its natural space, breathe, set your crown to gold, explode pictures—whatever seems appropriate.
8. Ground out any energy that isn't yours from the emotion.
9. Release any excess energy down your grounding cord.
10. Create a new male or female grounding cord.
11. Replenish your entire aura with golden sun energy.
12. Bring up just the right amount of earth energy for your body and aura at this time.
13. Thank your body for being willing to change and grow.
14. Take a few refreshing breaths and when ready stand up, gently stretch, and reverse polarities.
15. You may find it useful to make some notes of your experience.

Conscious Breathing

If you can consciously breathe and count your breath when angry or stressed, even for thirty seconds or a minute, you will naturally become more present, resourceful, and calm. You can think of your breathing as a barometer for where you are placing your consciousness. Chances are that your consciousness will not be in your body if your breathing comes from high in your chest. When you can breathe gently and deeply into your belly you'll be more present, more grounded, and more in touch with your resourcefulness and who you are. We've included two variations: one technique to use during your busy day, the other for when you have twenty minutes to dedicate to yourself. If you lose count simply begin again.

EXERCISE 88: Counting Your Breath to Reduce Stress Quickly (one minute)

1. Breathe gently and deeply, and with openness be in the center of your head.
2. Explode your old grounding cord and male- or female-ground.
3. Become conscious of your breathing.
4. Count your breath for 30 seconds to 1 minute, or for as long as you need to feel less angry or stressed. If you lose your place, simply begin again.
5. To help you maintain this calmer state, when finished explode your old grounding cord and again male- or female-ground.

EXERCISE 89: Counting Your Breath Extended Meditation (20 to 30 minutes)

1. Breathe gently and deeply, and with openness be in the center of your head.
2. Explode your old grounding cord and male- or female-ground.
3. Become conscious of your breathing.
4. "For 10 to 30 minutes do the following: Count your breath beginning with 1. When you get to 10, start over at 1. (The

counting is just to help you maintain focus, the count itself is unimportant). If you lose your place, simply begin again."

5. When through, create and destroy roses for any pictures that lit up, and recycle the energy back through your crown.
6. Explode your old grounding cord and male- or female-ground.
7. Replenish your body and aura with golden cosmic energy.
8. Bring up just the right amount of earth energy for your body and aura at this time.
9. Thank your body for being willing to change and grow.
10. Breathe gently and deeply, stand up, stretch, and reverse polarities.
11. You may find it useful to make some notes of your experience.

CHAPTER 24

Self-Evaluation

People often ask us: "How can I come to feel good about myself?" Embedded in this question is usually an underlying goal. From a clairvoyant perspective, the person usually seems to be seeking an effective way to argue with other people's voices in his or her head. Thus the question more accurately seems to be: "How do I justify my existence?" No one has to justify their existence. Being who we are with healthy boundaries, following our desires with the understanding that the purpose of our desires is to bring us into engagement with life, and cultivating kindness, generosity, and authenticity are their own justification and a natural path to happiness. The quest to feel good about oneself can too easily be a quest to overwhelm the energy of feeling bad about oneself. Instead of overwhelming energy blocks, we try to understand them, find their intrinsic meaning, and clear them.

It is, however, important to be able to evaluate yourself, to be open to knowing what your strengths and weaknesses are. The game of golf provides a very good model for how to use self-evaluation, because the self-evaluation in golf can also be part of a larger experience of how to enjoy yourself in the middle of success and failure.

You Engage the World, Making the Best Choices You Can Make

Hitting a particular shot requires a complex suite of emotional and intellectual skills. First you are called upon to accurately evaluate your overall skill and how you are playing this day. It's important to neither underestimate nor overestimate your skill. Second, you are called on to evaluate the course, the playing conditions, your strategy for the round, and your strategy for the moment given the particular ball placement you face. Once you decide what shot to hit, you will perform your best only if you let go, to the best of your ability, of thinking about the outcome. For the moment, if you are mentally skillful, you are neither optimistic nor pessimistic, neither confident of the outcome nor frightened, because you aren't focused on the outcome at all. If you are a good golfer you commit to the shot you have decided upon. With a trusting blend of conscious and unconscious mental and physical processes, you focus only on your swing in the moment you hit the ball.

As soon as you hit the ball, another cascade of emotions and thought occurs. If the shot you hit looks good, you let yourself enjoy that; if it looks bad, then you can let yourself grieve that. If you are to have fun with your emotions and let them be helpful to your game, the key is to have your emotions without them having you; letting your emotions be exactly what they are without spinning elaborate stories you then get lost in.

As you walk to your ball for the next shot, you evaluate your last shot, your overall game, your play this day, and begin to get ready to evaluate your next shot. Perhaps you enjoy the beauty of the course, enjoy the weather and the walk, and enjoy talking with your playing partners. When you get to the ball, its position may be better or worse than you expected. You can have lucky or unlucky breaks. Luck, both good and bad, is part of golf and part of life.[1]

Whatever is the case, whatever is your next shot, you will do best if you have your emotions, let them go, evaluate your next shot, commit to your best decision, and hit the ball. Then once again you will experience pleasure or regret, and this is the way golf works ideally, and this is the way life works ideally.

We engage the world, making the best choices we can make. We rejoice or grieve at what we think are the results. We plan our next shot at engaging the world. When we move smoothly and in relative balance through the ups and downs of daily life, then we can have outcomes we want and outcomes we dislike. We experience success and failure, within an overall sense of meaning, reliable happiness, even joy.

Mistakes

The word "mistake" gets improperly associated with guilt or punishment. As a result, the mere mention of the word "mistake" or even the idea of making a mistake becomes painful for many people. Since mistakes are inevitable, it is useful to clear your aura of pain and restriction around the concept of mistakes; to become comfortable and able to continue running your energy freely when you've made a mistake or when someone claims you've made one.

Avoiding the word "mistake" and using euphemisms like "I gave myself a learning opportunity" can be helpful in cultivating the wisdom that all experience is important and sacred and integrating your experience from mistakes, but the euphemism can also cover up pain or resistance that's still held in your aura around the idea of making a mistake. Odds are, if you can't look at some event in your life and openly say, "I made a mistake there," then you are still in resistance to accepting yourself as fallible.

Some people argue, "Every experience is sacred so how could it be a mistake?" Our answer is, every experience is sacred. Experience arising from mistakes is just as sacred, if often less pleasant, than experience arising from excellent judgment. It is profoundly life-enhancing to know and feel the absolute sacredness of every event even while having the practical wisdom and skill to evaluate which choices are poor choices in a relative world.

In the following exercises recall what you consider to be the biggest mistake you've ever made, however grave the consequences. With compassion for yourself, please acknowledge the event, accept that your life is what it is, let go of comparing how your life might have been (even while you acknowledge that you wish you hadn't made a mistake), and explore your mistake from a perspective of meaning. (To review this concept of meaning see Chapter 20, "Pleasure, Happiness and Joy"—in particular Exercise 66, "Finding Your Meaning Space About Three Inches Above your Crown," and Exercise 67, "Finding an Event's Essential Meaningfulness.") You might affirm to yourself, "Yes, I made a mistake. Yes, I could have made a better decision. I wish things were different." Or try creating personal affirmations that will allow you to compassionately accept your mistake. Repeating this exercise over a period of weeks or months will help you deepen your acceptance and understand the mistake's intrinsic meaning.

EXERCISE 90: Accepting a Personal Mistake and Exploring Its Meaning

1. With openness, from the center of your head male- or female-ground.
2. Create a rose out in front of you and allow the energy of the biggest mistake you've ever made to fill the rose. This will probably light up lots of pictures, so begin creating and exploding roses.
3. Breathe gently and deeply into your belly, and with compassion for yourself simply acknowledge the event—let it be real, let it have all the space it needs.
4. Affirm to yourself, "Yes, I made a mistake. Yes, I could have made a better decision. I wish things were different." Or experiment with personal affirmations that might work better for you.
5. Acknowledge any guilt, shame, disbelief, fear, regret, etc., and continue to explode pictures.
6. Acknowledge the consequences of the event as you continue to explode pictures.
7. Vacuum out any energy that belongs to others and remove any cords that light up. Use any of the tools you might find helpful to address the various energies of your mistake.
8. Spend however much time seems helpful in accepting your life as it is, letting go of comparing how you believe your life might have been.
9. When comfortable with your progress, observe your grounding and update if necessary.
10. Next, to find the space in which to explore the event's meaning, allow your awareness to rise up into your crown, then move about 3 inches above your crown.
11. In that meaning space find an energy that is yours, an energy that, like a lullaby, assures you that all is well.

12. Continuing to observe carefully, see if you can find the infinite resiliency of the meaning space, and its unceasing expansion in all directions.
13. Rest in that meaning space for as long as you'd like.
14. When through, explode the rose holding the energy of your mistake and recycle the energy back through your crown.
15. Explode your old grounding cord and male- or female-ground.
16. Come fully back into your body and the center of your head.
17. Replenish your body and aura with golden cosmic energy.
18. Bring up just the right amount of earth energy for your body and aura at this time.
19. Thank your body for being willing to change and grow.
20. Breathe gently and deeply, stand up, stretch, and reverse polarities.
21. You may find it useful to make some notes of your experience.

Often when you make a mistake, or if someone believes you've made a mistake, you will find a punishing energy in your space. Punishment energy comes from others, as your authentic energy won't seek to punish you. (You may recall from Chapter 19 that guilt that arises spontaneously from our own inner knowing is a form of healing called "natural guilt," which redirects us to break free of our limitations, expand consciousness, and create new meaning.) The following exercise will help you identify who the punishing energy comes from, explode matching pictures, and cultivate healthier boundaries.

EXERCISE 91: Clearing Punishment Energy Out of Your Aura
1. With openness, from the center of your head male- or female-ground.
2. Create a rose out in front of you and allow the energy of your mistake to fill the rose.
3. Breathe gently and deeply into your belly, and with compassion for yourself acknowledge the event—let it be real, let it have all the space it needs.

4. While intending to explode matching pictures, ask that any punishing energies around your mistake light up and see if you can identify who the punishing energy comes from.
5. If you cannot identify who the punishing energy belongs to, simply give your rose a grounding cord and drain the punishing energy from your rose, allowing Mother Earth to recycle it for you.
6. If you can identify who the punishing energy comes from, send (or breathe) it back to him or her (or his or her guides), intend to pull your energy out of his or her space, continue to explode matching pictures, and remove any cords you have created with him or her.
7. When through, explode your rose and recycle your energy back into your crown.
8. Create a new male or female grounding cord.
9. Replenish your entire aura with golden sun energy.
10. Bring up just the right amount of earth energy for your body and aura at this time.
11. Thank your body for being willing to change and grow.
12. Take a few refreshing breaths and when ready stand up, gently stretch, and reverse polarities.
13. You may find it useful to make some notes of your experience.

CHAPTER 25

Difficult Conversations

Most of us listen with the intent of determining who's right, and we stop listening as soon as we've determined that we are.

"True encounter" doesn't come from the initial, relatively easy relationship developments like falling in love. True encounter grows when relationships are supported by deeper communication skills and commitment to the give and take of long-term interactions. Take the following example: John's client, Cara, was told by her husband that she was unforgiving. She was really hurt and puzzled. She was in fact a very forgiving person. Why would he say she was unforgiving?

Often in such a situation her friends might advise her to stick up for herself and demand better treatment or to tell him how much he had hurt her. Depending upon how she implemented such advice, it could perhaps lead her into a skillful encounter. But that advice doesn't address developing a deep curiosity as to what her husband meant and what experience led him to say such a thing; nor does it call upon Cara to take unconditional responsibility to find her power to change herself rather than looking for all the change in him.

Cara did decide to take unconditional responsibility and committed herself to grounding, pulling her energy out of her husband's space, closing her second chakra to 15% and moving to the center of her head, amongst other psychic preparation. She then cultivated a deep curiosity about what his thoughts and experience had been that led him to feel that she was unforgiving. Most of us listen with the intent of determining who's right, and we stop listening as soon as we've determined that we are. But a much more effective purpose in listening is to understand the other person, whether they are right or not. As she used her psychic tools and talked with her husband and others, Cara came to understand several things—she was very forgiving, but only after she had taken time to process all of her emotions, talked through the issues, and reconnected with whoever had hurt her. But those things often weren't happening with her husband because they had different styles of forgiving and reconnecting, in large part because of male/female differences. It wasn't about who was right or who was wrong; was she forgiving or not; was what he said fair? It was about deeply engaging a hurtful conversation without rigidity, without black and white, without winners and losers, when neither of them was initially at their best or particularly collaborative.

This kind of interaction, some far less dramatic but always with contrasts, ambiguities, and ambivalences, is the most important skill for happiness, meaningfulness, and joy. Anyone can fall in love—the trick is to build ever more subtle, flexible, and direct relationships.

A Paradoxical Goal

For the authors, when we are successful in engaging in a difficult conversation (which isn't always the case, especially in the early stages of conversation), we find that a paradoxical shift in attitude is the most important single step. When we give up trying to win and stop getting caught up in what we might be entitled to or deserve, we become more effective. The objective in a difficult conversation is to understand the other person in his or her own terms, values, and meanings while being understood in your own terms. Then the creative work of looking for solutions and building relationships occurs.

You will be greatly aided in making this shift if you are grounded and neutral and practice acknowledging the other person. Still, under stress, it's easy to overestimate your neutrality and narrow your acknowledgment to those energies in the other person that you feel are justified.

EXERCISE 92: Exploring Your Anger at Not Getting What You Felt Entitled To

In the next exercise you'll imagine either a past conversation or make one up in which you got angry because you were not given the money, respect, love, time, or whatever you thought you deserved. Then you'll track your sensations, emotions, and thoughts, as well as how your chakras and aura react.

After you note your responses, adjust your attitude by using your psychic skills to find neutrality. Explore the stories you are telling yourself, especially your shoulds, have tos, and oughts (see Chapter 22, "Self-Talk and Stories"), until you can move from feeling "entitled" to just knowing what you want and becoming deeply curious about the other person's thoughts and feelings around the subject. Then re-imagine the conversation proceeding with your new attitude and repeat the self-reflection process described.

Please note your sensations, feelings, and thoughts and write them down. It's also important to track whether you were trying to coerce or punish the other person to drive them into doing what you thought was right. (From a spiritual point of view, coercing or punishing to get what you feel you are entitled to is always a bad strategy.)

Monitor how your chakras and aura react—which of your chakras are tight and which chakras are excessively open; which are performing well. Check to see whose energy you're using. As always, please monitor whether or not you are jumping into the other person's space.

1. From the center of your head, male- or female-ground.
2. Imagine either a past conversation or make one up in which you got angry because you were not being given the proper money, respect, love, or whatever you thought you deserved.
3. With openness to what you might find, explore your sensations, emotions, and thoughts.
4. Then explore how your chakras and aura responded.
5. Check to see if you were jumping into the other person's space.

6. Monitor to see if you were trying to coerce or punish the other person to drive them into doing what you think is right.
7. Then adjust your attitude by using your psychic skills to find neutrality or by addressing your self-talk until you can move from feeling "entitled" to knowing what you want and becoming deeply curious about the other person's thoughts and feelings.
8. Now re-imagine the conversation from your more resourceful attitude and repeat the self-reflection process described above.
9. Explode any remaining pictures, recycle your energy back into your crown, and release any excess energy down your grounding cord.
10. Create a new male or female grounding cord.
11. Replenish your entire aura with golden sun energy.
12. Bring up just the right amount of earth energy for your body and aura at this time.
13. Thank your body for being willing to change and grow.
14. Take a few refreshing breaths and when ready stand up, gently stretch, and reverse polarities.
15. You may find it useful to make some notes of your experience.

EXERCISE 93: Exploring Why Someone Behaved As They Did

In the following exercise you will imagine a past difficult conversation in which you could not understand why the person behaved as they did or why he or she argued for certain points. Use your internal awareness. Rather than using your imagination to score points, note where you get lit up. Explode your matching pictures and make a special effort to explore the other person's emotions or ideas. This will almost always involve looking at emotions or ideas that lie outside the emotional and intellectual energy range you usually explore. For example, if you engage people primarily through emotional connection, you may find yourself having difficulty with people who engage primarily though their rationality. To understand them it helps to stop, take a deep breath, and recognize that they will not reach out to others through their emotions. So it will help if you work very hard to listen to and acknowledge their ideas and intellectual arguments. Without giving up your own ideas, unless they change as part of your growing understanding, continue to listen to the only communication they're likely to share—their ideas—and continue to clear and self-reflect until you can engage the other's ideas respectfully, even though you may continue to disagree. As your neutrality and openness grow, you can engage the other person if that is an option.

Psychic skills often aren't enough. We suggest you study books like *Difficult Conversations, The Power of a Positive No,* and *Nonviolent Communication.*[1]

1. From the center of your head, male- or female-ground.
2. Imagine a past difficult conversation in which you could not understand why the person behaved as they did, or why they argued certain points.
3. Using your creative imagination and self-reflection, explore where in your aura pictures light up, and explode your matching pictures.
4. Make a special effort to explore the other person's emotions or ideas.
5. When through, recycle your energy back into your crown, and release any excess energy down your grounding cord.
6. Explode your old grounding cord and male- or female-ground.
7. Replenish your body and aura with golden cosmic energy.
8. Bring up just the right amount of earth energy for your body and aura at this time.
9. Thank your body for being willing to change and grow.
10. Breathe gently and deeply, stand up, stretch, and reverse polarities.
11. You may find it useful to make some notes of your experience.

EXERCISE 94: Bring into Current Time a Specific, Subtle Energy Related to Desire—Turning Off Your Perfect-Picture Energy

In the following exercise you'll acknowledge and bring into current time a specific but subtle energy related to desire, such as getting a raise in a job you currently have or improving a friendship. What makes it subtle is that you will not be running a perfect picture about how abundant the universe is or the fact that love is everywhere. You will be looking at a real interaction between two human beings—you and your boss or you and your friend.

1. From the center of your head, male- or female-ground.
2. Create a rose out in front of you and let it fill with the energy of your getting a raise in the job you currently have, or your improving a relationship, or a similar scenario of your choosing.
3. Acknowledge the other person at an energy level.
4. Hand the rose to them and observe their response. Create and destroy roses for any pictures this transaction lights up.
5. Attend very carefully to the energy of their response.
6. Hold off responding to their response until you've taken much longer than you think you need to try to fully understand the other person's values, attitudes, and goals.
7. Spend time figuring out their goals.
8. Work on your neutrality until you can, at an energy level, respond to them with unconditional respect, even if your response is to oppose them. Even in that case, make certain you address all their concerns.
9. Now do the entire cycle again, numbers 4 through 8, until you are comfortable that you have addressed skillfully both the other person's concerns and your own.
10. Later, you can work on your grounding, neutrality, listening skills, and goals so that when you do interact physically, you do so skillfully.
11. Explode roses and recycle your energy back into your crown.
12. Explode your old grounding cord and male- or female-ground.
13. Replenish your body and aura with golden cosmic energy.
14. Bring up just the right amount of earth energy for your body and aura at this time.
15. Thank your body for being willing to change and grow.

16. Breathe gently and deeply, stand up, stretch, and reverse polarities.
17. You may find it useful to make some notes of your experience.

What makes a difficult conversation authentic and exciting is that it requires you to engage a specific person about a specific issue. You can't rely on abstractions such as how abundant the universe is or that love really does pervade all interactions. These truths can form an unalterable base of support, but the human uniqueness of the encounter that adds to the joy that is everywhere present in the universe comes from the specifics of a very human interaction. It's that specificity and contrast that you incarnated for in the first place.

CHAPTER 26

Affirmation and Visualization

We use affirmation (repeating phrases that a person wants to convert into a belief) and visualization (picturing a desired outcome) very carefully. We actively avoid using affirmations or visualizations to overwhelm any internal opposition to goals. Spiritual freedom, the ability to run more and more colors and qualities through one's aura, is more important than a short-term outcome of achieving goals that a person thinks he or she wants.

Instead, internal opposition—that is, a person's own resistance to his or her goals—is to be addressed and cleared. Unaddressed resistance hardens and restricts the aura's ability to run energy, lessening one's spiritual freedom.[1]

Nonetheless, affirmation and visualization can be useful and powerful. We encourage their use in three ways: to sample or experience what an energy feels like even if it's not an energy you can sustain congruently; to light up resistance, which can then be addressed; and to help you acknowledge ambivalence and complexity.

The first two uses are quite straightforward. Our favorite affirmations are Louise Hay's affirmations for health.[2] Visualization uses the same process, visualizing rather than describing what you want. Hay's affirmations are an invaluable aid in our healing practice. For example, if someone has a congested spleen, we might have him or her repeat the affirmations: "I love and approve of myself. I trust the process of life to be there for me. I am safe. All is well." The ailing person has two objectives in mind. First, they are to learn to feel, hear, or see the energy of that affirmation in their aura when they say the words, even if the energy doesn't yet flow smoothly and sustainably throughout their aura. The second step, then, would be to feel, hear, or see where there is resistance in the aura to the flow of that affirmation, and to address that resistance, learn from it, and clear it where appropriate.

The third use we encourage is to help you acknowledge your preferences, ambivalences, and complexity. Perhaps the easiest example is one we often see in our consultations. People frequently say (largely to themselves) something like "I don't want to hear 'so-and-so' complain ever again" or a similar comment about not hearing. Such self-talk, repeated over decades, can have the unexpected consequence of (for example) turning off one's hearing. Since people will probably continue saying things you wish they didn't, the only way not to hear them is to not hear, period. Their self-talk is a form of resistance, and part of the underlying belief structure of a person intensely resisting different opinions is that different opinions harm them. What you resist, you become, hence the harm to the ability to hear.

Simply affirming that you want healthy, clear hearing is not as effective as an affirmation that acknowledges and helps you address your own ambivalence about the inevitability of some conversations containing content you'd rather not face. That is, people will sometimes be unhappy with us, or give us bad news, although we might wish people were always happy with us or always gave us good news. An affirmation acknowledging that you'd prefer people to be happy with you, and then continuing to affirm that, nonetheless, you want to hear everything that is said, helps you ready yourself emotionally to listen to everything, pleasant or not.

CHAPTER 27

Manifestation

If you can vibrate your desires as energies smoothly in your aura, they will manifest. To vibrate your desires smoothly requires the emotional and mental congruence that comes from engaging life, finding your resistance, and releasing it. This engagement of life not only helps you manifest your goals, it makes you more authentically open to life and relationships. Your external goals become training opportunities for your real goals, such as spiritual freedom and reliable happiness.

Over the course of the following four exercises on manifestation you'll first clear and refine the energy of a goal then release it as a rose, a tone, a feeling, or a beam of cool blue light into the dreamstate for manifestation. As you clear your goal, please pay particular attention to any resistance you may find, being careful not to treat resistance as a problem. Your resistance may hold a point of view that would be useful for you to attend to—for example, entering into a relationship that you had reservations about.

That's not to say that you're ever likely to be authentically without ambivalence; however, if your goal is an authentic goal, it won't be stopped by the ambivalence you allow yourself to be aware of. Squashing ambivalence because you don't approve of it can lead to disaster.

For the first exercise in this series, you'll create a rose for your goal, let it light you up, and simply explode pictures.

EXERCISE 95: Letting a Goal Light You Up So You Can Clear Pictures

1. From the center of your head, male- or female-ground.
2. Create a rose and let it become saturated with your goal.

3. Let your goal light you up and explode pictures.
4. Recycle your energy back into your crown.
5. Explode your old grounding cord and male- or female-ground.
6. Replenish your body and aura with golden cosmic energy.
7. Bring up just the right amount of earth energy for your body and aura at this time.
8. Thank your body for being willing to change and grow.
9. Breathe gently and deeply, stand up, stretch, and reverse polarities.
10. You may find it useful to make some notes of your experience.

EXERCISE 96: Sorting Out Energies from Your Goal

For the second exercise in the series you'll create a rose for your goal, give it a grounding cord, and drain any energies that are not authentically yours.

1. From the center of your head, male- or female-ground.
2. Create a rose and let it become saturated with your goal.
3. Begin to create and destroy roses (pictures).
4. Give your goal rose a grounding cord and drain the energies that are not yours.
5. Explode your rose and recycle your energy back into your crown.
6. Explode your old grounding cord and male- or female-ground.
7. Replenish your body and aura with golden cosmic energy.
8. Bring up just the right amount of earth energy for your body and aura at this time.
9. Thank your body for being willing to change and grow.
10. Breathe gently and deeply, stand up, stretch, and reverse polarities.
11. You may find it useful to make some notes of your experience.

EXERCISE 97: Vibrating Your Goal Throughout Your Aura

For the third exercise in the series you'll observe how the energy of your goal vibrates in your aura, first noticing where it vibrates comfortably, then noticing where it meets resistance. Remember not to treat any resistance as a problem. Pay careful attention to see if the resistance contains a point of view that would be useful for you to attend to. Ask how much of the resistance is your energy, and drain off the energy that isn't yours. Any remaining resistance will be your personal resistance, so bring the energy into current time by exploding your pictures. Then look at it, understand it, and see if you have anything to learn from it.

1. From the center of your head, male- or female-ground.
2. Having refined the energy of your goal, allow it—as a color, feeling, or sound—to come into your crown chakra then flow throughout your body and aura.
3. Notice where it vibrates comfortably and freely and where it meets resistance.
4. Turn your attention to the resistance. Drain any energy that isn't yours, and explode pictures for any remaining resistance to bring it into current time. If there is any resistance left after you've removed other people's energy and brought your own resistance energy into current time, pay attention to that resistance. Search to see if that resistance has useful information for you.
5. Explode pictures and recycle your energy back into your crown.
6. Explode your old grounding cord and male- or female-ground.
7. Replenish your body and aura with golden cosmic energy.
8. Bring up just the right amount of earth energy for your body and aura at this time.
9. Thank your body for being willing to change and grow.
10. Breathe gently and deeply, stand up, stretch, and reverse polarities.
11. You may find it useful to make some notes of your experience.

EXERCISE 98: Releasing Your Goal into the Dreamstate for Manifestation

In the fourth and final exercise in the series, after having clarified the energy of your goal and addressing your resistances to it in the previous three exercises, you'll now bring it into your crown chakra, then down into your third chakra, then allow it to move out into manifestation in your dreamstate as a rose, a tone, a feeling, or a beam of cool ocean-blue light. We suggest using a cool ocean blue because it goes out into the dreamstate as an invitation, a conversation, rather than a set of instructions.[1]

Critical to manifestation are your first- and second-chakra contributions as your physical activity in the world. People sometimes have the idea that events will manifest like lottery winnings, which only happens with certain kinds of karma. Your waking contribution to life as a conversation is physical activity like learning how to create value, improving your communication skills, or exercising.

1. From the center of your head, male- or female-ground.
2. Having clarified your goal in the previous exercises, bring the energy of your goal (as a color, sound, or feeling) down into your crown and let it permeate your crown. Explode roses until the energy is clear and flows unobstructed.
3. Next, let the energy of your goal move down into your sixth chakra. Explode roses until the energy is clear and flows unobstructed.
4. Then let the energy of your goal move down into your fifth chakra. Explode roses until the energy is clear and flows unobstructed.
5. Next let the energy of your goal move down into your fourth chakra. Explode roses until the energy is clear and flows unobstructed.
6. Then let the energy of your goal move down into your third chakra and permeate it. Explode roses until the energy is clear and flows unobstructed.
7. From your third chakra allow your goal—as a rose, a tone, a feeling, or a beam of cool blue light—to flow out into your dreamstate.
8. Explode roses (pictures) and recycle your energy back into your crown.
9. Explode your old grounding cord and male- or female-ground.
10. Replenish your body and aura with golden cosmic energy.

11. Bring up just the right amount of earth energy for your body and aura at this time.
12. Thank your body for being willing to change and grow.
13. Breathe gently and deeply, stand up, stretch, and reverse polarities.
14. You may find it useful to make some notes of your experience.

CHAPTER 28

A Good Life

Desire has such wild yet subtle creativity that when you engage it with courage and unconditional responsibility, it leads you from the surface of your longing to the depths of meaning.

One of the principal objectives of this book has been to explore the place of desire in a world in which we create but do not control our reality. If you are unhappy there's a natural tendency to think that if you get love, money, or health you will become happy. The expectation that the fulfillment of your desires will bring you happiness is surely built into your body and psychology, or otherwise you would not go out into the world pursuing your goals. But unhappiness arises from an inner alienation. Unless in pursuing love, money, or health you change that inner alienation by growing and clearing your own inner barriers, you will not have reliable happiness. Even if you get your desires without inner change, your happiness is likely to be short term. Fairly quickly your inner alienation is likely to regenerate your unhappiness. You can clear that inner alienation by pursuing your goals, which works reliably because, but only because, that pursuit brings you into relationship and communication with life.

As you look to your future and decide your goals, it is impossible to know just where meaning and satisfaction will emerge. While some of our clients make a great deal of money in glamorous jobs and that's great, we think the following examples are more often the kind of good lives people are likely to create. David, John's client, stayed engaged and committed, exercised unconditional responsibility, and thereby developed spiritual freedom and depth, and success and meaning, that he could never have consciously known to value before the fact.

David had spent his young adult life getting an MBA, studying various spiritual systems deeply, and making a living in small businesses whose goals he supported. When he started studying with John, his ambition was to form an ecological consulting firm and make a real impact on bettering the planet. He didn't have any special expertise in ecology, nor a plan to gain any special expertise. He and John were unable to come up with any high-tech, or low-tech, management contribution he might make directly to ecology. Everywhere he looked there were many people already more qualified. To prepare himself to be able to enter another graduate school so he could make a real contribution to the planet, David got an entry-level job in computer programming in a large organization. Immediately he faced challenges interacting with a coworker. Taking unconditional responsibility, David worked hard to understand and develop strategies to cope with the coworker. David was quite successful, and though challenged and aggravated, he also had fun coping with the difficulties.

After a few years David was promoted to management. Now his work became really challenging. His boss pushed hard for David to get more productivity from the people he supervised, who in turn often pushed back; and it was David's responsibility to satisfy internal "clients" who could be demanding without understanding what might take months to program when only weeks remained on the deadline. At times David thought he might never make it in management; but year by year using the kinds of psychic and practical approaches discussed in this book, David became more and more skillful in difficult conversations, more comfortable in his job, and more appreciated by his boss.

Stepping back to look at this decade-long process, both David and John think that David has accomplished something more satisfying than the romantic idea he started out with about environmental consulting. David had been challenged to go deep within himself in ways he could not have imagined to even want before his experiences and the development they engendered. In meeting his challenges, David has achieved a kind of spiritual integration that neither his imagination nor his earlier spiritual journeys suggested was possible. His spiritual integration isn't the kind where David is always loving and his spiritual energy fills the room. It's a quieter, more personal spiritual integration in which he can treat himself and others with respect as they encounter very specific conflicts and interests. Those conflicts aren't glossed over; they are addressed in emotionally satisfying ways that are productive for the business.

David's enormously exciting and satisfying outcome did not manifest at all in the manner one might expect for someone who was busy using all his resources to create his desired reality. People don't normally, with ego awareness, seek a job with real year-in year-out difficulties. People don't normally seek a job that illuminates real aura blocks, but ones that their friends wouldn't notice as being personality issues. As a practical matter, David could never have developed the freedom he created without the challenges and scares he endured. Yet, looking back, it's plain to see just how David did inwardly seek and manifest his challenges. David has spent decades (and lifetimes) studying various spiritual paths. Yet something continued to be missing from his relationships. Authentic intimacy just wasn't there. David's inner self knew that the fastest, easiest path towards his goal of an authenticity he'd never gained in other lifetimes was right through the experience of a stress-filled job. David could have failed at that job, but even then, he'd be further along the path to a new kind of authenticity than the earlier lifetimes of meditation had developed. He always had a good chance of succeeding in the job, as well as learning. He stayed resilient and did learn.

What's also really wonderful is that when you look at what is happening in inner dimensions, David is directly contributing to the inner energies that will bring environmental healing. He's contributing to environmental healing to an extent he would not have been able to even if he had managed to make a living as an environmental consultant. Instead he learned the "ecology" of interacting smoothly and productively with a boss, with people he supervises, and with clients. In the not-always-obvious logic of spiritual energies and their impact in the physical world, learning to work both productively and harmoniously is a skill that will support environmental solutions in the external world. David has truly meaningfully engaged his physical and spiritual dharma.

The gifts of the ego, with its sharp contrasts, require that the ego have limitations on its knowledge. Desire can only know its present; it lacks the experience to understand the consequences of desire's fulfillment. Nevertheless, if your ego is in flow with your inner ego, your desire itself will naturally flow and change easily, making space for vital transformations not recognized as vital by the ego. But if the ego grasps its desires too hard, it will lose contact with the very sources of flow.

A certain humility towards your desires is a useful skill to cultivate. It is possible to want what is bad for you, and the passion or intensity of your desire is no guarantee of its inner truth. In fact, very often your own resistance and fear are what you interpret as passion or intensity, and consequently those emotions can actually be a counter-indicator of the authenticity of your desire. With a certain humility, desires carry you flowingly into the future.

In this book we have stressed the human waking consciousness, but each night you shift your awareness into the parts of you that do know your own greater self-interest. Through the play of a flexible ego engaging life through the rhythms of days, seasons, and years, a conversation goes on between your ego self and other parts of yourself and All That Is. Only the playing out of desire as you seek your goals allows you to have that conversation so that Mother Earth, your soul, and the multiple voices of other people and other beings get woven into your personality with a uniqueness that comes from your engaging life, as it is.

Desire has such wild yet subtle creativity that when you engage it with courage and unconditional responsibility, it leads you from the surface of your longing to the depths of meaning. Desire, courageously engaged, transformed David's wish to have an official position as an ecological consultant into spiritual depth that genuinely contributes to the inner ecology of humanity; it transformed Cara's desire to have a loving supportive relationship into her ever-increasing ability to lovingly and supportively engage her partner when neither of them are at their best; and it transformed Sarah's wish to be a retired poet into a vital, exciting, and challenging job, filled with the poetry of her desire to help others, augmented with growing skill in difficult conversations.

Engaging the chaotic, divine dance of life as fearlessly as you can, with kindness and generosity, promotes pleasure, generates happiness, and allows you to become ever more aware of the joy and meaning that are always and already fully present, yet miraculously and mysteriously also always growing.

Notes

Chapter 2: Perceiving Energy

1. Some of our favorite CDs of the mantras: *Sounds of the Chakras* by Harish Johari, Destiny Recordings, 2004, www.sanatansociety.com; *Bija Mantras, Chakra Tuning* by Vyaas Houston, American Sanskrit Institute, 2002, www.americansanskrit.com; and *Chanting the Chakras: The Roots of Awakening* by Layne Redmond, Sounds True, 2001, www.layneredmond.com.

2. We often use the phrase "body and aura" for focus purposes, so that people remember to address both inside and outside the space of their physical body.

Chapter 3: Whose Energy Is It? An Elegant Path to a New Kind of Authenticity

1. Regarding energy bodies intermixing: In fact, a person's personal psychic energy is called his or her "information," which refers to the fact that energy carries emotion and impulse.

2. There are some subtle points concerning neutral energy that we won't elaborate in this book.

3. *Difficult Conversations: How to Discuss What Matters Most* by Douglas Stone, Sheila Heen, and Bruce Patton (New York: Penguin Books, 1999).

4. *Nonviolent Communication: A Language of Life* by Marshall B. Rosenberg (Encinitas, CA: Puddledancer Press, 2003).

5. Though the saying "No matter where you go, there you are" is attributed to many, it is believed to originate with Confucius (551–479 BCE). In 1994, Jon Kabat-Zinn published a wonderful book called *Wherever you go there you are: Mindfulness Meditations* (New York: Hyperion Books, 1994).

Chapter 4: Pictures

1. In collaboration between your sixth and seventh chakras, pictures are naturally created and destroyed in an automatic, spontaneous, and continuous process.

2. You can use smaller or larger roses, place the rose closer, or even put your picture on a screen, a concept we explain in *Basic Psychic Development: A User's Guide to Auras, Chakras & Clairvoyance* (York Beach, ME: Samuel

Weiser, Inc., 1999). We've chosen this method because it facilitates your learning to explode pictures, even before you have a lot of neutrality. Exploding pictures inside the aura without neutrality can result in tearing parts of the aura.

3. Getting lit up: Running energy also lights up energies that aren't yours.

Chapter 5: Grounding and the Center of the Head

1. There are many methods in which to ground, depending on the purpose and the energy range in which a system works. The style we employ for personal aura work is profoundly and uniquely oriented towards everyday relationships and experience. John learned it from Lewis Bostwick at the Berkeley Psychic Institute in 1973.

2. *Gloria: "Even though I had been meditating for years I had never learned to ground until I began studying with John. After about a month of grounding practice I noticed many great changes. One unexpected and delightful change was that my lifelong nail-biting habit was simply gone."*

3. There are several important times when we suggest that people *not* use grounding as part of their strategy, such as when feeling severe depression, disassociation, or suicidal tendencies. In such cases, we recommend that you seek conventional therapies directed towards extreme distress.

4. We suggest having a grounding cord except when accessing more transcendent states, or experiencing the conditions in note 3 above. For example, when channeling you will deliberately release your grounding cord so that you can vibrate at a less physical vibration.

Chapter 6: The Energy of Biological Differences

1. In academic writing biological differences are referred to as "sexual" differences. "Gender" is used to denote more flexible affiliations, but we think there are too many readers who would be unfamiliar with the academic usage. Therefore we have chosen here to use the word "gender."

2. Neither maleness nor femaleness is to be preferred to the other. We'll all have male and female incarnations in our incarnational cycle; we'll all have straight and gay, lesbian, bisexual, and transsexual lifetimes. Although we the authors have seen great benefit through our study of gender energies and gendered grounding, we are unconditionally committed to people having their full individuality and free will.

3. The institutes in the lineage of Lewis Bostwick give a lot of attention to exploring male grounding and the very interesting energy in the pituitary gland.

4. Though our gender strongly directs us according to our physical biology, the authors know at least one male-born transgendered friend who finds it very useful and important to female-ground, even though he doesn't have the physical or etheric analogs of a female reproductive system.

5. Men jump into women's space as much as women jump into men's space. The energy they use to jump into a woman's space comes primarily from their third chakra and is not a biological energy.

6. For serious depression in either men or women, we recommend that you first seek conventional therapies directed towards extreme distress.

7. For uncontrolled anger in either men or women, we recommend that you first seek conventional therapies in anger management.

Chapter 7: The Seven Major Western Chakras: Psychic Centers of Awareness and Healing

1. The front first chakra is really more complex than we can address here. We've chosen to clear it in a simplified way, which is perfectly adequate for the purposes of this book.

2. We work with a different first-chakra orientation than some other systems. For example, Barbara Brennan's "Hands of Light" healing system, when contrasted with ours, provides a great example of how different chakra orientations suit different purposes. The downward-facing orientation of the first chakra is perfectly suited for working at a body/healing level, which is Barbara Brennan's foremost focus. We work with the horizontal (to the floor) first-chakra orientation because it is perfectly suited to engage the personality, aura, and emotions. The downward first-chakra orientation vibrates beneath the frequency range of emotions, thus wouldn't align with our purposes. Barbara Brennan's system addresses emotions in depth, simply in a different manner.

3. "Czar of the Universe" is an amusing phrase used by one of John's law professors, Philip Areeda.

4. In the area of the sixth chakra you will find the energy coming from the analytical part of the brain. We prefer not to include this analytical intellect as part of the sixth chakra. In fact, to use the sixth chakra well requires that you learn to find a quite separate energy of clairvoyance. You can learn to use the analytical intellect along with your clairvoyance, but they are two separate energies. Additionally, there is a synthesizing energy involving the sixth chakra that isn't really available to humans in this time period. This is the energy that Seth calls the *spacious intellect*, and it requires the collaboration of many people.

5. There is no one "right" energy to use to clear the chakras. As you explore you will become more able to discern the difference among these subtle energies and to make choices based on your personal experience and preferences.

6. Three of our favorite mantra recordings: *Sounds of the Chakras* by Harish Johari, Destiny Recordings, 2004, www.sanatansociety.com; *Bija Mantras, Chakra Tuning* by Vyaas Houston, American Sanskrit Institute, 2002, www.americansanskrit.com; and *Chanting the Chakras: The Roots of Awakening* by Layne Redmond, Sounds True, 2001, www.layneredmond.com. The practice and study of the mantras is a journey of beauty and subtlety. We explore the more subtle energies of the mantras in our advanced classes, and will do so in future books. We suggest you read the collected works of chakra scholars Harish Johari and Anodea Judith.

Chapter 8: Tools for Large-Scale Changes

1. The analyzer: When you get very serious your awareness moves forward and out of the center of the head into a space called the *analyzer*. It's hard to find neutrality from the analyzer space. In our book, *Basic Psychic Development: A User's Guide to Auras, Chakras & Clairvoyance*, Chapter Five, page 81, you will find exercises to explore the analyzer more deeply.

2. Contract cords are not as easy to remove as regular cords. There are a number of techniques for clearing contracts, some advanced. You don't need the advanced techniques. Simply by staying patient and removing your energy from the cord, or by exploding the pictures it comes in on, eventually even the most stubborn contract will dissipate, even if it takes days or weeks. We will address contracts in depth in future books.

3. Just because you perceive something in the greatest detail in someone else's aura does not mean you have permission to remove or heal it. It takes experience, but you will eventually become skillful at recognizing what changes another person is comfortable making. You will learn to assess their comfort by observing them at an inner level, including the feelings of both the personality and the soul.

Chapter 9: Opening to Life As It Is: Resistance and Neutrality

1. In the divine scheme there's no such thing as intrinsic evil. "Evil" is a word we use to criticize certain behavior, and our assessment is always an opinion. Nevertheless in the relative world there are objective differences in culpability, and it is to this that we are trying to refer. You can match pictures with people who, in the relative world, are objectively bad even if you are a very good person.

2. We often characterize pictures by their content—for example, bully-ing—not by who did the bullying. Thus if you had pictures relating to your bullying or your being bullied, they would nevertheless be charac-terized as bullying pictures.

Chapter 11: Humanity Has Chosen to Have a Self-Reflective Ego

1. As we move outside of linear time we move to a more rambunctious, multidirectional creativity that will lead in the next few hundred years to the development of what we are calling the "spacious ego."

2. *The "Unknown" Reality, Volume One,* by Jane Roberts (San Rafael, CA: Amber-Allen Publisher, Inc., 1977); and *The "Unknown" Reality, Volume Two,* by Jane Roberts (San Rafael, CA: Amber-Allen Publisher, Inc., 1979).

3. Mystics continued to break through the walls of ordinary consciousness and through the stark barriers of what is inside a person and what is out-side. A new myth arose, not universally but pervasively, that there was a height of consciousness accessible only to humans called enlightenment or nondual awareness, and seeking it became the goal for generations of mystics. Many subsidiary notions such as the divinity, omniscience, and omnipotence of the guru became attached to the enlightenment quest. We discuss enlightenment in Chapter 12.

Chapter 12: What's New About the New Age? Enlightenment, Mastery, and the Spacious Ego

1, 2. *The Nature of the Psyche: Its Human Expression* by Jane Roberts, pages 110 and 96 (Englewood Cliffs, NJ: Prentice-Hall, Inc., 1979).

3. The nature of those structures has changed over time as the ego itself has changed. To the authors, as they have been trained by their guides to see the psychic structures of the ego, the structures are composed of small filters. While none of the traditions that we know of discuss non-dual awareness or enlightenment in terms of these filters, most do talk in terms of destroying the ego. Those traditions destroy the self-reflective ego. They do not, in most cases, destroy all sense of individuality.

In a particular instance we know of, a guru had spouses live apart for a long time because their love, centered as it was in the self-reflective ego, was an impediment to nondual awareness. Clairvoyantly, we can see that the separation was a deep, elegant, "correct" move to promote nondual awareness, because true nondual awareness at this time in humanity's development is inconsistent with the self-reflective ego.

Our guides say that both nondual awareness and enlightenment, to whatever extent they are different, require large-scale alterations of the etheric body whether the nondual/enlightened person tries for these changes or is even aware of them specifically. The traditions that do use systematic alterations of the etheric body are usually addressing various yoga *nadis*. Our guides have trained us in terms of etheric filters because according to them, seeing the etheric body in that way will facilitate the changes that will lead to the new consciousness of the Aquarian Age. The important point is that any tradition seeking to destroy the self-reflective ego, whether or not the aim is to blot out all sense of individuality, would be destroying something of inherent value and the foundation for the coming age (according to our guides). In the future, our guides say, humanity will find ways—with each individual's self-reflective ego intact—to participate in group consciousness and thereby directly arise knowingly in nondual awareness.

4. The person attaining nondual awareness merely experiences what was always and already present, what was merely camouflaged by the etheric filters. From a Sethian perspective, even that awareness is new. It's an intellectual paradox (the universe is full of them) that everything that ever could be already is, *and* each moment is completely and unpredictably new. Not even God knows the next moment as it is lived out in human experience. Uncertainty is not a constraint on God; it's the source of creativity that All That Is seeks in experience.

5. *A Simple Feeling of Being: Embracing Your True Nature* by Ken Wilber (Boston, MA: Shambhala Publications, 2004).

6. *Zen Flesh, Zen Bones* by Paul Reps (North Claredon, VT: Tuttle Publishing, 1957).

Chapter 13: Rambunctious Multidirectional Time

1. We explore the frequency range as discrete notes because those discrete frequencies are important in studying the human energy field. Psychic energies tend to coalesce at those discrete steps. But just as a singer can make sounds anywhere between two notes in a way a piano cannot, so all the frequencies between the steps in the Theosophical system also exist and can be accessed.

2. John's four-CD set is entitled *Navigating the Seven Planes of Consciousness: Advanced Skills (Psychic Psychology)* (Berkeley, CA: North Atlantic Books, 2011).

Chapter 14: The Reincarnational Process and the Eternal Validity of the Personality

1. Buddhists apply the truth of impermanence to the soul. While impermanence applies to everything, even the soul, in the ever-expanding universe, gestalts like the soul have a recognizable eternity even while they are always transforming.

2. Human consciousness itself is changing. The authors expect that in the future many of us will track more of our experience even while we're alive that occurs in interactions with other dimensions and as part of larger, exquisitely fascinating consciousnesses.

3. *Seth Speaks: The Eternal Validity of the Soul* by Jane Roberts (Englewood Cliffs, NJ: Prentice-Hall, Inc., 1972), p. 416. Seth is not a physical being. He is a being who completed his physical incarnations and now teaches in many dimensions. Seth regularly spoke through the first modern channel, Jane Roberts, from September of 1963 to her death on September 5, 1984.

4. More distant personalities from the same soul can also be co-personalities, maybe not in so close a manner. Again, the multidimensional world is so free that our description must simplify.

5. To learn more about the world-famous healing community founded by Brazilian channel John of God, go to: www.johnofgod-healing.com.

Chapter 17: Creating Your Own Reality According to Your Aura

1. A full discussion of this idea is for another book.

2. Four excellent books for exploring soul age, as well as many aspects of the soul, are listed below:

   The Michael Handbook: A Channeled System for Self Understanding by José Stevens and Simon Warwick-Smith (Sonoma, CA: Warwick Press, 1988).

   Transforming Your Dragons: How to Turn Fear Patterns into Personal Power by José Stevens, PhD (Rochester, VT: Bear & Company, 1994).

   The Journey of Your Soul: A Channel Explores Channeling and the Michael Teachings by Shepherd Hoodwin (Laguna Beach, CA: Summerjoy Press, 1999).

   Your Soul's Plan: Discovering the Real Meaning of the Life You Planned Before You Were Born by Robert Schwartz (Berkeley, CA: Frog Books/North Atlantic Books, 2009).

3. Sometimes your spiritual freedom seems to move backwards, but this is an illusion.

Chapter 22: Self-Talk and Stories: Conversations vs. Commands

1. *How to Stubbornly Refuse to Make Yourself Miserable about Anything (Yes Anything!)* by Albert Ellis, PhD (New York: Kensington Publishing Corp., 1988). Albert Ellis lived from 1913 to 2007. Two excellent websites on Dr. Ellis's work are www.rebtnetwork.org, and that of the Albert Ellis Institute, www.rebt.org.

2. We refer to this region as *the telepathics,* which involves the energies of the fifth and sixth chakras, as well as the jawline and ears. See Chapter 7.

Chapter 23: Anger

1. *Responding to Anger: A Workbook* by Lorrainne Bilodeau, MS (Center City, MN: Hazelden, 2001).

Chapter 24: Self-Evaluation

1. We're not saying you don't create your own reality, just that there is spontaneity to outcomes that can seem a lot like luck, so it behooves you to accept that open-endedness.

Chapter 25: Difficult Conversations

1. *Difficult Conversations: How to Discuss What Matters Most* by Douglas Stone, Sheila Heen, and Bruce Patton (New York: Penguin Books, 1999).

   The Power of a Positive No: How to Say No and Still Get to Yes by William Ury (New York: Bantam Dell, 2007).

   Nonviolent Communication: A Language of Life by Marshall B. Rosenberg (Encinitas, CA: Puddledancer Press, 2003).

Chapter 26: Affirmation and Visualization

1. Every action, skillful or not, ultimately adds to the eternal expansion of each consciousness, so in some way every action adds to the overall spiritual freedom. However, unskillful action can clog the aura, making it less available temporarily, and thus lessening one's experience of his or her own spiritual freedom. Also, unaddressed resistance may contain corrective information.

2. *You Can Heal Your Life* by Louise L. Hay (Carlsbad, CA: Hay House, 1984).

Chapter 27: Manifestation

1. John's teacher, Lewis Bostwick, as well as others, suggest sending it out as a pink-colored energy. Our guides say that color acts like a set of instructions to the dream self. Thus they suggest using a cool ocean blue because it behaves more like an invitation, a conversation.

Index

Endnotes are referred to by page, the letter n (for note), and the note number.

A

absolute meaning, 244–45
acceptance, unconditional responsibility and, 236–37
affirmations, 307–8
Ammachi (the Hugging Saint), 184
analyzer, the, 324n 1 (ch. 8)
angels, consciousness and development of, 179
anger
  becoming skillful with, 281–83
  behavior of others, understanding, 302–3
  compressed anger, 288–90
  conscious breathing and, 290–91
  escalating, 272–73
  giving space to, 146–47
  mechanics of, 283–88
  not getting what you want, exploring, 300–302
  observing changes in your aura during, 264–65
  observing the space of, exercise for, 143–45
  responses to, imagining, 266–67
anxiety
  and the aura, 263–64
  female, grounding and, 84
Astral Plane, 196

aura, global reality, 222, 223–24
aura, personal
  anger and, 282–84
  changes in, awareness of, 264–67
  clearing, and pursuing desires, 224
  cords in, understanding and removing, 129–36
  ego, how it functions in, 207–12
  energies of others, sorting out, 21–29
  energy/attention getting stuck in, 30–32
  excess energy in, cords and, 131
  experience, as vibrating in, 142–43
  feeling tones and, 276–77
  goals, vibrating in your aura, 310–11
  grounding energies out of, 128–29
  male and female, differences in, 67–68
  mechanics of, and the third chakra, 107
  monitoring, as core skill, 261–64
  pain and, 239, 240–41
  in past time, awareness of, 259–61

pictures in, lighting up, 50–52
in present time, awareness of,
    42–43, 257–59
punishment, clearing from your
    aura, 297–98
purpose of, 196
resistance and neutrality, effects
    of, 141–42
self-organization of, 274
seniority and, 151–52
skills in learning to perceive, 5
spiritual freedom and, 166–69,
    227
stories as organizers of, 273
unconditional responsibility for,
    232–34
uniqueness of, 17–18
authenticity
    boundaries and, 32–33
    as distinct energy, 17–18, 27
    healing and, 89
    Mother Earth and, 56–57
awareness
    aura changes, in specific situa-
        tions, 264–67
    center of the head, cultivating,
        64–66
    in current time, 257–59
    monitoring your whole aura,
        261–64
    in past time, 259–61

B
babies
    grounding cords and, 134

sense of "I," development of, 208
Bostwick, Lewis, 10, 254
boundaries
    authenticity and, 32–33
    of children, 133
    collapse of, triggers for, 283–84
    healthy, the power and freedom
        of, 137
    second chakra and, 104, 105
breathing techniques
    breathing energy out of a pet-
        peeve picture, 48–49
    conscious breathing, exercises
        for, 290–91
    removing cords, 135
Brennan, Barbara, 103, 133, 134,
    323–2 (ch. 7)
brown color, grounding and, 58
Buddhist traditions
    cords in, 133
    impermanence, 327n 1 (ch. 14)
    nondual awareness and, 189

C
caretakers, grounding cords and, 134
Causal/Mental Plane, 196
cetaceans, consciousness of, 179
center of the head, 64–66
chakras
    cords in, 132
    function of, 104–13
    further studies, 103
    mantra meditations for, 120–22
    opening and empowering of,
        113–20

placement of, 100, 102–3
understanding, 99–101
See also clearing the chakras;
    specific chakras
challenges
    blame *vs.* taking responsibility,
        232–34
    difficult conversations, 299–305
    meaning and, 253–54
    responding to, 231–32, 315–17
clarity, male. *See* male clarity
clearing the chakras
    boundaries, power and freedom
        of, 137–38
    cords, clearing, 129–36
    daily practice, suggestions for,
        138–39
    grounding energies in, 128–29
    roses, creating and destroying,
        124–27
    vacuuming energy, 127–28
    See also chakras; specific chakras
codependency, 88–90
collaboration
    cords and, 130, 131
    of energies, 30–32
colors
    challenges, changing the color of,
        159–60
    grounding and, 57–58
    spiritual freedom and, 166–69
    See also specific colors
communication, effective, 32–33
compassion, cultivating, 155–56
complexity, female, 72–79, 80–81

compressed emotions, freeing,
    289–90
consciousness, group, 180–81
consciousness, human. *See* human
consciousness
contracts, cords as, 133, 324n 2
    (ch. 8)
conversations, difficult, 299–305
co-personalities, 202–5
cords
    beneficial, 134
    recognizing, 131–33
    removing, methods for, 134–36,
        138
    results of, 133
    understanding, 129–31
cosmic energy. *See* golden
    cosmic energy
courage, desire and, 318
creative energy, female, 87–90
creativity, spontaneous, 173–74
crown chakra. *See* seventh chakra
    curiosity, development of psychic
    skills and, 3–4
current time, 42–43

D
daily practice, recommendations for,
    138–39
death
    personality development after,
        193
    and the reincarnation process,
        199–205

desires
  ego flexibility and, 211–12
  exploring, and turning off perfect
    picture energy, 303–4
  good life, living, 315–19
  life complexities and, 228
  manifesting, 309–13
  pleasure and, 243
  polarities and, 222
  pursuing in everyday life, 224
  reincarnation and, 202
  spiritual freedom and, 166
  trust and, 213–20
dharma, personal, 17–18
difficulties. *See* challenges
  disease, understanding, 37–39
distance from challenges, creating,
  160–64
dream state
  global aura and, 223
  human consciousness and, 177–
    78
  releasing goals into, 311–13
dreaminess, perfect pictures and,
  165

E
earth energy
  exercise to experience, 12
  grounding and, 56–57
Eastern mystical traditions
  nondual awareness and, 185
  transcendence of self-reflective
    ego and, 183

See also Buddhist traditions
ego, self-reflective
  vs. enlightenment, 174–75, 325n
    3 (ch. 12)
  expanding consciousness of,
    190–91
  humanity's choice of, 177–81
  inner ego, 211
  limitations and assets of, 207–12
  purpose of, 196
  systems demanding the
    transcendence of, 183–86
Ellis, Albert, 269, 270, 328n 1
  (ch. 22)
emotions
  hidden and compressed, freeing,
    289–90
  skillful handling of, 137, 231
  vibrating in the aura, 143
  you are not your emotions,
    148–49
  See also specific emotions
emotions, perceiving
  anger, giving space to, 146–47
  comparing how emotions occupy
    space, 145–46
  difficult emotions, observing the
    space of, 147–48
  exploring, 7–9
  observing the space of anger,
    happiness, impatience, love,
    143–45
empowering and opening the
  chakras, 113–20

energy, personal
    comparing your energy with dif-
        ferent consciousnesses, 19–20
    comparing your energy with
        respected others, 18–19
    constrictions as pain, 240–41
    as "information," 321n 1 (ch. 3)
    learning to perceive, skills
        involved in, 5
    moving from inside to outside
        the aura, 143
    pulling your energy out of some-
        one's space, 36–37
    separating energy, methods for,
        23–27
    sorting out from goals, 310
    taking back, questions about,
        27–29
    understanding, 29–30
    uniqueness of, 17–18
    See also aura, personal
energy, vacuuming, 127–28, 138
energy of others
    enmeshment with a parent, 22–
        27, 31–32
    exploding pictures, other
        people's, 52–53
    giving energy back, questions
        about, 27–29
    matching energies, dealing with,
        34–35
    respect and gentleness toward, 21
    sorting out from your aura, 21–
        29, 30–32

enlightenment
    vs. keeping the self-reflective ego,
        174–75, 177, 325n 3 (ch. 11),
        325n 3 (ch. 12)
    limitations of, 187–89
    as nondual awareness, 184–85
enmeshment
    and anger, exploring, 286
    causes of, 31, 34
    parental, exploring, 22–27, 31–
        32
    taking responsibility for, 36
Etheric/Physical Plane, 194–96
evil, 324n 1 (ch. 9)
exercises
    anger, exploring, 146–47, 285–
        86, 287–88, 300–302
    aura, clearing using your ground-
        ing cord, 129
    aura, how it changes in specific
        situations, 264–65
    aura, running the colors of the
        rainbow through, 167–69
    aura, the effects of anxiety on,
        263–64
    behavior of others, understand-
        ing, 302–3
    beliefs to bring different groups
        together, brainstorming,
        234–35
    breathing, conscious, 290–91
    challenges, exploring, 158–60
    changes, your aura's response to,
        262–63

comparing your energy with different consciousnesses, 19–20

comparing your energy with someone you respect enormously, 18–19

crown to gold without clearing, 157

current time, noticing in, 257–58

desire, turning off perfect picture energy, 303–4

dislikes, dwelling on, 150

emotions, observing and exploring, 7–9, 143–45, 145–46, 147–48, 148–49, 289–90

energies, separating, 22–27, 25–27, 36–37

energy field, noticing in current time, 258–59

experience, seeing as sacred and an opportunity for growth, 155–56

feeling tones, finding, 277

female energies, acknowledging the complexity of, 78–79, 80–83

female grounding cord, creating and challenging, 75–77

female grounding for male grief in a woman's space, 90–91

fifth chakra, exploding roses, vacuuming energy, and removing cords, 138

fourth chakra, vacuuming energies, 127–28

goals, working with, 309–13

golden cosmic energy, experiencing, 11

golden crown in ten seconds, 157

green earth energy, experiencing, 12

grounding and grounding cords, working with, 60–63

head, finding the center of, 65–66

inner landscape, changing, 278–79

inner wisdom, consulting, 216

intrinsic you, finding, 247–48

life interpretations, exploring, 277–78

lighting yourself up intentionally, 153–54

love, imagining, 214–16

male energies, acknowledging the simplicity of, 79–83

male grounding cord, creating, 71–72

meaning, observing from two perspectives, 248–49

meaning space, finding above the crown, 250–51

mistakes, exploring, 296–97

moving something further away, 157–58

neutrality, in-the-body exercises to gain, 156–60

neutrality, out-of-body exercises to gain, 160–64

non-judgmentalness, 154–55

"Om," experiencing the energy of, 9–10

pain energy, separating, 38–39

parents and in-laws and self-talk, 271

past times, reconnecting with, 260–61

pet-peeve pictures, breathing your energy out of, 48–49

pictures, exploding pleasant and unpleasant, 45–47

pictures, finding matching, 235–36

responses of others, imagining, 265–67

second chakra, creating and destroying roses, 125–27

self-talk, examining, 270–71

seniority, 152

third chakra, removing cords from, 135–36

today, reconnecting with, 259–60

expansion, subjective, 173–74

experience
  as energized by meaning, 253–54
  everyday, the importance of, 222
  finding the larger context of, exercises for, 250–53
  sacred and meaningful nature of, 155–56

exploding pictures
  collections of pictures, 52
  difficulties with, 52

new levels of meaning, 50

other people's pictures, 52–53

polarity and, 54

spending time with pictures, 50–51

tools and process for, 44–50

understanding, 43–44, 53

See also pictures; specific exercises

F
fantasies, perfect pictures as, 164–65

father, separating your energy from, 23–25

fear
  present time and, 43
  resistance as a form of, 152–53

feeling tones, finding, 277

feet chakras
  functions of, 112
  location, illustration of, 101
  opening and empowering, 116–17
  placement, 102–3

female energies
  complexity of, acknowledging, 78–83
  as different from men's, 67–68
  female and male grounding, differences in, 69–70
  female guilt, 92–94, 97
  female responsibility and male rage, 94–96
  grounding cord, creating, 75–76
  grounding cord, creating and

challenging, 76–77
male grief, experiencing, 87–90,
    97
perfect pictures and, 84, 165
two drives of women, 83–87
understanding, 72–74
female grounding
    examples of, 98
    perfect pictures and, 86, 165
    understanding and working with,
        72–77, 86–87
    when experiencing male grief, 97
fifth chakra
    exploding roses, vacuuming
        energy, and removing cords,
        138
    functions of, 109
    location, illustration of, 101
    mantra meditation for, 122
    opening and empowering, 118
    placement, 102
    self-reflection, evaluation, and
        interpretation, the generation
        of, 208–9
    stories as structured in, 275
filters
    of cetaceans, 179
    as generating the self-reflective
        ego, 174–75
    retaining, and mystical engage-
        ment, 189–90
    shattering, in enlightenment,
        185, 187
first chakra
    functions of, 104

location, illustration of, 101
mantra meditation for, 121
opening and empowering, 117
placement, 102, 103, 323n 2
    (ch. 7)
fourth chakra
    functions of, 108–9
    location, illustration of, 101
    mantra meditation for, 122
    opening and empowering, 118
    placement, 102
    vacuuming energies from, 127–
        28
freedom, spiritual. See spiritual
    freedom
frequencies
    of cords, 132, 135
    exploring the psychic energies of,
        197, 326n 1 (ch. 13)

G
gender energies
    complexity of, appreciating, 78,
        80
    understanding, 67–68, 322n 2
        (ch. 6)
gestalts
    developmental vision of, 191–92
    inner ego, 211
    as self-organizing systems, 174
goals, working with, 309–13
gold color, working with, 57, 156–
    57
golden cosmic energy
    dissolving events with, 49–50

exercise to experience, 11
exploding pictures with, 44–45
green earth energy, 12, 57
grief, male. *See* male grief
grounding
   advantages of, 56
   breaking, to explore ungrounded
     anger, 285–86
   cautions, 322n 3 (ch. 5)
   colors and, 57–58
   feet chakras and, 112
   first chakra and, 104
   male and female, understanding,
     68, 69–70
   quick grounding, 62
   removing energies out of your
     body and aura, 128–29
   See also female grounding; male
     grounding
grounding cord
   creating, 58–62
   female, creating and challenging,
     75, 76–77
   grounding energies out of your
     body and aura, 128–29
   male, creating, 71–72
   mental image of grounding,
     creating, 63
   quick grounding, 62
   transcendent states and, 322n 4
     (ch. 5)
   understanding, 55–56
group consciousness, 180–81
guilt, 92–94, 97, 240
gurus, problems with, 187

H

hand chakras
   functions of, 112–13
   location, illustration of, 101
   opening and empowering, 119
   placement, 103
happiness
   desires and, 211–12, 214–16,
     220
   distinguishing from pleasure and
     joy, 243–45
   finding through meaning,
     252–53
   generating, as spiritual freedom,
     166
   observing the space of, exercise
     for, 143–45
Hay, Louise, 307
head, center of
   centering and, 64–66
   finding your intrinsic self,
     246–47
headaches, causes of, 131
healing
   affirmations and, 307–8
   chakra meditation for, 113
   disease, understanding, 37–39
   hand chakras and, 112–13
   healthy boundaries and, 137
heart chakra. *See* fourth chakra
helping others, female grounding
   and, 83–87
hormonal balance, feminine, 86,
   165
Hugging Saint (Ammachi), 184

human consciousness
  breathing as barometer for, 290
  as the center of the universe,
    190–91
  development of, 177–81
  and nondual awareness, 184–
    85, 187–89
  seven planes of, in Theosophy,
    194–97
humility relative to desire, 318
hysterectomy, female grounding
  and, 72

I
identification with emotions,
  noticing, 148–49
impatience, observing the space of,
  143–45
impermanence, 327n 1 (ch. 14)
industriousness, 108
internal awareness, 257
  See also awareness
interpretation
  generation of, 208–9
  life interpretations, exploring,
    277–78
  stories, as gatekeepers, 276
intimacy, honoring boundaries and,
  28–29
intuition, trusting, 217–19

J
joy, distinguishing from pleasure
  and happiness, 243–45

judgmentalness *vs.* non-resistance,
  154–55

K
Krishnamurti, J., 190

L
life interpretations, exploring,
  277–78
lighting up
  intentionally lighting yourself up,
    152–54
  pictures in the aura, 50–52,
    322n 3 (ch. 4)
liver, clearing anger from, 287–88
losses
  grieving, the importance of,
    231–32
  pain and punishment, 239–41
  See also challenges
love
  fourth chakra and, 108–9
  observing the space of, exercise
    for, 143–45
  personal aura and, 274

M
male clarity, cultivating, 88, 91–92
male energies
  as different from women's,
    67–68
  female and male grounding,
    differences in, 69–70
  grounding cord, creating, 71–72

male clarity, 88, 91–92
perfect pictures and, 84–85
simplicity of, acknowledging,
    71–72, 79–80, 82–83
male grief
    dynamic of, 87–90, 97
    female grounding for, 90–91, 97
male grounding, 71–72, 98
male rage, understanding and
    working with, 94–96, 98
manifestation of desires, 309–13,
    329n 1 (ch. 27)
mantra meditation on the chakras,
    120–22
mantras, recordings of, 321n 1
    k(ch. 2), 324n 6 (ch. 7)
matching energies, 33, 34–35
matching pictures
    exercises for exploding, 234–35,
        265
    finding, exercise for, 235–36
    magnetism of, 234
    proportionality and, 236
    understanding, 53–54
    See also pictures
meaning
    essential, finding, 251–52
    everything as full of, 253–54
    finding, exercises for, 248–51
    happiness, finding, 252–53
    spiritual, 219
    strategic and absolute, 244–45
meditations
    ancient, to open psychic aware-
        ness, 6

counting your breath, 290–91
daily practice, 139
mantra meditation for the
    chakras, 120–22
setting the chakras, 115–19
See also exercises
men's energies. See male energies
Mental/Causal Plane, 196
mirror neurons, 265
mistakes, 295–98
moods, passing through the aura,
    246–47
mother, separating your energy
    from, 25–27
Mother Earth, 56–57, 223
    See also earth energy
Mother Meera, 187

N
nadis, 99
neutral energies, 10–11
    See also golden cosmic energy;
        green earth energy
neutrality
    in-the-body neutrality, cultivat-
        ing, 156–60
    out-of-body neutrality, 160–64
    pain and, 241
    sacred nature of experience,
        cultivating, 155–56
    sixth chakra and, 110
    understanding, 141–42
Niebuhr, Reinhold, 237
nondual awareness
    limitations of, 187–89

paradox of, 326n 4 (ch. 12)

personality, the process of
redemption, 203–5

and the self-reflective ego,
184–85, 325n 3 (ch. 12)

non-judgmentalness, 154–55

O

obstructions, overwhelming vs.
addressing, 229

"Om," exercise to experience the
energy of, 9–10

opening and empowering the
chakras, 113–20

openness, development of psychic
skills and, 3–4

opposition vs. resistance, 151,
154–55

ovaries, perfect pictures and, 84,
165

P

pain

educating the soul, 210

as indication of a cord, 131

nondual awareness and, 189

and pleasure, 243–44

present time and, 43

punishment and, 239–41

understanding and working with,
37–39

white light and, 57

parents

enmeshment with, 22–27, 31–
32

and in-laws, exercise to explore
self-talk, 271

past time, becoming aware in,
259–61

perfect pictures

as comforting fantasies, 164–66

female, understanding, 84

male, understanding, 84–85

turning off the energy of, and
exploring desires, 303–4

See also pictures

personality, reincarnation and,
199–205, 327n 4 (ch. 14)

pet-peeves, breathing your energy
out of, 48–49

Physical/Etheric Plane, 194–96

pictures

clearing, goals and, 309–10

clearing cords, 130

collections of, 52

lighting up, 51–52, 152–54

other people's pictures, 52–53

and polarity, 54

present time, 42–43

spending time with, 50–51

understanding, 41–42

See also exploding pictures; matching pictures; perfect pictures

pineal gland, as location of center of
the head, 64

planes, Theosophical system of,
194–97

playfulness

development of psychic skills
and, 3–4

in exploring biological differences, 96–97

pleasure, distinguishing from happiness and joy, 243–45

polarities
matching energies and, 35
pictures and energy, 54
taking responsibility for, 36

present time, understanding, 42–43

proportionality, letting go of, 236

protection, white light and, 57

psychic skills, process of, 3–4, 6–7

punishment
clearing from your aura, 297–98
pain and, 239–41

purple light, lighting something up with, 287, 288

purpose of life, present and future, 254

R

rage, male. *See* male rage

reality, creating your own
auras, according to, 223–24
desires, life complexities and, 228
energy flow through the aura, 226–27
obstructions, overwhelming *vs.* addressing, 229
paradox of, 221–22
progress, slipping backwards, 229–30
proportionality, letting go of, 236

spiritual freedom, challenges to, 226, 227
structural integration and, 223

reincarnation, processes of, 199–205

relationships
conversations, difficult, 299–305
difficult, understanding and working with, 36–37
third chakra and, 106–7

reproductive system, female
auras and, 67–68
perfect pictures, and the urge to help others, 84–86, 165
See also female energies

resentment
and anger, finding, 287
clearing from the spleen and liver, 287–88
cords and, 133
See also anger

resistance
as attachment or aversion to change, 31
cords and, 131
letting go of, 43–44
vs. non-judgmentalness, 154–55
vs. opposition, 151
releasing, as spiritual freedom, 166
understanding, 141–42, 149–51, 307, 308

responsibility, unconditional, 231–34

rigidity, 255

Roberts, Jane, 15, 188, 201
    See also Seth
roses
    creating and destroying, 124–27,
        321n 2 (ch. 4)
    exercise to separate energies,
        25–27
    the rose vacuum cleaner, 127–
        28, 138
    See also pictures; specific exercises

S
sacredness of experience, 155–56,
    295
sciatic nerve, female grounding and,
    73, 74
second chakra
    enmeshment and anger, explor-
        ing, 286
    functions of, 104–6
    location, illustration of, 101
    mantra meditation for, 121
    opening and empowering, 117
    placement, 102
    roses, creating and destroying,
        125–27
self
    deeper, core, or intrinsic self,
        246–47
    paradox of, 173–75
    self-reflective ego, humanity's
        choice of, 177–81, 207–8
self-evaluation, 293–98
self-reflection, generation of, 208–9
    See also ego, self-reflective

self-righteousness, 275–76
self-talk
    conversation vs. commands, 269–
        71
    and hearing, 308
    stories and, 271–73
seniority, understanding, 151–52
separateness
    humanity's choice of, 177–81
    the soul's experience of, 210
Seth
    exploration of psychic energies,
        197
    on his incarnations, 200
    introduction to, 15–16, 327n 3
        (ch. 14)
    quotations, 171, 183
    reality, creating your own, 173
    Sethian synthesis, 175
    See also Roberts, Jane
Seven Planes of Consciousness,
    194–97
seventh chakra
    challenges, dealing with, 160–61
    functions of, 111–12
    location, illustration of, 101
    meaning space, finding above,
        250–51
    neutrality and, 156–57
    opening and empowering,
        118–19
    placement, 102
sexuality, second chakra and, 105
Shirdi Sai Baba, 190
silver color, grounding and, 58

simplicity, male, 71–72, 79–80,
    82–83
sixth chakra
    energies of, 323n 4 (ch. 7)
    functions of, 110–11
    location, illustration of, 101
    mantra meditation for, 122
    opening and empowering, 118
    placement, 102
soul
    global reality aura and, 223–24,
        327n 2 (ch. 17)
    reincarnation and, 199–205,
        327n 1 (ch. 14)
    in Theosophy, 186
souls, younger vs. older, 225
space, psychic
    anger, giving space to, 146–47
    difficult emotions, observing the
        space of, 147–48
    emotions occupying space,
        comparing, 145–46
    neutrality and, 142, 143
spaciness, perfect pictures and, 165
spiritual freedom
    challenges to, 211–12, 226, 227,
        328n 1 (ch. 26)
    understanding the mechanics of,
        166–69
spleen, clearing anger from, 287–88
stagnation, cords and, 133
stories
    as gatekeepers, 276–79
    kinds of, 274–75
    as organizers of the aura, 273

self-talk and, 271–73
strategic meaning, 244–45
stress, exercise to reduce quickly,
    290
stuck, working with being, 211–12
subjective expansion, 173–74
subplanes, Theosophical system of,
    194
suffering, pain and punishment as,
    239–41
    See also pain
T
Theosophy, 183–84, 185–86,
    193–94
third chakra
    anger and, 283
    functions of, 106–8
    location, illustration of, 101
    mantra meditation for, 121
    opening and empowering, 117
    placement, 102
    removing cords from, 135–36
time
    multidirectional reality of,
        193–97
    past time, becoming aware in,
        259–61
    present time, understanding,
        42–43
    unidirectionality of, humanity's
        awareness of, 180, 197
transcending experiences
    anger, 281–82
    vs. letting go of resistance to, 44
    white light and, 57

trust
  desires and, 213–20

U

unfairness, revisiting, 235–36
unhappiness, understanding, 315
Unity level, 204–5, 282
universe, planes of, 194–96

V

vacuuming energy, 127–28, 138
vibrations, soul, 224
vibrations of the physical plane, 196
victimization, understanding,
  31–32, 33
visualization, 307–8

W

white light
  perfect pictures and, 165
  personal preferences and, 151
  working with, 57–58
wisdom
  inner, consulting, 216
  practical, defined, 255
women's energies. *See* female energies

Y

Yin-Yang symbol, 174

About the Authors

John Friedlander grew up in Georgia and graduated from Duke University and Harvard Law School. He began his metaphysical education in 1969, studied meditation during two trips to India in 1971 and '73, trained with Lewis Bostwick in 1973 at the Berkeley Psychic Institute in California, and joined Jane Roberts's seminal Seth class in 1974. He practiced law from 1974 to 1989 but began to teach classes in psychic awareness in 1975, gradually phasing out his legal work in favor of his busy metaphysical practice. Friedlander and his wife live in Saline, Michigan.

Gloria Hemsher was born in New Jersey and grew up in Delray Beach, Florida. She majored in art and graduated from Santa Fe Community College in Gainesville, Florida. Naturally intuitive as a child, she grew up with a clairvoyant mother in a family environment where psychic awareness was the norm. Hemsher began structured studies in yoga and meditation in the early '70s, living for several years in an ashram. Gloria coauthored *Basic Psychic Development: A User's Guide to Auras, Chakras & Clairvoyance* with John Friedlander in 1999, and began a career as a psychic awareness teacher and personal coach. She lives in Cincinnati, Ohio, with her husband and two children.

Please share your thoughts...
To share your comments or questions, or to sign up for our newsletter, *The Grounding Cord*, please contact us at psychicpsychology.org

We anticipate that some readers will find some of the material confusing and others may disagree with the some of the material. While we won't be able to respond to each person individually, questions and issues of general interest will be addressed on our website or in future books and classes.

About North Atlantic Books

North Atlantic Books (NAB) is a 501(c)(3) nonprofit publisher committed to a bold exploration of the relationships between mind, body, spirit, culture, and nature. Founded in 1974, NAB aims to nurture a holistic view of the arts, sciences, humanities, and healing. To make a donation or to learn more about our books, authors, events, and newsletter, please visit www.northatlanticbooks.com.